FRANK B[...]
A LIFE BEYOND [...]

Brian Mooney

THOROGOOD

Thorogood Publishing Ltd
10-12 Rivington Street, London EC2A 3DU
Telephone: 020 7749 4748 • Fax: 020 7729 6110
Email: info@thorogoodpublishing.co.uk
Web: www.thorogoodpublishing.co.uk

A CIP catalogue record for this book is available from the British Library.

ISBN 1 85418 741 4 • 978-185418741-3

Book designed and typeset in the UK by Driftdesign

Printed in the UK by Ashford Colour Press

Front cover photograph
Frank Baines in Market Hill, Coggeshall, 1971
© Anglia Press Agency.

CONTENTS

INTRODUCTION
LIFE BEYOND THE SEA

I FIRST MET FRANK WHEN LIFE WAS ETERNAL. Like me he was going to be around for ever, and in the full flood of youth I presumed that the world would always be awash with just such dazzling people. Forty years on, when life seems far from eternal, I see things differently.

In all my travels and reporting assignments around the world, I have never met anyone quite like Frank – but, despite many charmed hours in Frank's company from our first meeting in 1969, I am now sure that in many ways I barely knew him at all. A puzzle to others and a riddle to himself, there were many faces to Frank Baines – Able Seaman and Chindit officer, Hindu monk and antique dealer, businessman and journalist, author and painter, lover and son. Even he at times did not know in which role he was most at home. He compartmentalised his life and rarely let anyone into more than one tabernacle. You could never quite pin him down.

Frank used various first names – Francis, Frank, Frankie, and Hector – and at least three versions of his surname – Baines, Baynes and Beans. In the army he was Captain Baines, with the number 201689. He was later known under the alias of Peter Maine, and the Sanskrit name Govinda Priya, and as Prisoner Number 101747, and he wrote a newspaper column in the *nom de plume* of Merlin.

He achieved fame in his lifetime for his haunting memoirs of a Cornish childhood and for a stirring account of a voyage under sail to the Southern Oceans; but he is as well remembered for being outrageously outspoken, wildly entertaining and unabashedly homosexual. He travelled around the globe for much of his life and spent long periods in India and Italy; but Essex was his home for more than 50 years.

Frank published four books – *Look Towards the Sea* (1958), *In Deep* (1959), *Culture of Bacillus* (1962) and *Officer Boy* (1971) – for the most part imaginative biographies, or artfully fictionalised narratives of an adventurous and singular life.

Aside from Frank's service in the army, he never held a serious fulltime job. His first work was as an apprentice seaman; his last as a *plongeur*, washing dishes. As a boy, Frank ran away from boarding school; the rebel emerged early. As an adult, Frank went to prison for refusing to pay his National Insurance; the rebel never died.

Frank had an extraordinary influence on people and was revered and feared in equal measure. Some people, including Frank himself, thought he was psychic; throughout his life he saw and wrote about ghosts. He loved birds, plants and trees and he had a special affinity for animals. For much of his life he would find himself in close proximity to them – pigs, horses, dogs, mules, elephants, buffaloes, even a slow loris. Indeed he was as much at home with nature as with humanity, and was as perceptive an observer of flowers and trees as of people.

His father was a knight of the realm, honoured by the King, and an acclaimed architect, and both father and son died virtual paupers. His mother was a maid-servant when she married and a Lady living in a substantial house when she died. Frank's life was full of contradictions and, although he never resolved any of them, nor perhaps ever wished to, he lived them to the full. In the end he was happy to be a misfit.

He was a man of action, as sailor, soldier and traveller, but he spent much time in introspection as a monk and living alone. Although he was immensely attractive to men and women alike and enjoyed the company and intimacy of both, he was in essence a man's man. His sexual and emotional preference was for boys and young men, particularly those from the Orient. His first passionate love affair was with one of his Gurkha riflemen behind enemy lines in Burma.

He had English upper-class attitudes and prejudices, but was prone to social pretensions that sprang from an inferiority complex about his quite modest ancestry. He mixed freely and easily with people from all nations and backgrounds. Indeed he probably felt more at home with foreigners – in his application for registration in the Army Officers' Emergency Reserve, he specified 'any non-white regiment', adding that he had 'never been with white troops'.[1]

Frank made many friends and cherished them, but he was also careless with his friendships and broke them. He liked provoking people and often he did not know when to stop. He went out of his way to shock but was himself pretty well unshockable. He was marvellously entertaining, and a great raconteur; he was never boring.

He was learned and well read, but his thinking was at times muddled and he could trip up over his own words. He was a writer with a strong visual sense, but his prose could sometimes run away with him, leading him into near-incomprehensible jungles of verbiage. He was a cultured and cultivated man. His writing was dotted with references to Classical, Eastern and European literature, religion, and opera and with images from painting and architecture, and he painted well himself.

He was trained as an artillery officer, but he was not confident with the science of gunnery. 'I have no confidence in my abilities in that direction,' Frank wrote in his application for the Army Officers' Emergency Reserve. 'I am a rotten calculator.' But he went to war, and bravely did his duty – indeed he was pretty much fearless.

He lived in India through independence and afterwards, but he was not sympathetic to either the Indians or their new nation, and he always said that General Dyer was right to open fire on unarmed protesters at Amritsar.[2]

He loved style and loved living in style, and he had exquisite taste. He was a grandee manqué, but he could also survive quite happily on virtually nothing.

---

1   Army Personnel Records.
2   In 1919 General Reginald Dyer gave orders for his troops to fire on unarmed protesters, killing at least 379 of them.

He lived his many lives richly and to the full, and when he was done with each he self-destructed and followed his own motto: he walked on. He was at some periods in his life a rich man, but his money disappeared because he was both generous and a spendthrift. Although he published four books, much of his best work remained unpublished.

Frank spun his life into many tales, and conjured his own truth out of fiction; he buried his tracks in the sand, but the traces he left behind were authentic. This is an attempt to unravel the yarn and uncover the tracks, an imperfect fulfilment of a promise I made to him that I would one day write his biography. It has taken me on a journey full of surprises and unexpected turns, and I could not have undertaken it without the unstinting assistance of his family and an army of Frank's friends and admirers, too numerous to mention all by name.

I thank especially Frank's relations, Jill Baines, Avis Baines, Douglas Oldham, Robert Oldham and Win Oldham, and Frank's close friends who shared their memories of him, among them his literary executor Dan Sansom, Lesley Driscoll, John Grimsey, Matthew Screaton, Simon Ward, Jeremy Hill, Julian Birch, Elizabeth Cannon, Pamela Harper, Maggie Brown, Mark Stimson, David Robinson, Richard Goss, Geoffrey Angold, Ray Pluck, Kate Leatherdale, and Stanley Haines. Former colleagues have also provided immeasurable help, including Frank's fellow Chindit officer Richard Rhodes James, a contemporary journalist on the Calcutta *Statesman* Philip Crosland, and his publisher Maurice-Temple Smith. Dubby Bhagat, Sunanda Datta-Ray and Dev Ashish have been extremely generous in providing invaluable insights into Frank's life in India. David Clement, a tall ships expert, and Hanna Hagmark-Cooper of Ålands Sjöfartsmuseum helped with Frank's days as a sailor. I have been assisted and advised professionally by Richard Tames, Chris Pond, Gail Turner and Jean Cannon, and I have been helped in numerous other ways by Lawrence Fort, Sophia Mooney, Katherine Bright-Holmes, Oliver Everett, Nancy Langston, and John Elliot. I am also indebted to the archivists at the Methuen Archives at the Random House Group Archive & Library in Rushden and the

Harry Ransom Humanities Research Center, The University of Texas at Austin, for their courteous assistance. Both archives contain literary material and correspondence between Frank and his publishers, Eyre & Spottiswoode, and between Frank and his literary Agents, David Higham Associates, and I am grateful for their permission to quote extensively from these sources, and from Frank's published work. My biggest debt is to Antony Edmonds, my editor, whose thoroughness, enthusiasm and good judgment have contributed so much to this book in its final form.

Coggeshall – March 2011

ONE

THE FOSSE WAY TO MILE END ROAD

FOR SOMEONE WHO WAS TO LEAD SUCH AN exotic life, Frank started out in a far from glamorous suburb of south-east London. He was born in Clapham on 24 September 1915, but if his birthplace was unremarkable there was more than a degree of mystery and intrigue surrounding his entry into the world.

Frank's birth was recorded in the Wandsworth registry, in the sub-district of Clapham, under the name of Francis Trevean Baynes, and his father was listed as Frank Baynes. In later life, they were both known as Baines – Sir Frank, the architect, and Francis (Frank), the author. On his death, Sir Frank was registered as Frank L. Baynes, but he was born Baines. This intentional muddling of the family name is a constant and unexplained feature of Frank's childhood; and it was to leave its mark on him.

According to family tradition, the Baineses were descended from Huguenot silk weavers. There is no surviving evidence of this. Frank's paternal grandfather, Samuel Baines, was born in Bermondsey in South London in 1841. He became a coppersmith and worked in the part of London's industrial East End, which was then Middlesex, where railways, boiler-making, shipbuilding and brewing ensured steady demand for copperware – pipes, cylinders and vats.

Samuel Baines married a girl from Stepney, Elizabeth Ann Coates, who was born in 1844, and they lived in a three-storey house in Stepney Green at No 1, Maria Terrace, a stone's throw from the Blind Beggar pub on the Mile End Road. Here they raised six children – two sons, Hubert (born 1874) and Frank Lloyd (1877), and four daughters, Rosa (1869), Alice (1871), Ethel (1876) and Dorothy (1888). There was a Coates family in another house in Maria Terrace, which is today a row of elegant red-brick town houses, with their surviving gothic arches above the front doors and white gables over the second floor windows. The area was heavily bombed in World War II and largely rebuilt in faceless concrete in the 1950s and 1960s. The two boys, Hubert and Frank, attended the nearby People's Palace School, a pioneering and innovative nineteenth-century institution that was a forerunner of the twentieth-century technical colleges.

Even though Samuel Baines was only an employee,[3] the family evidently prospered, and in the mid or late 1880s they were living just round the corner in a larger house at 64 Beaumont Square, and by 1900 they had moved about a mile further out of London to the more salubrious district of Bromley-by-Bow, to a rented house at No 7 Wellington Road. The three daughters, still at home, were by then school teachers; Hubert, who had started out as an apprentice coppersmith,[4] was by now in South Africa where he made a good living in diamonds and earned his spurs in the Boer War; and Frank's father, Frank Lloyd, was an architect's draughtsman. Samuel Baines, by then a widower, was sufficiently well off to afford a live-in servant. The house they occupied, No 7, is now demolished, but three like it remain, gothic-gabled with mullioned windows and angled chimney stacks in what is today Wellington Way (the name of the street was changed by the London County Council in the 1930s). Their distinct Arts and Crafts features would certainly have made their mark on the young draughtsman.

What was behind the seemingly innocuous double identity at Frank's

---

3   Samuel Baines is recorded as an employed coppersmith in the 1891 census.
4   Hubert Baines is listed as an apprentice coppersmith in the 1891 census.

birth? There is some suggestion that the future Sir Frank came under pressure for social reasons to change his name when he married Frank's mother, and this could well be true, although such a move would have been remarkably petty – even for that time – and hypocritical. There is also a story in the family that he tried to keep his marriage secret from his sisters, and just a hint that he may already have been married. He certainly went out of his way over the years to conceal his past. His listing in *Who's Who*, for example, stated that he was 'privately educated' which was simply not true. The People's Palace School was anything but private.

Frank's mother, Rhoda Oldham, was a well-educated country girl who became a housemaid in Chigwell. The second of 11 children, she was born in 1889 in Combroke, a tiny 'estate' village in Warwickshire in the heart of England, just a few miles from Shakespeare's birthplace, Stratford-upon-Avon.[5]

Combroke is a village which has changed little over the years. Nestling in a small valley, the village is approached by two roads, both down steep hills, one of them leading off the ancient Roman road, the Fosse Way. One mile away, as the crow flies, is Compton Verney, the ancestral home of Lord Willoughby de Broke. Combroke was originally built to house the estate workers of Compton Verney, and over the decades a number of Oldhams were employed there.

Rhoda's father, Edward Fines Oldham, was a carpenter and wheelwright who made his way into farming by trading up on the profits from an apple orchard and from piglets – the progeny of a particularly fertile sow he had acquired at market. Born in Combroke in 1865, he was evidently enterprising and thrifty and by the end of his life he was farming 300 acres of local land and living at Green Farm, the biggest farm-house in the village. Several of his sons worked on his land. Edward's sister Mary was the village school teacher and another sister, Caroline, ran the village post office. When Edward died in 1939 he

---

5   The village was spelt as Combroke when Frank was a child, but is now commonly known
     as Combrook.

was a prosperous yeoman farmer; his estate was valued at £3,282, enough to buy half a dozen decent suburban 'semis' at the time. His wife, Rebecca (née Hughes), who used to drive the pony and trap for the local vicar, was also a country girl. She was born in nearby Preston-on-Stour, and died in 1968, just one month short of her 100th birthday. In a newspaper interview on her 99th birthday she attributed her long life to hard work and love.

'We had next to nothing when we started, only love, but we pulled together and made a success of things,' Rebecca Oldham told the *Coventry Evening Telegraph*.[6] She recalled helping on the farm, and baking her own bread, churning butter and curing bacon.

The Oldhams were upright, hard-working country folk. Their original house opposite the church – No 15 Combroke – is still there (although three cottages have been knocked into one dwelling) and one member of the family was still living in the village in 2010.[7]

Rhoda attended the local school until the age of 12 when she was certified as having reached the National Standard. She later went into service and moved to London. In the national census of 1911 she was registered as a household servant with the Abbott family in Oakwood, Chigwell, just across the River Roding from Loughton, where Frank Baines was living with his brother, sisters, father and three servants. Presumably it was in this well-to-do corner of Essex, on the fringes of London and Epping Forest, where she met her future husband.

Rhoda was aged 24, and 11 years younger than Frank's father, when they married on 13 June 1914, a few weeks before the outbreak of the First World War. Five years later, at the end of the war, her husband was a Knight of the Realm and she was a Lady.

Frank Lloyd Baines and Rhoda Oldham married at Southwark Register Office, and the marriage certificate shows that they were both supposedly living at the time at No 76, Crampton Street, just off the

---

6   13 May 1966.
7   Two of Rhoda's nephews, Douglas and Robert (Bob), shared their family memories with the author. Winifred Oldham, the widow of her youngest brother, Ernest, was still living in Combrook in 2010.

Walworth Road – a part of London known as Newington Butts. It was then common practice to adopt 'suitcase' residences, giving a temporarily rented address to make the formalities of marriage easier and cheaper, so it is by no means certain that they were already living together. The marriage appears to be the start of the Baynes deception. The letter 'i' in both Sir Frank's and his father's family name was scored through on the marriage certificate and replaced with a 'y'. Samuel Baines had died in March the previous year, so he never witnessed the deception. Instead he was himself the beneficiary of a minor deceit at his death. Under 'Occupation' on his father's death certificate, his son Frank listed: 'of independent means'. The former coppersmith from the East End, who had died in Loughton, had been socially elevated in death.

But the mystery and deceits do not stop there. The future Sir Frank Baines, by now an established Crown servant and architect, listed his profession on the marriage certificate as 'commercial traveller (motor oils, etc)'; and while he described his wife's father, quite correctly, as a 'farmer', he entered his own father, the coppersmith Samuel Baines, as a 'civil engineer'. On 24 February, three months before the commercial traveller's wedding, the civil servant had attended a Royal levée at Buckingham Palace – no doubt resplendent in levée dress – a far cry from Southwark Registry Office and peddling oils suitable for the Panhard-Levassors and de Dions of the day.[8] He had been appointed a member of the Royal Victorian Order by the King in 1911.[9]

The future Sir Frank does indeed appear to have made strenuous efforts to keep his marriage secret, certainly from his sisters. Avis Baines, Sir Frank's niece by marriage, says that for many years the sisters were not told, adding that he was 'a very odd man, very secretive'.[10]

Frank Lloyd Baines was aged 38 when his son was born; his wife Rhoda just 26.

---

8   *The Times*, 25 February 1914.
9   *London Gazette*, 25 July 1911.
10 Avis Baines, who married Hubert Baines's son Ralph, interviewed by the author in 2010.

By most accounts it was not a happy marriage. Frank said it seemed to have been 'more or less a runaway marriage',[11] and he recalled some bitter rows, with more than a suggestion that his father had an affair with one of Rhoda's sisters.[12]

The couple seems to have spent a lot of time apart, leaving Frank to grow up mainly with his mother. Sir Frank was often in Loughton, which was something of a Baines fiefdom, and long-term place of residence of his brother and sisters. The family seems to have moved there from the East of London in 1906. Professor Clyde Binfield, in his biography of James Cubitt the architect, *The Contexting of a Chapel Architect*,[13] portrays Edwardian Loughton as a modish place, which indeed it was, and Chris Pond in his *Buildings of Loughton and Notable People of the Town*[14] describes an interesting network of literary, scientific and artistic people who lived there at the time – mostly nonconformist or heterodox in outlook and religion, and many of whom Baines knew. They included the physiologist Sir Leonard Erskine Hill; the pioneer medical researcher Major Greenwood; Millais Culpin, the London Hospital psychological and occupational therapist; and Arthur Bacot, a forensic entomologist. Some of these collaborated with Baines in his interest in the social and environmental aspects of architecture. Arthur Morrison, the journalist and Essex novelist, another East End lad removed to Loughton, was every bit as anxious as Baines to conceal his origins.[15]

Sir Frank built several houses in Loughton, including one for his sister Ethel – Hillside, the Uplands – and two others at Traps Hill for himself and his brother, Hubert. It was in Loughton, at his sister's home Hillside, that Sir Frank made and signed his final will in 1928. The family also had another substantial property in Loughton, Tree Tops on Park Hill. Sir Frank's houses in Loughton were all called 'Alicon' – the Muslim Seventh Heaven to which Azrael, the Angel of

---

11   *Look Towards the Sea* (Eyre & Spottiswoode, 1958), p. 138.
12   Frank himself hints at this in *Look Towards the Sea*, pp. 130-32.
13   The Chapels Society, 2001.
14   LDHS publications, 2003.
15   S. Newens, *Arthur Morrison*, 2008.

Death, conveys the spirits of the just.

Curiously in all his writing, the young Frank never once mentioned Loughton. Perhaps, as the scene of his father's other life, he did not know about it. Certainly, Sir Frank kept his existence in Loughton well guarded from his wife and child.

Sir Frank may have been a maverick, but for all that he had a hugely successful career. Even though he had no formal architectural qualifications, he worked his way up to become Principal Architect and then Director of His Majesty's Office of Works, in charge of royal palaces, the Houses of Parliament, and all public and historic buildings. He was on intimate terms with King George V, and once installed a marble bath for him at Buckingham Palace. His appointment as a Knight Bachelor in the Birthday Honours of 1918 cited his 'important and valuable works to the Office of Works, the Ministry of Munitions, Admiralty, War Office and Air Ministry'.[16]

This was Baines's second honour in six months, as he had been appointed CBE in the 1918 New Year's Honours List. He was made CVO in December 1922.

The Office of Works was almost a family business. Sir Frank's brother Hubert, who had had a colourful youth fighting in the Boer War and diamond mining in South Africa, was its Chief Mechanical and Electrical Engineer, and during the First World War Hubert was also in charge of civil defence for London. In fact during the war both Baines brothers wielded enormous influence; the two boys from the East End had done well.

Among Sir Frank's many celebrated works were a monumental office building, Imperial Chemical House; its sister, Thames House on Millbank, now headquarters of MI5; the Well Hall garden suburb in Woolwich, built for munitions factory workers; Roe Green estate in Kingsbury, built for aircraft workers; and the Sunray estate in Camberwell, built as homes 'fit for heroes'. A pupil of the Arts and Crafts Architect C. R. Ashbee, his style was Late or High Imperial. But he

---

16   *London Gazette*, 31 May 1918.

could build not only with grandeur but also – in his suburban estates – on a more human scale. In these estates, he replicated the traditions and vernacular of the almost accidental shape of the English country village, with its variety of shape and materials, but on a mass-produced scale with standardised units. He also pioneered the mass production of pre-fabricated factory sheds for which there was huge demand during the 1914-18 war.

His conservation and preservation work, for which he had a world-wide reputation, included restorations at Westminster Hall (where he saved the great hammer beam roof by inserting a complex support of steel rods), Hampton Court, Tintern Abbey, Bylands Abbey, and Melrose Abbey. He assisted the French sculptor Auguste Rodin on the installation of his cast of the Burghers of Calais in the Victoria Tower Gardens next to the Houses of Parliament. He also designed the stage props for the future King Edward VIII's investiture as Prince of Wales at Caernarvon Castle in 1911 and the regalia in London for the victory celebrations at the end of the First World War. During the war he was responsible for a huge construction programme – munitions and armaments factories, hospitals, army camps, and accommodation blocks – and his wartime work took him on a number of secret missions to continental Europe.

Arthur Pillans (A. P.) Laurie, who, before he went on to a distinguished academic career, was one of Sir Frank's teachers at school, wrote a glowing account of his former pupil's war work in *Pictures and Politics,* which was published in 1934.[17] The future Principal of Edinburgh's Heriot Watt College told how Frank's father was kissed by France's First World War hero, Marshall Foch.

Sir Frank Baines was one of the most remarkable personalities connected with the War. I had known him as a boy attending the People's Palace

---

17   A. P. Laurie (1861-1949), for many years Principal of Heriot-Watt College, Edinburgh, was a chemist who specialised in the analysis of painting and pigmentation. His books include *The Painter's Methods & Materials* (1926) and an apologia for Adolf Hitler, *The Case for Germany* (1939).

School. He entered the Office of Works as an architect draughtsman, and ultimately became Chief Architect. During the War, he did excellent service, erecting factories for the Ministry of Munitions with a staff working against time, and often working almost continuously night and day. He was responsible for the timber contracts, which saved this country many thousands of pounds, and roused the wrath of the timber merchants, who had hoped to squeeze the government unmercifully. They finally organised an attack on him by name in the House of Commons, an unprecedented business. He was in France during the attack on Verdun,[18] and on his own responsibility diverted ships loaded with timber – from Norway to France – timber which was urgently needed for the trenches. Foch was so pleased with him that he kissed him on both cheeks. He came home to be faced with dismissal, which was averted by a special message of thanks from the French Government to the Office of Works. Here and there, scattered throughout our Civil Service, smothered in routine, there were men like him who broke through all precedent and pulled us through.

Indeed during the war, the future Sir Frank earned the epithet 'the busy henchman'. This was in relation to one of his more unusual wartime tasks – arranging to store works of art from the national collections in the Strand Underground Station during the Zeppelin air raids.[19]

On leaving the Office of Works in 1927, Sir Frank was made Knight of the Royal Victoria Order (KCVO) for his services to the Monarch, and he became a consultant for ICI where he was a close friend of Lord Melchett, the founding father of the modern company, for whom he had designed a new headquarters, Imperial Chemical House.[20]

ICI's impressive riverside location at Millbank and its advanced internal features led to it being described in the 1930s as 'the finest office building in the British Empire'. The building's agents advertised

---

18   The German attack on the French lines at Verdun in February 1916 resulted in one of the biggest and most decisive battles in the First World War.

19   C. J. Holmes wrote in his memoirs, *Self & Partners* (1936), that Frank Baines helped transform the station into 'a perfect underground fortress', p. 327.

20   Lord Melchett, Alfred Moritz Mond, a British industrialist, financier, politician and Zionist (1868-1930), was the creator of ICI.

it as 'represent[ing] the last word in modern business efficiency'. However, the design was not universally praised; the architectural historian Sir Nikolaus Pevsner wrote of his dislike for Thames House's 'nasty cheese-coloured roof'.[21]

The building was on such a scale and its costs so enormous (£800,000 at the time) that questions were asked in Parliament about Sir Frank's involvement, with the suggestion that a Crown servant should not have undertaken such a huge private project; he resigned soon afterwards to take on the consultancy role with Imperial Chemicals.[22]

Sir Frank Baines had seemingly boundless energy and he threw himself into many causes in the defence of buildings – from the use of lime mortar in restoration and the prohibition of lead in paint and the effect of atmospheric pollution on building stones, to 'twin gravity grouters' and the Royal Society for the Arts (RSA) campaign for 'the preservation of the cottage architecture of Great Britain'.

Sir Frank was very active in the RSA, and was particularly supportive of its campaign to save England's rural cottages. 'This cottage architecture is a part of the great general tradition of architecture, a tributary of the broad stream of craftsmanship which flowed through medieval England,' he wrote. 'The heedless wastage of work of historic, artistic and intrinsic value must be stopped. The inroads of the speculator, ruthlessly destroying what he is powerless to create, must be limited.'[23]

He also – prophetically – threw himself into the RSA's involvement in 'the protection of the civil population from hostile aerial attack'. His notes, reviewing the RSA's 1927 competition for Industrial Designs, display a mordant wit, and a sentiment which would strike a heartfelt note with millions of his compatriots for generations to come.

'It is a pity,' he wrote, 'that some of the competitors did not consider how they would like to live with their designs before attempting to inflict them on the public.'

---

21 MI5 website.
22 Hansard, Vol. 207, 22 June 1927.
23 Notes prepared for the Prime Minister, Stanley Baldwin, December 1926.

Sir Frank was a furious worker. Within a day of being given the brief for his Well Hall housing estate for munitions workers in Eltham, he had carried out an inspection and plotted the hills and trees around which he would run his lanes and paths. He worked through the night to produce the layout, and had the drawings and specifications for the first 40 buildings out to tender in 10 days.

Sir Frank was never afraid of being controversial – a characteristic he passed on to his son. He caused a furore in 1920 with his proposed design for a 160-foot high Egyptian-style pylon war memorial – like a monumental entrance to an ancient temple – at Hyde Park Corner. The scheme was quietly abandoned in the midst of a storm of criticism.

Sir Frank's late work included a redesign of the Olympia Exhibition Hall in London, and towards the end of his life he also advised Mustafa Kemal Atatürk on the rebuilding of Istanbul.

A keen gardener, Sir Frank was also a prolific writer – another gift inherited by his son. The picture of Sir Frank that emerges from his writings is of a highly intelligent, cultured and sensitive man. He wrote a book on gardening and several plays in Shakespearean style. He also contributed widely to journals, and in 1929 he was appointed to the editorial board of a new monthly journal, *The Realist*, along with, among others, Arnold Bennett, Aldous Huxley, Julian Huxley, H G Wells and Herbert Reid. He wrote a lengthy article for the first edition in April 1929, *Architecture and Sculpture: An Intimate Relation*, in which he argues that good architecture is a fusion of all the arts:

Architecture, more than any other craft, needs the stimulus of public opinion, based on knowledge and sympathetic interest, to keep it healthily active and sane. No other craft is so primarily, so vitally, so intrinsically, the concern of us all. We are all its critics. All of us live in, work in, and pass by its erections. We are all influenced by, even if we are not conscious of, the failures, successes, and great achievements of architecture. It is far more fundamentally the proper subject of concern of the people generally than is often admitted; and the fact that people have often neglected it, is due to effects, the causes of which rest with architects and their practices, rather than those arising out of the alleged insensibility and ignorances of the mass of the people.

Sir Frank expresses the view that England has lost touch with the relationship it once had with its buildings and that mass production has killed individual craftsmanship:

The eye has assumed a blankness of vision as if to save itself from ill-usage. It seems evident that architecture, unless of outstanding excellence and quality, has not been clearly seen – certainly not apprehended – and today is largely ignored by most of us.

We can readily get away from a picture or a piece of sculpture, but it is difficult to get away from the modern architecture of our streets, and the towns in which we live. This has been accomplished by complete inattention amounting to blindness, by erecting a blank shutter in the mind, and by a definite if instinctive refusal to perceive. This method is indeed the only safe manner to obliterate a large proportion of the 'architecture' of our modern towns and bungaloid villages of recent and monstrous growth.

He goes on to define what he means by architecture and what it means to mankind:

Architecture may be said to comprise the great scroll of humanity, being the chief expression of man in all his stages of development; every tradition is contained within some monument; and architecture, or structure-building, developing side by side with human thought and capacity, has involved a changing yet true symbolism transfixing in some palpable form the records and tradition of the time. Architecture is thus the very script of history, and every thought finds its special page in the monumental record.

The architect, however, is not the overlord, or should not be the overlord. In Medieval England he did not in fact exist; certainly not as we know him today.

Sir Frank takes the view that there is a special relationship between the individual crafts that make up a building and he is especially interested in the synthesis of architecture and sculpture:

> If it is to be believed that all phenomena are utter illusion, even so, an art utilising a three-dimensional method of representation may be held to be more nearly approximating to the illusion itself. If indeed life and all that constitutes life are an illusion, then all the 'facts' that are apparently presented in some orderly sequence in the mind are illusion also.

In the August issue of the same year (1929), Sir Frank advocates the case for conservation and denounces the 'vandal restorers' of the nineteenth century:

> The essential principal of the rights of our people to conserve, and to retain unaltered and undebased, their ancient and historic monuments, is one which Parliament cannot afford to disregard, particularly with the present Government in power, with its Prime Minister,[24] who has shown repeatedly his intelligent, keen and enthusiastic interest in the preservation of all the historic records of our British civilization.

Sir Frank rails against the lack of statutory powers to protect ancient buildings (ecclesiastical buildings, dwelling houses and castles in private occupation had not been included in the 1913 Act of Parliament designed to protect ancient monuments). He writes that, in the last century, many great churches had been 'restored', a process that involved incalculable damage. The Royal Fine Art Commission had failed to campaign

---

24 He was referring to Stanley Baldwin (1867-1947), who was Prime Minister at the time he wrote the article.

against the new Sacristy at Westminster Abbey, and he asks sarcastically who had been the 'eminent ecclesiastical architect' who saw fit to 'restore' St Albans Cathedral and Westminster Abbey – and Southwell Minister, where sham Norman windows replaced late fourteenth-century ones. He describes the restoration of Lichfield Cathedral as 'outrageous' and the work on Truro Cathedral 'senseless vandalism'.

Sir Frank had an intellectual reach which went far beyond his professional work. The remnants of his library, which Lady Baines kept and which was sold after her death, attest to a wide range of interests – many of which he passed on to his son. There were books on southern Andalusian rock paintings, on botanical gardens, birds, fish, the wild flowers of Kashmir, Far Eastern paintings, the Greeks, and Cornwall and its antiquities; and on the works of Freud, Vasari, Shakespeare, Pepys, Voltaire, Dickens, and Agricola.[25]

Although very much a public figure, Sir Frank remained highly secretive about his past – even to his own family. He was aged 38 when Frank was born and he appears to have remained remote and rather distant from his son. His entry in *Who's Who* gave no clues about his forebears, and he remained tight-lipped even with his son: 'as close as an oyster concerning where we sprang from,' Frank wrote.[26]

The legacy of mystery surrounding his father was to leave its mark on Frank, as did his father's unconventional ideas and his readiness to court controversy.

---

25 Philips, Son & Neale auction catalogue, 17 July 1963.
26 *Look Towards the Sea*, p. 74.

TWO

CHILDHOOD IN CLAPHAM AND CORNWALL

FRANK HAD GOOD RELATIONS WITH BOTH HIS PARENTS, and his childhood seems to have been genuinely happy. It was certainly full of romantic adventure. He was always tumbling in and out of love with little girls his age or with matronly figures – on occasions even with the matrons at his schools. He had a craving for affection and attention which never left him, and which in later life found explicit expression.

Frank wrote about being raised almost entirely in Cornwall, but in fact he had as much a Clapham childhood as a Cornish childhood. He grew up in 1920s London in a redbrick Victorian mansion block in Venn Street at No 5, Grafton Mansions, a short walk from Clapham Common and next door to a Post Office sorting depot. The three-bedroom flat is airy and spacious, but far from grand.

Frank also spent many days at his mother's family village in Warwickshire, and in *Look Towards the Sea* he writes with pride about his 'ancestral home' there and about his maternal grandparents: 'Granny was herself exceptionally beautiful … Grandad, who was the handsomest young man I had ever known.'[27]

---

27 *Look Towards the Sea*, p. 157.

Frank therefore had three very different childhood homes – in London, in Warwickshire and in Cornwall. His muddled identity, which started with a seemingly innocuous change of names, grew roots in this splintered upbringing.

Frank's mother took him on frequent trips to Combroke, where he enjoyed the life of a traditional English yeoman farming community. His grandfather kept a treasure trove of ancient farm implements and a penny-farthing bicycle. The Oldhams were regular churchgoers, and Frank would have been familiar with the tiny nineteenth-century church of St Margaret's in the centre of the village just opposite his grandparents' home. Made from local grey stone, the simple church has very few monuments to catch a child's eyes, but there are two memorials which Frank could not have failed to see every time he entered the building.

A framed parchment scroll by the porch commemorates the nine sons of Combroke who died in the First World War, among them a relation, Herbert Oldham. A brass plaque on the northern side of the chantry chapel records the fate of John James Hewson, Captain in the Royal Artillery, who was killed by a fall from a horse at Bellary in Southern India on 1 October 1887, aged 31. Such a fate would surely stir the heart of any young child – especially one who loved riding.

In *Look Towards the Sea,* Frank describes life in both London and Warwickshire with lively interest, his account often spiced with stories about his mother's brothers and sisters, his uncles and aunts, including Violet (who had a black child); Gertrude, Auntie Em, with whom he hints his father was romantically involved; and Uncle Ted, who was courting one of the servant girls up at 'the big house'. In London, there were rides on trams and omnibuses, and genteel tea parties with his relations, and in Combroke happy hours playing with other children in the woods by the brook which gave the village its name and which flows from the big lake at Compton Verney through the valley to the River Dene.

Frank attended a kindergarten in London attached to what is now Streatham and Clapham High School for Girls, before being sent away to boarding school. He recalled with affection the three years he spent at prep school in East Anglia, where he won a History Prize, but he dismissed his spell at Oundle in a few disparaging pages:

> I was driven to Euston in the taxi with my mother as if I was going to execution in a tumbril ... It was evident that even at Euston, even before the train had departed, one had suddenly become sub-human, something that was being mass-produced, churned out. One was no longer an individual, one was a product in the process of evolution, an egg in an incubator ... I began glancing around desperately like a trapped animal for some means of escape.[28]

Frank's four years at Oundle (1929-33) were, however, notable for one encounter. It turned out that he was there at the same time as two cousins he did not know. They were Hubert's sons, Roy and Ralph Baines. Ralph was Head Boy. Frank literally bumped into Roy, one year his senior, on the rugger field. They instinctively recognised each other as cousins, but while together at Oundle they never spoke to one another. Frank recorded the incident and the even more bizarre moment, a few weeks earlier, when he had first discovered that his father was not as he thought Mr Francis Baynes, but was in fact Sir Frank Baines. This was when they moved into their new holiday home in Cornwall in 1929.[29]

The discovery came about because one of the workmen at their new house referred to 'Sir Frank' – and Frank, his son, could not understand who the workman was talking about. Sir Frank's real identity had only been revealed in Cornwall because he had signed the deeds to the new house in his real name.

It was not therefore until he was aged 14 that Frank really knew who he was. He writes of this in 1958 in *Look Towards the Sea*:

> I still don't know what it was all about. Later on, when I got to know him,

---

28 *Look Towards the Sea*, pp. 198-9.
29 *Look Towards the Sea*, pp. 76-80.

H.B. [Hubert Baines, his uncle] told me nothing. He just used to prevaricate, and if I pressed the matter ended up by waving his arms. Auntie Ethel, my father's sister, was worse. She clothed the matter in such a mass of philo-sophical-sounding verbiage that I choked on it and had difficulty in fighting my way through to air. Auntie Babs, H.B.'s wife, made a joke out of it. Gran, Bab's mother, could never be kept to the point. Ralph and Roy drowned the matter in beer. Mother – my own mother – hedged and I didn't like to press her on account of some obscure, last-minute fear. I think she was being loyal to my father. So all my enquiries have always come to nothing and I shall never be able to find out now.[30]

Nothing in Frank's youth quite equals the spell that Cornwall cast on him, and it is for his evocation of coming of age there that he is most remembered as a fine writer. He carried Cornwall with him for the rest of his days. What happened there shaped his destiny; and in many ways he saw his life after Cornwall as a progression downhill.

Cornwall was his father's gift; family life, such as it was, was focused almost entirely on holidays together in Cornwall. Frank's father enjoyed spending time in south Cornwall, which he had first visited as a young man and where he habitually took holidays, and when he became suc-cessful and prosperous he acquired a large estate there.

Frank's middle name, Trevean, is Cornish. It is a homestead in St Keverne, the southern Cornish parish, mid-way between Falmouth and Lizard Point, where the family first rented a number of holiday farmhouses and where they finally bought their dream home by the sea, Trenoweth.

Look Towards the Sea, Frank's first book, is centred around the house, which his father purchased in 1929 on the proceeds of his com-mission from Thames House. Then and today it is a place of unsurpassed beauty. Frank wrote the book some 20 years after he had left his child-hood paradise, and he begins his account of the house on a note of yearning:

---

30 *Look Towards the Sea*, p. 239.

I find it very difficult to write objectively about Trenoweth. It was the climax of my life and of my ambitions. From Trenoweth everything has just been one long, heart-breaking, miserable, pitiful and sometimes degrading recession. During the twenty years or so that we have left I have returned three times, and on each occasion have been not only overcome but overwhelmed with emotion. So that I have come to realise that Trenoweth is something very important in my life – a sort of perennial archetype from which everything else is measured and found wanting; a standard from which all other values more or less inevitably regress.[31]

The rambling white painted house, neither modest nor grand, nestles in the cup of a dale, and from it there are uninterrupted views through the green V of a valley to the blue sea below. The house and grounds were substantially rearranged and redesigned by Sir Frank, and in the twenty-first century they have been painstakingly and sympathetically restored by their current owners. Around and below the house, a rich profusion of bamboo shrubs and trees tumble into the valley where two streams join before flowing on to the sea. The paths that wind down the sloping ground are still there, as is the rockery, which was hewn from local stone and carried laboriously across country under the orders of Sir Frank and his wife.

All the Baines's holiday homes were within the Parish of St Keverne, the southernmost in England, and birthplace of Michael Joseph, a blacksmith who led the ill-fated Cornish rebellion against the Tudor King Henry VII in 1497.[32] The surrounding country is criss-crossed with narrow lanes and paths sunken in wooded vales where the high steeple of St Keverne church stands out above the open farmland fields. Valleys fall away gently from the town towards the sea to small ports and hidden coves carved out of the cliffs. The young Frank regarded

---

31 *Look Towards the Sea*, p. 81.
32 Michael Joseph (An Gof), together with Thomas Flamank, a lawyer from Bodmin, led an army of some 15,000 Cornishmen to London in 1497 to protest against taxation. They were routed at Blackheath, and Joseph and Flamank were hung, drawn and quartered. Joseph is commemorated in a statue at St Keverne.

the country from there to the Lizard as his childhood domain, as he makes clear in the opening paragraph of *Look Towards the Sea*:

> I made the country entirely my own. I never feel any strong, damp wind in my face, even the hot, monsoon gales of the tropics, but I am transported there. And I stand in imagination on Manacle Point, or in the ruined farmhouse at the Gillie High Rocks, looking out across the Atlantic. With the sea at my feet.[33]

The Baines family lived extremely well in Cornwall. In fact they appear to have had a lavish time there. Frank writes about importing wines and fruit from London, about sailing, horse riding, hunting and servants, all in contrast to their much more humdrum life in Clapham. The family owned a yacht, the *Seabright*, and Frank became both an accomplished sailor and a good horseman. He enjoyed hunting, shooting and deep sea fishing. 'Our life was – ambiguous,' he writes. 'In Cornwall, super-abundance and a good deal of waste, with yachts, horses, family retainers, drinks and big tips. In London, the middle-class virtues of thrift, not talking to the neighbours, and sometimes doing your own washing.'[34]

Unsurprisingly it was to Cornwall that Frank and a school friend fled when they ran away from Oundle in early December 1933. The two boys initially made for Tilbury with the intention of boarding a ship, but they ended up in Cornwall, where they hid out in a boarding house at Mousehole until found by their parents. The upshot of his escape from Oundle was that Frank was summoned to meet his Uncle Hubert, his father's brother, for the first time. Hitherto he had not been introduced to any of his father's relations; Frank said they had been carefully segregated.[35] Hubert's daughter-in-law, Jill Baines, believes that the subterfuge was indeed to do with Sir Frank wishing to keep his marriage secret.

---

33   *Look Towards the Sea*, p. 11.
34   *Look Towards the Sea*, p. 138.
35   *Look Towards the Sea*, p. 239.

Jill Baines says that for reasons she was never been able to fathom, he just did not want his sisters to know and that for a long time they knew nothing about Auntie Rhoda. The Baineses were certainly a very eccentric family.[36]

The meeting with Hubert took place in Sir Frank's London office in Henrietta Street, close to the old Fruit Market in Covent Garden, and it was not a success. It seems to have determined Frank on making good his plans to escape. But before that happened tragedy struck.

Frank's father died suddenly at Trenoweth on Christmas Day in 1933. Wild rumours accompanied him to the grave. According to Frank's account, his father's investments had been suffering badly in the global meltdown that followed the 1929 Wall Street Crash; he had also been recently diagnosed with a serious illness and had looked increasingly grey.

Violet Bean, a native of St Keverne, who knew the family, says that Frank's father died in strange circumstances.[37] Cornwall in those days was very different and odd things sometimes happened at Trenoweth. She thinks that Sir Frank committed suicide. [This is a belief shared by Hubert's son, Roy.[38]] She says that, although the doctor said he died in his sleep, it always seemed suspicious. There had been some stealing and skulduggery on the estate.[39]

Sir Frank bequeathed his entire estate to Hubert.[40] His will had been written in Loughton on a stationer's threepenny will form in 1928, five years before he died. It was perhaps odd that he did not leave anything to Rhoda, but in the event it was just as well that he passed this responsibility to his older brother. Frank and Hubert were very close, and Frank would certainly have trusted Hubert to do the right thing.

---

36 Jill Baines, married to Hubert Baines's son Roy, interviewed by the author in 2009.
37 Interviewed by the author at Trenoweth in 1995.
38 Roy Baines's wife, Jill, interviewed by the author in 2009.
39 The death certificate in the name of Frank Lloyd Baynes records heart attack brought on by degenerative heart failure.
40 Sir Frank Baines's will, dated 22 February 1928.

The probate indicates that something calamitous had indeed happened to Sir Frank's finances. Sir Frank left £65,826 gross, then a princely sum, but this small fortune netted down to a mere £808 – presumably after meeting massive debts.[41]

Frank records a little of his father's road to ruin in *Look Towards the Sea*:

> He used to write me about it at school and it was faintly worrying. I knew things had gone very wrong for him. He was somehow involved with the German Chancellor, Dr Brüning.[42] And when Dr Brüning fell he had a bad moment. Lord Melchett's death hit him very hard.[43] Besides being very good friends, he was a staunch patron. Hitler's coming to power just about put the lid on it. I think Father kind of lost hope in anything ever working out. I gathered that the speculations had gone to pieces too.[44]

Frank and his mother stayed at Trenoweth while the house was sold and Hubert made suitable financial arrangements for them. Frank had a small endowment of £250, and the following summer, having endured two terms at a crammer, he abandoned the idea of trying for Oxford and instead invested £50 to become an apprentice at sea.

Who was this would-be sailor? A sallow youth, certainly, but immensely good looking and bursting with enthusiasm and energy. He had brown curly hair, pale blue eyes, and sumptuous lips. He was very conscious of his fine, almost beautiful features, and as such he would invariably focus on the way other people looked and introduce people in his writing by describing their faces. He had developed into a very visual person: thanks to his father's love of gardening, he knew the names of countless flowers and trees. He observed what he saw, and

---

41 Probate of Sir Frank Baines's will, 26 January 1934.
42 German Chancellor whose fall in 1932 paved the way for the rise of Adolf Hitler.
43 Lord Melchett was a close friend and had commissioned Sir Frank to design the new ICI company headquarters in London.
44 *Look Towards the Sea*, p. 209.

learned from it. Later, when he came to write, he would deploy this powers of observation, and a prodigious memory for detail, to good effect. He had a rich baritone voice which he would use with increasing effect as he developed into a garrulous talker.

Although by no means a scholar, Frank had acquired a good education and he was well read. In characteristic self-parody, he would say that he did not like being taught, but that he liked learning. He knew the Bible and could quote widely from it, and he had read extensively both the classics and the usual staples of English literature. He was familiar with opera and knowledgeable about painting and architecture.

Frank was athletic, and by his own account a fine horseman, a good sailor and an excellent marksman; and he was slender and fit. He was apparently fearless and could put on an impressive show of bravura. But inwardly, he was already fighting demons. He had been brought up in a protected middle-class and privileged environment, and in some respects he was very much of his class – a snob who admired good taste, good looks and the good things of life. But beneath this thin veneer, which would wear thinner over the years, lurked a rebel and a would-be revolutionary. He was also highly emotional, very sentimental and a bag of nerves, a young man who could get very wound up, and who in turn and over time would learn how to wind up other people. It became one of his specialities – a calling card. And on top of it all, he was unsure of his manhood. He longed for and sought after other people's affection, but he had not yet discovered how to return it; he was sexually aware, precocious almost, but as yet unawakened. He was still an innocent, and this youthful innocence was about to be tested on the high seas.

THREE

VOYAGES

IN FRANK'S MIND HE HAD BEEN RUNNING AWAY to sea since childhood. His prep school in East Anglia was by the sea, and in Cornwall he was surrounded by it. His flight from Oundle was based on a plan to find a berth on a ship at Tilbury, a plan which in the event proved futile. From an early age Frank had felt that the sea was in his blood; he had even made a link in his imagination with someone he thought of as a distant sea-faring ancestor. This was James Baines, owner of the first English clipper ship, the English-owned *Marco Polo*, and the founder of the Liverpool-based Black Ball Line, which claimed to be the first scheduled passenger line in the world.

'I have often wondered whether the terrific compulsion I felt for going to sea, which dragged me around the world in ships' fo'c'sles, was an inheritance from James Baines,' Frank writes. 'If so, he owed me four years.'[45]

Frank quotes his father as saying that they were indeed related to the Liverpool Baineses, but that he did not wish to broadcast the fact since he didn't 'want everybody to know we are connected with trade'.[46] This statement is highly revealing about his father's social pretensions and also about his self-delusion, because a descendant of the Liverpool Baines family, Richard Daglish, has concluded that there was almost certainly no connection whatsoever with Sir Frank's family:

45   *Look Towards the Sea*, p. 75.
46   *Look Towards the Sea*, p. 75.

After more research, including close study of census and other returns, I have reluctantly concluded that Frank Baines was not, after all, a cousin and that his supposed family connection with James Baines was dreamed up in one of his romantic moments. It is a pity to lose such a black sheep from our flock.[47]

But whatever the merits of this presumed family connection, Frank certainly felt the pull of the sea; and also of sailing ships. In *Look Towards the Sea*, he describes a scene off Lizard Point in which the reader can sense a sailing ship working her spell on Frank:

Things draw to a close. Spring with its brilliant early flowering was gone; summer too was over. But it was autumn, still ripe and mellow. We spent a lot of time on the boat. The *Seabright* could make about 10 knots when flat out and was a very seaworthy vessel. She had a commodious cabin and a roomy cockpit. She was also fitted up with a nice lavatory. As my father aged, anxieties thickened, he spent more and more time on her. When he was on the *Seabright* I think he really felt he was away from things.

I have so many memories of autumn and the boat. They crowd upon me. Steaming across glassy seas towards Land's End. Lamorna cliffs, pink and apricot. The Wolf lighthouse with its restless and turbulent swell. Loneliness. Hot days ripening in the sun. Mother frying mackerel. Truro River and the oak woods at King Harry Ferry. Lying off Gillan all Sunday afternoon, visitors on the beach and some pretty girls, me showing off. Up to Gweek, we land at Bosane quay and walk through the yellowing woods, my father a trifle breathless. Fishing for conger. Mother hooks a hundred-pound shark and lands it after an hour and a half. I try to gaff a sun-fish. Basking shark. Hauling nets at night by lamplight, a great sting ray swims into the beam but we miss it. Fog. Loneliness. The awful, reverberating echoes of

---

47   In correspondence with the author, 2009. James Baines of Liverpool in fact hijacked the name and flag of the original Black Ball line from its New York founders.

the Lizard foghorn. Loneliness. Hot days. Boiling hot days; and more loneliness. It goes on and on.

The swell used to rise and fall around Carn Dhu with sucking noises. At
low water springs the whole extent of Manacle Reef would be exposed
as much as it ever was. Great, glabrous, brown wads of indecent-looking
seaweed wallowed around the thighs of the rocks and spread out upon
the surface of the water like pubic hair. It had the bald, naked look of
things which never see daylight. Looking down into the water you could
see the seaweed move like tentacles. They reached up towards the bottom
of the boat, reaching and stretching. One would edge away from the side
apprehensively and in another minute one would be back. They possessed
a strange fascination. 'One day,' I said to myself, 'these things are going
to get me.'

Sometimes it would be so hot fishing, we up-anchored and ran about.
Making out to sea, the shore would disappear into a haze. When we got
out beyond Black Head we would catch the swell. It came sweeping in,
indescribably majestic ...

Long, hot, breathless, slightly boring days in the sun.

One morning we were fishing for plaice and whiting off Coverack and
were awfully fed up. It was not very exciting. All the forenoon a big sailing
vessel had been standing off and on beyond the Lizard, just below the
horizon. She was under topsails ...

About an hour's run brought us up with the ship, which was an enormous
five-masted barque, the *Magdalene Vinnen*, registered at Bremen.[48] They
were very excited at seeing us, and an officer hailed us through a megaphone
in guttural English and asked us to come alongside – which we did. Where-

---

48 She in fact had only four masts and was renamed the *Sedov* in 1948. Now based in Murmansk,
she is the largest sailing vessel afloat.

upon they threw down a bulky packet of letters for us to post – none of them had any stamps on – and offered to shake out all her sail for us to photograph. We sheered away and lay off a bit. Her crew swarmed into the rigging – men on every mast. And the operation was conducted with the most wonderful precision. Sail after sail fell and filled; they hoisted upper topsails, they hoisted top gallants, they shook out royals, they set staysails on practically every stay. The jibs on her jib-boom flowered like lotuses. In fifteen minutes she carried everything. And she began to move. There wasn't a breath of wind on the water. The whole circle of sea and sky was encircled within a globe of airlessness. But all her sails filled. There was plenty up there. She heeled to it. The breeze was west. She set course east and squared up. A crinkle of foam appeared at her foot.[49]

Frank is using poetic licence here because no sailing ship of that size could break sail and get underway in such a short time; it normally took a good six hours to shake out every sail.[50] But the experience of being at close quarters with one of these ships left its mark; and when Frank decided to go to sea, he chose a similar sailing ship. He signed up to sail on one of the last grain ships – the four-mast steel barque *Lawhill*, owned by the Finnish shipper Gustaf Erikson of Mariehamn. It was a good choice.

Built in Dundee in 1892, originally as a jute-carrying ship, the *Lawhill* was 317 feet long and sported a full classic topgallant sailing rig – with five square sails on each of the fore, main and mizzen masts, a brailing spanker and jib headed topsail on the jigger, three jigger staysails, two mizzen staysails, two main staysails, and a fore staysail, inner and outer jib and flying jib. Fully canvassed she carried 38,000 square feet of sail. Her three main masts topped out 190 feet above the keelson, and the yards across them, on which seaman had to tend sails and bunt-lines, stretched far out over the open sea. Named after Law Hill in Dundee and with a figurehead representing Mary, Queen of Scots, she was the last large sailing ship to be built on the Tay.

---

49 *Look Towards the Sea*, pp. 205-207.
50 David Clement, Tall Ships expert, in a note to the author, 2009.

Under her first owners, the *Lawhill* made several voyages to South-East Asia and one run carrying jute from Chittagong to Dundee. She was then sold to the Anglo-American Oil Company to transport case oil and general cargo, and for 12 years was commanded by the renowned Captain Jarvis, inventor of a brace winch which bears his name and which took some of the sweat out of hoisting sails and yards. Erikson acquired her in 1917.

It is remarkable that these ships were still sailing commercially in the 1930s. High-pressure engines, developed in the 1880s, made steam ships faster, more economical and more reliable, and had all but put paid to sail. But the old ships clung on in new clothes, built of iron and steel, with wire rigging and powered by canvas sails from metal masts, and they could still just about compete transporting non-perishable cargoes on selective routes, particularly across the Southern Ocean where it was expensive to provide bunkering for steam ships and where the wind was constant and cost nothing. Moreover, sailing ships had smaller crews, and on a run to Australia a good master could make the same average speed as a steam ship. Gustaf Erikson was the last great owner of commercial sail ships, and he continued to operate these floating warehouses throughout the 1930s, long after every other major shipping company had gone over to steam. The *Lawhill* was the pride of his fleet.

Under Erikson's ownership, the *Lawhill* made many successful and profitable voyages, and in the inter-war years lifted more grain from Australian ports than any other square-rigger. Never described as beautiful, she was sturdy and reliable, and despite storm damage, collisions, groundings, and the Depression, she earned herself the sobriquet 'Lucky Lawhill'. In 1904 she had survived a dismasting and in 1912 she ran down a fishing smack from Rye with the loss of two lives. In 1932 she sank the Polish steamer the *Niemen* in a collision in the Skagerrak Straits between Sweden and Denmark, although she was subsequently cleared of responsibility. She was seized as an enemy ship by the South African government in 1941, and ended her days in 1957, broken up for scrap in Lourenço Marques. By then, she had completed 50 voyages, including 18 round trips to Australia.

Frank had arranged through Erikson's London agents, Clarkson's, to take an indentured apprenticeship on one of his ships, and they had offered him a berth on the *Lawhill*.

Frank's uncle Hubert took him down to inspect her at Millwall Docks on the Isle of Dogs, then a bustling basin in London's inner port and today transformed and overshadowed by the giant office towers of Canary Wharf. They travelled there by taxi. It must have been a poignant journey for Hubert Baines. Now a successful civil engineer, with bowler hat and rolled umbrella, living in a substantial house in Loughton with a wife and two adult sons, he was escorting his breakaway nephew to a sailing ship just over a mile away from where he was born and brought up in Stepney. Frank described his uncle's disdain for the state of the ship, with its disorderly and drunken crewmen, and his horror at seeing a woman's brassière and a policeman's helmet hanging up as trophies in the sail-locker. There was no hint, no understanding, that his uncle, who was strangely silent during the entire visit, was just a short walk away from his own child-hood home and that his thoughts might have been there and not on the *Lawhill*. And because he knew nothing about his father's family history, Frank could not have reflected on the irony that he was embarking on a new life – in effect running away to sea – only a short distance from the very spot where his paternal grandfather had worked all his life.

'I saw at once that she was no dream boat,' Frank writes. 'A great scab of red rust disfigured one gorgeous cheek.' Once he was on board things seemed no better: 'The ship was a wreck given over apparently to scenes of squalid debauch at night.'[51]

But the inspection was not in the end a total disaster – ships and men rot in port – and Frank was cleared to go by his uncle, who was

---

51   *In Deep* (Eyre & Spottiswoode, 1959), pp. 13 & 15.

most probably relieved at the prospect of being shot of him. 'On the way home I experienced a strange sensation of fulfillment as if I had partaken of a communion,' Frank writes. 'H.B. (Uncle Hubert) never spoke.'[52]

Frank joined the *Lawhill* a week later, shortly after his nineteenth birthday. His mother saw him off. While being shown his quarters she mistook the enormous tin of very greasy, yellow margarine standing on the apprentices' half-deck table for engine grease.

'I have never known what my mother actually thought about the whole business,' Frank writes in the closing pages of *Look Towards the Sea*. 'She has never said. Mother never opposed me in anything which she divined I felt absolutely essential for me to do. She never interfered with my internal compulsions ... She acted in this way like the House of Lords, and I must say that her function has been entirely beneficial.'[53]

Barely out of school, Frank plunged into his new life, trawling the bawdy bars around the docks with his new crewmates. On his first night ashore, he found himself in an unfamiliar world:

In a side-alley a pale, haggard man caressed his girl's throat, fingered a razor. Behind me in the bar an effeminate boy, smiling at being called a pansy, emptied his beer under the counter on to the sawdust, snapped off the top of his glass leaving lovely jagged edges, rammed it in his opponent's face, walked out in the shocked silence – only the wounded like the low note of a bird sobbing. Razor gangs ranged Commercial Road, scoured Limehouse Causeway, and the cosh-boys with bicycle chains beat up a lone drunk on Wapping Old Stairs. Somewhere a sex-maniac is slowly ravaging a virgin – who says the kids of today have a prerogative of violence? My evening out had been better than a night at Grand Guignol. I returned to the ship and blissfully fell asleep.

---

52 *In Deep*, p. 19.
53 *Look Towards the Sea*, p. 251.

On the following day, with all hands, I am chipping rust in the hold. It is vast and shadowy as a whale's belly.[54]

Frank gradually got to know the ship and his fellow crew over the next few days as they prepared for sea and took on ballast. They were towed down river where they rode anchor off Gravesend, waiting for an easterly wind to sail out of the Channel; and they finally set sail on 8 October 1934.

On a blustery cold night, three days later, the *Lawhill* tacked by the lights of a local fishing fleet bobbing off the Lizard, and the young apprentice, frantically hauling lines on deck, bade symbolic farewell to his youth in Cornwall and headed with his ship towards the Bay of Biscay – and to Australia and adult life.

Frank wrote a vivid account of the outward voyage to Australia in his second book, *In Deep*. Like his first, it was written and published many years after the events it describes, and it is also partly, and intentionally, fictionalised. In the Foreword he writes:

This story is based on a real voyage of the four-masted barque *Lawhill*. But because I have included in it some incidents which never happened to me while I was on her but to me on other ships, and because I have included in it some incidents which never happened to me at all but to other seamen from whom I had them during those long interminable yarns which seamen are always exchanging, I thought it best to make this clear, and to signify the fact by giving my ship the fictitious name of *Mathew Scobie* in the story.

But of course, it has all happened, even if it didn't happen on *Lawhill*.

Frank sailed under Captain Artur Alexander Söderlund. A native of Åland, Söderlund was one of the last of a breed, a Baltic sailor, man and boy. He was 35 when he took command of the *Lawhill* in 1933

---

54 *In Deep*, pp. 24-5.

and he was to sail her almost to her graveyard, giving up command in 1947. He died in 1954. Frank describes the Captain and officers as 'fine seamen' and, although exactly half Captain Söderlund's age, Frank refers to him throughout the voyage as 'the Old Man'.

The log of what was to be the *Lawhill*'s thirty-sixth voyage records that she arrived at Port Victoria on 5 January 1935. She dumped most of her ballast there and then sailed up the Spencer Gulf to Wallaroo to load grain, sailing for England on 19 February. She arrived back in Falmouth in June 1935, and by then Frank was an experienced hand.

For neither the first nor the last time in his life Frank sailed under a different name. His crewmates called him Hector and, more formally, Mr Beans. In his book, they are a motley selection: the Master, 'alone, aloof, unapproachable'; a half-crazed Finnish donkey-man[55] who looked like Frankenstein and behaved like a survivor from the Copper Age; a Mate who was always drunk; a young apprentice called Moses; Swedes of all shapes from Åland; a German; a Belgian; a Laplander; two Australians; a British Able Seaman who was tattooed from head to foot; and an upper-middle-class English boy called 'the Admiral' who had been sent down from Oxford. The names Frank gives do not correspond with the crew manifest, which is preserved in the Ålands Maritime Museum. He transformed them into composite characters and gave them fictitious names, but they emerge as fully authentic creatures of flesh and blood.

His first, humiliating, trick at the wheel is described equally vividly:

'South by East!' Quietly suppressing my excitement I applied myself to getting the hang of *Mathew Scoble* – no yacht, but one hundred yards by twelve yards and thirty-two thousand square foot of canvas, all of which she was now carrying. It took me the whole of my trick. Very soon I was spinning the wheel a couple of turns to port to arrest her and then a couple of turns to starboard to bring her back. I was in a lather of sweat, pretty exhausted, very discouraged and, I felt, near to tears as well. For some

---

55 The donkey-man looked after and operated machinery and engines on the decks of sailing ships.

time the Mate had been standing gazing not forward or to windward, as I thought he ought to, but astern. I couldn't think why. I thought I would find out and greatly daring, peeped round the side of the wheel-house and looked out aft, along our wake. The wake was clearly demarcated in the autumn sea-glow and sky-glow from its disturbed water. It delineated a graceful zig-zag and was the worst tell tale a bad helmsman ever needed for his recommendation. The Mate came out of contemplating my handi-work and came over.[56]

Later Frank drescribes cleaning the heads, one of the many dirty jobs assigned to the apprentices:

The heads were two very primitive cubicles on the port side under the fo'c's'l-head. They were designed with divine simplicity on the principle simply of two cones with pipes at the bottom that let out over the ship's side. The only trouble was that the pipes had never been conceived as accommodating the Homeric Nordic stools deposited there by our Scan-dinavian sailors and as a result were permanently blocked. A curved iron rod, almost six feet long, had been forged by the donkey-men to unseal these stoppages. You plunged the rod into the mouth of the cone and even-tually found the pipe vent at the bottom. Then you worked it up and down like mad to the accompaniment of a very sinister sucking noise from the conglomerate excreta. If you were unwise you poured down a bucket of water. This simply squirted back into your face. Success was achieved by main force and no refinements. As the whole thing was of solid Swedish iron and must have been designed and made in an era before they discovered these sorts of uses for porcelain, you could give it the hell of a whacking. In rough weather a really good sea was just able to make the outside of the vent pipes which it entered with terrific gurgling force and roar, splattering the contents all over the place. One these occasions the crew preferred to remain constipated.[57]

---

56 *In Deep*, p. 65.
57 *In Deep*, pp. 69-70.

Frank could be at different times matter-of-fact and lyrical. Here he describes the first time he is sent aloft to clear the main upper t'gallant bunt-lines:

As I went up I became more than ever aware of penetrating into a densely populated area where, on the higher levels, life became for the inhabitants more attenuated perhaps but certainly fiercer. It was subjected to keener draughts of competition, tensions more intense. The evidence of occupation which from on deck and in the lower rigging were but a murmur as of highly civilized communities living in integrated cohesion with each other, muted and gentle, here had a strain of hysteria. It was like a sort of inverted underworld where ruled the knife, the razor and the broken bottle. And above the crosstrees lurked sinister entities, dealing out death. Once or twice, when I was tempted to look down, I was overcome with vertigo. The pressure on the wind of the body had increased and was inclined to pluck at clothes with an aggressive and resentful hand like a half-intimidated mob with the intention of lynching you yet lacks the courage to do so. But there was no mistaking its intent: there was no getting away from the presence of the wind. It had body, was solid ...

I reached the crosstrees and without pausing a moment to look around me or to take stock of my position, plunged into the t'gallant shrouds. I had not been in them a second before I realised that they were everything the Admiral had said. After the massive stability of the tubular steel topmasts and lowerm'sts it was with absolute terror one projected oneself on to the t'gallant mast to feel it whip and quibble. The t'gallant mast was a spar of massive Oregon stepped into the topmast below the crosstrees through steel rings. I couldn't make out where it was secured and in examining it I suddenly became aware I was gazing down a mast that bent and whipped like a hazel.[58]

---

58   *In Deep*, pp. 74-5.

Frank survived his blooding on the rigging, but only after being swivelled upside down some 160 feet above deck, and when he came down the Mate had angry words for him. He had taken too long.

In Frank's narrative, they had to tack from coast to coast to clear the Channel and then they ran into a great storm as they battled round Ushant, the rocky island off the western point of Brittany. The ferocious storm threw everything at them, including a near-fatal knockdown:

> The ship fell on her beam-ends about seven o'clock in the morning of 12 October. She inclined to an angle of about sixty degrees, dipped her courses, and sent every loose bit of gear tumbling into the scuppers. She remained in this position for about seven minutes and it was touch-and-go whether she would not go right over.[59]

The *Lawhill* did in fact run into a big storm on this voyage. But Frank was probably exaggerating when he described a sixty degree heel. Ships such as the *Lawhill* frequently heeled to forty five degrees (enough to dip their lower shrouds into the water), and survived, provided their cargo or ballast did not shift.

Frank certainly used his imagination, or rather borrowed from an episode on another voyage, when he describes the ritual ceremony performed by Neptune to mark the crossing of the line at the Equator. Young Moses was chased up the rigging and then fell to his death. A young apprentice was killed in just such an accident on a subsequent voyage.

But the bulk of the voyage was based on what actually happened to Frank: lazy days in the Horse Latitudes when they ghosted through light winds and the apprentices were sent into the holds to chip the rust; balmy nights on deck with sailors swapping tales and singing shanties; and the excitement of landfall in the Spencer Gulf.

It took a long time for these sailing boats to dump their ballast, or

---

59   *In Deep*, p. 89.

most of it, and then load up with grain at one of the jetties in the gulf. The grain was carried on in sacks and, as the holds filled, the remaining ballast could be dumped. It was a slow process. They took on their grain at Wallaroo, a one-horse port, where the crews of the *Lawhill* and other grains ships ran riot – apparently with the enthusiastic approval of the locals.

Frank, still a virgin, says that he fell in love with the daughter of the local hotel, the *Cornucopia*, a magnificent two-storey hotel, with open verandas, which is still the town's main social hub, and this is where the account of his first sea voyage ends:

> It's perfectly marvellous to have been fighting, to be seamen, to be drunk, to have watched horses race streets in sunlight, to go up to the *Cornucopia*.

> We sail in a week.[60]

The voyage to Australia had made a sailor out of a schoolboy.

---

60   *In Deep*, p. 222.

FOUR
APPROACH OF WAR

FRANK WAS TEMPTED TO JUMP SHIP IN AUSTRALIA, but he remembered a promise he had made to his Uncle Hubert and sailed back to England. There is no record of whether the *Lawhill* returned east, via Cape Horn, or west the way she had come, via the Cape of Good Hope, but Frank's name is inscribed among 'Cape Horners' in her crew list preserved in the Maritime Museum at Ålands, the *Lawhill*'s home port. In any case the *Lawhill* arrived back in Falmouth on 23 June 1935. For Frank it must have been a bitter-sweet moment to drop anchor there, so close to his lost world of Trenoweth, which had by then been sold. But Frank was now a grown man, sea-hardened, and ready for more adventure.

The widowed Lady Baines was living in Combroke: she had returned to her childhood village in Warwickshire to live with her parents. As the only child, Frank must have struggled with his conscience about what to do next, but in the event he spent only a few weeks with his mother before the call of the sea took him off again. In September 1935, he signed up to join the *Discovery II*, a royal research ship which carried out scientific and marine surveys in the Southern Seas around the British Antarctic Territories and which was then berthed in St Katherine's Dock by the Tower of London. But something untoward must have taken place, because by the time she actually sailed, on 1 October, Frank had signed off.

Lean times followed. Frank had recently turned 20 and just as his friends and contemporaries from school were starting out at university, or training to be officers in the armed forces, he found himself marooned back in Combroke with his mother, with no job. Being idle and unemployed was not an option with the Oldhams, and Frank became an estate agent in Warwickshire. It is not clear what work he did, but he spent a season riding with the Warwickshire hounds, crossed paths with the 'beautiful but evil Mrs C', and got himself embroiled with the local aristocracy by laying claim to a non-existent title. Trouble ensued, and he was blackmailed and then rescued by his Uncle Hubert. Frank summarises this period as follows: 'We spent a long summer in Combroke in 1936 but it became impossible, so I went house-hunting in Essex.'[61]

Moving to Essex was almost certainly his Uncle Hubert's suggestion. He and his sisters were well established in Loughton, in the houses designed and built by Sir Frank, and sufficient money had been rescued from the meltdown of Sir Frank's estate to purchase Lady Baines a decent home. Frank himself found a house which had style and elegance: The Cedars in Coggeshall, a small market town between Braintree and Colchester. Lady Baines moved there with Frank in February 1937.

Frank writes: 'My mother thought it was rather a come-down, although quite in keeping with an impoverished widow's status. The Cedars was then only regarded as a glorified villa.'[62] But he is exaggerating both the extent of his mother's social downfall and indeed the implication that she had that far to fall. She was in fact moving into one of the finest residences in Coggeshall, a Regency house in a walled garden with a *belvedere* rising above its slate roof. In any case she had of course come from a distinctly modest background, as had her late husband. However, Frank continues in the same vein:

Moving to Essex was naturally an admission of failure, for although the county was crammed with an incredible assortment of idiosyncratic

---

61 A biographical note Frank wrote for his literary agent, Paul Scott, dated 21 August 1956, in the David Higham archive at the Harry Ransom Center, University of Texas.

62 *A Memoir Concerning The Cedars* written by Frank in 1986 (in possession of the author).

squirearchy, the departure from Liverpool Street Station was not considered at all fashionable and the passage through the smoking chimneys of the East End was not thought to be very nice either. The train stopped for a considerable time at Harold Wood, where they coupled on a second engine to get it up the Brentwood Bank, and when you got down at Kelvedon it was like descending at the end of the world.

By moving to The Cedars, Mother had steeled herself to adapting to a sort of lower-class kind of life. She considered the house to be the very minimum requirement consonant with any sort of social respectability, and really only appropriate to small-time doctors or curates.

Mother arrived by train with 23 railway wagon-loads of possessions. These consisted of 19 wagon-loads of furniture and household accoutrements, four wagon-loads of shrubs and plants, 20 chickens, three geese and one horse. This created quite a sensation.

I mounted the horse and rode into Coggeshall.

Thus Frank entered the town as he would live in it – in some style. Coggeshall was to be his home base, albeit with long furloughs abroad, for the remainder of his life, and, until her death in 1963, was his mother's home: 'Mother possessed £800 a year, and settled down at The Cedars to genteel poverty with two maids and a gardener, and managed very well.'

Writing in *Officer Boy* some three decades later, Frank describes the period that followed as 'my locust years of semi-delinquency', from which he was saved only by the outbreak of World War II:

So it would be small wonder if, frequently having found myself in desperate straits, I should seek, as has every respectable nihilist, to pull the pillars of the house down on top of me in the hope of perishing among the ruins.

Such an attitude is sufficient, without further elaboration, to explain the futility of my achievements during this period, which reads like the catalogue of the crimes of some juvenile delinquent.[63]

In the narrative at the start of *Officer Boy*, Frank reduces his adventures during this period to a few lines:

Managed to be an Able Seaman on a haunted brigantine yacht whose owner died on the voyage round from Hull to participate in the Coronation Review at Spithead ... Tried to set sail for the Seychelles on own yacht and failed. Went on the bum in Cornwall ... Deserted an oil tanker in Montevideo.[64]

In fact a lot happened between his leaving his mother in Coggeshall in the spring of 1937 and his returning there from Montevideo just before Christmas the following year. For much of the time Frank was at sea.

The 'haunted brigantine' was the *Lady of Avenel*, a majestic two-masted wooden square rigger measuring just short of 100 feet, which Frank joined in March 1937. Built in Falmouth in 1874 as a trading vessel, she began her life delivering granite from Cornwall to all parts of the world.

The Lady of Avenel is a character in Sir Walter Scott's novel, *The Monastery*, who pines away in her castle awaiting the return of her husband from the wars. After she dies, her ghost haunts the estate. *The Lady of Avenel* was thus a ghost ship from the moment she was named and, after a life of carrying granite, her decks had a shiny lustre from the dust which added to the sense of her ghostliness.

In 1925 she became a support vessel for a British Arctic expedition, and on her return she was abandoned at Leith in Scotland and left to rot. She was then acquired by Wilfred Dowman, a retired windjammer captain, who also owned the *Cutty Sark*, and a Leeds businessman, Mr F S Jackson, and brought south to Bridlington with a new crew,

---

63 *Officer Boy* (Eyre & Spottiswoode, 1971), p. 9.
64 *Officer Boy*, p. 9.

among them an old Cape Horner, Ernest George Musselwhite, who became her boatswain. *The Lady of Avenel* was given a partial refit in Bridlington and a local carpenter, Alf Wright, was hired to replace all the oak panelling in the saloon. He later confessed that he had felt a woman's presence as he worked, and heard a voice.

The ship, now with its Bridlington crew, headed to Looe in Cornwall, its county of origin, for a major re-fit. On the first night out when the watchman, Tom Hutchinson, lit the oil lamps, they suddenly dimmed and he, too, heard a woman's voice cursing him. He refused to go on board alone ever again.

After the refurbished ship once again entered Bridlington harbour the crew planned a party on board to celebrate. The local men went ashore to see their families, leaving the ship's cook alone in the galley. He heard the light footsteps of a woman up on deck and went to investigate. He found no-one there, but he heard a woman's voice and was so terrified that he left the ship and waited on the south pier for the crew's return.

The legend grew more sinister when George Musselwhite, the Boatswain, fell ill on the very day he started making a model of the ship and died a few days later, aged only 54. The *Lady of Avenel's* co-owner, Wilfred Dowman, also died, in 1936 and the crew were paid off and she was put up for sale. Amy Johnson, the pioneer woman aviator, looked over her but she was eventually purchased by another, though unknown, wealthy lady.

It was at this point that Frank Baines entered the story. Summoned by a friend, Paddy Rust, he signed on as a crew member of the *Lady of Avenel* and was appointed watchman, the job that Hutchinson was doing when he died unexpectedly. Frank joined her in Hull and they set sail to take part in George VI's Coronation Review at Spithead, which was planned for 20 May 1937. But the mystery lady owner died on the short passage, and Frank wrote cryptically about a 'ghostly visitation in the North Sea'.[65]

---

65   The biographical note of 21 August 1956.

The *Lady of Avenel* took part in the Review and was then sailed to Cowes, on the Isle of Wight, where Frank's notes only hint at what happened: 'May blossom; yearning; a madman and a lecherous woman.'

That may well have been a reference to the next woman to be involved with the *Lady of Avenel,* Frances Day – Britain's original blonde bombshell. This flagrantly bi-sexual American-born cabaret dancer, the country's first stage and screen sex symbol, chartered the *Lady of Avenel* for the summer.

Day's wide eyes, sultry lips and swept-back blonde hair turned the heads of men and women alike. At various stages she was the mistress of four royal princes and of the future British Prime Minister Anthony Eden. She also inspired the passionate admiration of America's bi-sexual First Lady, Eleanor Roosevelt, as well as tantalising George Bernard Shaw, who wrote one of his last plays for her.

'We sail for Deauville with a cargo of film stars,' Frank, the Watchman, wrote.[66]

Known as the Lady of the French Coast, Deauville was a famed and fashionable playground in the 1930s, favoured by the French and English alike for its casino, horse racing, golf and beaches.

'Love in Deauville,' Frank continues. 'The Tigress Mother. Hot weather stimulates sex. I get drunk and dance a hornpipe over Frances Day's head. Passage of arms with John Mills.'[67] Then an up-and-coming film and stage actor, who went on to a successful film career and was knighted in 1976, Mills had starred with Day, and he left an alluring account of the diva:

> She was what in those days one called a knock-out. She was small with blonde hair and so well endowed up front that, frankly, to put it in Army terms, she sported the largest pair of 'Bristols' it has ever been my pleasure to set eyes upon.[68]

---

66 The biographical note of 21 August 1956.
67 The biographical note of 21 August 1956.
68 Frances Day's star-studded career went into decline after WWII and she eventually retired, changed her name, and died in obscurity aged 75 in April 1984.

She was devastatingly attractive, and I discovered later on, when I was in a show with her that the men in the audience simply couldn't take their eyes off her ... Men adored her, but women disliked her – she became a permanent threat to their happy marriages from the moment the curtain went up.[69]

Mills recorded that on the passage over to Deauville, Day was the only member of her small party with sea legs sufficient to enjoy their roast pork lunch in a Force Eight Gale. The group included another British actor, Anthony Pélissier, and the lawyer and racehorse owner, Isidore Kerman:

The rest of the short holiday was so marvellous that the few hours of torture were soon forgotten. We swam, sunbathed and gambled. The voyage home too was perfect. The Channel behaved itself; I fell in love with boats and the sea.[70]

Back in England Frank signed off the *Lady of Avenel* and met up with another old seadog, Captain Cornell, with whom he bought a share in a sailing boat, the *Fair Maid*, with plans to sail her to the Seychelles. But they nearly came to grief on a trial run when they almost wrecked her, and the voyage never happened.[71]

At the end of 1937, Frank spent his first Christmas in Coggeshall with his mother at The Cedars, and not long afterwards he was off to sea again. This time he teamed up with a young American sailor, Dwight Long, who was on the home leg of a circumnavigation on his 32-foot ketch *Idle Hour*. Long sailed up the Thames to London, where he spent the winter moored in St Katherine's Dock while he travelled around Britain on a lecture tour and wrote a book – *Seven Seas on a Shoestring* – about the voyage which would make him the youngest sailor at the

---

69   *Up in the Clouds, Gentlemen Please* (Weidenfeld & Nicolson, 1980), John Mills's autobiography, pp. 37 & 134.
70   *Up in the Clouds*, p. 134.
71   *The Lady Avenel* ended her days in Poole where she was abandoned and scuttled in 1939. There is no record of the *Fair Maid*.

time to circumnavigate the globe. Frank joined the *Idle Hour,* recording that it was 'more by luck than good management' that he successfully helped sail her to Torquay, ready for her final push across the Atlantic.[72]

He was back in Cornwall and it was summer, and he 'went on the bum' until he was rescued and befriended by Trenoweth's new owner. He called the visit to his father's old home 'embarrassing', but gave no further details. A few weeks later, he joined the *San Gaspar* oil tanker at Falmouth and headed for South America. The *San Gaspar* was a British-owned 13,000-tonne single funnel ship, with an accommodation block a quarter of the way back from the bows which made her look uncommonly ugly. She was certainly not the sleekest ship that Frank ever sailed on, nor the happiest; and he appears not to have enjoyed being on her.[73]

They fetched up in Curaçao in the Dutch Antilles, a major oil and refinery port, and then coasted down South America to Montevideo, the capital of Uruguay. Here Frank jumped ship, recording: 'I discover what I have let myself in for. I desert.'[74]

Frank spent three months 'on the run' in Uruguay, a period he summarised briefly in *Officer Boy*: 'Was imprisoned in Tacuarembó (up-country Uruguay); gave myself up for dead and buried; descended into hell! And was rescued in the third month by a visiting commissioner to whom I pleaded that I was a journalist. And fled back to Montevideo riding on the undercarriage of a Paraguayan Rail sleeping-car from Asunción.'[75]

What Frank writes is generally true or at least based on what happened. Allowing for the distortions of memory over time and for his instinctive tendency to dramatise, Frank always strives to be factually correct; and when he departs from the facts or exaggerates stories for effect, or changes names to avoid upsetting or libelling people, he is

---

72   The biographical note of 21 August 1956
73   Built in Tyneside in 1921, she survived a torpedo attack off Trinidad during World War II and was broken up in Osaka in 1954.
74   The biographical note of 21 August 1956.
75   *Officer Boy*, p. 9.

invariably honest and signals what he is doing. His description of those months on the loose in Uruguay is therefore, while incomplete, almost certainly truthful.

Back in Montevideo after his hobo-style train ride Frank was by now truly down and out. 'On the beach in Monte,' he writes in the brief biographical notes he prepared for his publisher many years later. 'I sleep in the town drains.'[76]

Frank appears to have thrown himself on the mercy of the British Consul, but not without a struggle. 'My last ice-cream and the British Consul,' his notes continue. 'On the mat in the Consulate, I refuse repatriation. Tears, despair and the last letter home in an ornate salon. Tea at the Seamen's Mission.'

As he records in *Officer Boy*, the Seamen's Mission was his salvation. It was patronised by the wife of the British Minister, Lady Effie Millington-Drake:

> Lady Effie (the ship-owner, Lord Inchcape's daughter, and much loved by seamen to whom she devoted a large part of her fortune) had all the ships' crews frequently to tea at her Seaman's Mission and tried to calm things down with huge helpings of fresh fruit salad.[77]

Largely through Lady Effie's influence, the British Consul found Frank a berth on a cargo ship, the *SS Harbury*, which was bound for London.[78]

Before they left Montevideo, Frank took part in some riotous assembly, carousing with the crews of HMS *Exeter* and *Ajax* at the height of the Munich crisis while the German pocket-battleship *Graf Spee* lurked threateningly over the horizon, and assisting a group of drunken sailors sing their way out of jail with a passionate rendition of the *Marseillaise*.

---

76 The biographical note of 21 August 1956.
77 *Officer Boy*, p. 10.
78 Owned by Harrisons, she was sunk by a German U-Boat on a convoy to Canada in 1943.

Frank's ship plied across the River Plate, through a *Pampero* storm, and then up-river to load cargo at the Argentine port of Rosario, before heading back out to the South Atlantic and home.

'Shadows of War,' Frank's biographical note continues, 'echoes of Munich. Dark thoughts at night. We sail finally for Europe. It is December 1938.'[79]

His account in *Officer Boy* is fuller:

As I did not want to spend all the war years in some terrible sardine-can as a sitting target for torpedoes, I left the sea when I got home, forever. I have never been back ...

I got back to England just in time for Christmas (1938). I spent it with my mother at Coggeshall in Essex.

The winter seemed to have arrived there early that year, for I remember all the ponds were frozen over and we went skating at the Abbey. Afterwards my mother provided a roast-goose lunch for us at The Cedars, where an exceptionally plump spider descended from the sculpted ceiling and hung, spinning its threat, immediately in front of the nose of Elizabeth Everard.[80]

On Christmas Eve, we all went carol singing with, among others in the village less noteworthy, Phyllis Wood,[81] who even then showed symptoms of becoming excessively respectable, so much so, she pretended to be shocked that I had tanked up with a bottle of gin, although of course she did not refuse any when offered.[82]

In the New Year Frank secured employment with the help of his mother, as a Conservative party agent. This was not as implausible as

---

79   The biographical note of 21 August 1956.
80   The Everards were at the time the owners of Coggeshall Abbey.
81   A local worthy who became chairman of Coggeshall Parish Council and was awarded an OBE.
82   *Officer Boy*, pp. 17-18.

it might appear. Despite his time below decks at sea, he was still very much part of the Establishment, the promising son of a respected county lady. He was recruited through the Junior Imperial League and started off with three months' unpaid work in Witham, which he described as 'a piece of sheer hell', and then transferred to a paid post in Wimbledon. The outbreak of war in September 1939 saved him by his own admission from being caught with his fingers in the till. He made a hurried exit from Wimbledon and returned to Coggeshall intent on enlisting.

FIVE

SOLDIER

FRANK WRITES IN *Officer Boy* OF HIS RESPONSE to the call to arms:

> Never one to relish just kicking my heels in Coggeshall, however, I was
> now consumed with cankerous impatience. Competition to get oneself
> into the armed forces was terrific! I made use of every gambit I knew, even
> to importuning my relatives to use their influence. The newspapers were
> full of notices instructing applicants to await their call-up papers, so
> naturally the only thing that never entered my head was the simple expedient
> of applying at the local recruiting office.[83]

It was the girl next door who finally propelled Frank into action.
She accosted him on the doorstep of The Cedars and declared her love:

> I sought refuge from her in the arms of the Colchester Recruiting Office
> which received me very generously. It was a gloomy building in a back-
> street, redolent of what have since become identifiable as National Assistance
> odours, or Social Security smells; the sort of stale, male, genital effluvia
> barely kept in abeyance by socks, soap and cigarette smoke and various
> secretions between the floor boards.

---

83 *Officer Boy*, p. 31.

By evening – although it was not a felicitous choice – I was in Clacton, enlisted as a gunner in what must have been the least glamorous Anti-Aircraft Battery in East Anglia.[84]

Frank joined up on 27 November 1939, recording his occupation on his enlistment papers as 'clerk' and describing his complexion as 'fresh'.[85] A few days later he was despatched to a Royal Artillery unit in Harwich where he found himself defending Parkeston Quay, which guards the harbour at the mouth of the River Stour. He was highly disdainful of the officers in command of his unit:

It had been formed on the eve of the outbreak of war by a bunch of upper-crust Clactonians on the basis of a sort of feudal levy. The upper echelons of the local gentry had all been its original officers. [Almost all] the founding fathers had long since fled, and indeed not long after its foundation the battery was heavily adulterated by an influx of the more pretentious sort of Clacton trader.[86]

The Sergeant-Major in charge of the unit was so unpopular 'that it would have been a grave risk for him to have gone into action'.[87]

Frank's first experience of war was semi-comic. Two enemy Heinkels landed in the sea in front of the battery to lay mines off Harwich, but it turned out that the guns guarding the entrance to the estuary could not depress low enough to fire at them because they had been sandbagged high to shoot at airborne aircraft.

Shortly afterwards, Frank's battery was transferred to Martlesham aerodrome where soon enough he had his first taste of action.[88]

The airfield on Martlesham Heath, just east of Ipswich, was a bomber base and during the war it was to play host not only to Frank

---

84 *Officer Boy*, p. 32.
85 Service records, supplied by the Army Personnel Centre.
86 *Officer Boy*, p. 33.
87 *Officer Boy*, p. 34.
88 While many of the original buildings remain, dotted about the area, much of the site was re-built as British Telecom's research and development centre.

but also to – among others – Ian Smith, who was to become Prime Minister of Rhodesia (now Zimbabwe) and unilaterally declare its independence in 1965; Group Captain Peter Townsend, the future lover of Princess Margaret; and World War II flying ace Squadron Leader Douglas Bader, subject of the film *Reach for the Sky*.

Frank, in his lowly gun battery on the perimeter of the airfield, would have had no contact with air crews. However he did fire his Lewis gun at some enemy aircraft on 15 August 1940, at the height of the Battle of Britain, when the airbase was attacked in broad daylight by German bombers and a squadron of 'little wasp-like' JU87 dive-bombers:

> The actual action was short-lived but, while it lasted, it was undeniably exciting. It was like an enormously blown-up grouse shoot.
>
> In the first place, Martlesham Heath is by no means dissimilar to what I imagine a grouse moor might be like. Then, the Lewis gun-posts with their small, camouflaged, sand-bagged emplacements are exactly similar to what one has seen illustrated in the papers, namely a sort of hide, when Harold Macmillan use to go shooting with the Duke of Devonshire.[89]

The bombers targeted the aerodrome, while the Junkers attacked the gun placements on the perimeters, making repeated diving passes. Then Frank opened fire:

> I surrendered myself to the spirit of this shooting and was soon surrounded with spent cartridges in my enthusiasm for the sport.[90]

The action intensified, and the Junkers lined up to strafe and bomb Frank's position. He kept firing, with his loader, Eric, working calmly at his side, until a bomb dropped nearby:

---

89 *Officer Boy*, p. 40.
90 *Officer Boy*, pp. 45-6.

The next minute the floor of the emplacement heaved, the sandbagged wall caved outwards, carrying us with it; and we found ourselves sprawled out into the open, completely exposed. The sensation was like being stripped naked ...

'Come on!' screeched Eric, without giving me time to get my breath back, 'here's another!' and we scrambled to the gun, still secure on its mountings, however, and pointing to heaven like an admonitory finger in an attitude of prayer, as if metal wouldn't melt in its mouth. While Eric clamped on another magazine, I started to level it at the succeeding Junkers which were marshalling in the sky for a second battle.

Altogether we survived three such attacks, but I do not think I could have stood another ... My legs ... doubled under me from the effects of sheer terror.[91]

According to the Martlesham Operations Record Book, the bombardment left two craters on the aerodrome, and wrecked the guardroom and stores and damaged other buildings; and a loaded bomber exploded close to the watch tower, taking out two hangars. Some of the gun emplacements were also blown out. There were seven casualties but miraculously no fatalities.

The official report on the attack also noted that the vegetable garden was partly smothered in debris, 'much to the distress of Squadron Leader Brice ... There was no panic although naturally everyone was badly scared.'[92]

Frank served as a gunner on the home front for just over a year and in late 1940, encouraged by a new commanding officer and sickened by soldiering in the ranks, he put in for a commission and was accepted for Officer Cadet Training in India – a move that was to transform his life. For the next 15 years India was to become his second home.

---

91 *Officer Boy*, p. 49.
92 Archives of Martlesham Heath Aviation Society.

Considerable preparations were needed, as he records in *Officer Boy*:[93]

> There was a huge list of equipment one was expected to take, which certainly included saddlery and may even have comprised polo sticks. Consequently I purchased in Coggeshall from Mr Birkin, our builder, a black-painted wooden blanket-box twice as roomy but just about the same shape as a coffin, especially to accommodate my boots and my saddles and bridles and my riding paraphernalia ... I was determined on cutting a dash with all this gear and impressing anyone open to conviction. My year of bottom-rank living had left me with delusions of frustrated grandeur, for which only the glamour of India would be able to compensate.[94]

Frank was shipped out to India with a pack of fellow officer cadets in January 1941, initially as far as Durban in considerable discomfort in the holds on an old meat carrier the *Highland Chieftain* – a steamship he had first encountered on the River Plate:

> It was like living in a great, pullulating dormitory full of puppies. As they romped, they sulked, they played, they quarrelled, they fought, they fed, they farted and finally they exuded that fulminating milky smell of young dog, so these youths exuded their own potent, stinging, eye-watering, acid stench like a particularly potent French dressing.[95]

The young cadets' lives were transformed on the last leg across the Indian Ocean: they completed the voyage in the comparative luxury of cabins on a passenger liner, the *Winchester Castle*. Frank saw the upgrade as a symbolic rite of passage in his transition from sailor to gentleman officer, and also as a statement about the British in India. A consignment of ragamuffins emerging from below decks would have struck an irrevocable blow at the British image!

---

93 *Officer Boy*, p. 51.
94 Birkin & Sons was still in business in 2010 as a building firm and also as Coggeshall's undertakers.
95 *Officer Boy*, p. 53.

We disembarked in Bombay on 3 March 1941, and went direct to the railway station. There our new role was demonstrated from the very outset by the slavish subservience directed towards us by the railway coolies and the carriage sweepers, one of whom immediately came forward and, without giving me a moment's respite, promptly informed me in broken English that I was a prince! [96]

They were despatched for officer training to Deolali, about 100 miles north-east of Bombay. This was an artillery school next door to a military sanatorium, which has come down in history as the origin of the expression 'to go Doolally'.

While evidently impressed, indeed at times overwhelmed, by the glamour of India, Frank was never duped by it, nor was he taken in by the British Raj:

The chief fault, according to my estimation, was that the British Raj was almost too good to be true. It was too like a plastic copy ... a pure parody ... Aldwych-farce-cum-country-house-party.[97]

Nor did he under-estimate the degree to which the British were hated and despised:

It was not possible at that time, for instance, to enter bazaars anywhere in the Orient, let alone India where British prestige had reached its nadir, without becoming aware of pair after pair of hostile eyes observing you, exploring your vulnerable places, boring incisively into your vitals.[98]

Frank would also come to see through the imperial veneer and appreciate the fragility of Britain's hold on its Asian colonies:

India, Burma, and Malaya were over-ripe fruits – imperial loot. They would

---

96 *Officer Boy*, p. 55.
97 *Officer Boy*, pp. 72-3.
98 *Officer Boy*, p. 142.

fall to anybody for the picking. All the more credit, then, to the Japanese for discovering this.[99]

Officer Boy relates Frank's training as an artillery officer and how he managed to pass out with a commission even after 'firing' on his own troops in his theoretical practice barrage. He was commissioned on 1 August 1941 as Second Lieutenant in the 21st Mountain Regiment and he joined its 6th Mountain Battery, a unit which was known as Jacobs. Frank was immediately posted to the Pathan tribal country in what was then the North-West Frontier with Afghanistan, an outpost of the Empire and an area seething with unrest. He writes that 'the tribes of Waziristan were stirring restlessly'.[100] In fact this fiercely independent region has been repelling outsiders for centuries – it is the local industry – and little has changed since Frank's time there: Waziristan is now the Taliban stronghold in Pakistan.

The tribes of Waziristan had been in a state of open rebellion against the British since an unfortunate incident in 1937 when the local Resident mounted an armed operation to rescue a Hindu girl who had been kidnapped by Pathans, converted to Islam, married a local boy and became pregnant with his child. She had taken the name of Islam Bibi, and when she was plucked, or 'rescued' from their midst, the tribesmen responded with fury to what they regarded as an unforgivable insult; and one of their religious leaders Mirza Ali Khan, who was known as the Fakir of Ipi, declared a Jihad against the British.

By the time Frank arrived in August 1941, the Fakir had acquired mythological status. Frank described him as a crossbreed of the German World War I Red Baron and Robin Hood. He was still fighting in the hills when he died in 1960.

Frank was plunged instantly into the cat-and-mouse war against Ipi's tribal warriors. Everything was astir, and Ipi had developed a huge cannon – a manly symbol of his defiance of the British, and the equivalent

---

99 *Officer Boy*, p. 56.
100 *Officer Boy*, p. 143.

of a modern-day 'weapon of mass destruction' – which had been firing nightly into the heart of the cantonment in the British garrison at Razmak.[101]

Frank took part in a major offensive against Ipi, and on 13 September 1941, just a few days before his twenty-sixth birthday, he went into action commanding a mountain battery in the nearby hills close to the Afghanistan border.

Despite some unorthodox artillery ranging from a hilltop, but not before Frank himself had had a taste of being bombarded by Ipi's cannon, his unit fired on a camel transporting the suspected weapon across the plain through an unseen gully below them and succeeded in putting the big gun out of action:

> It all sounds, I know, too like the autobiography of *Benvenuto Cellini*. But it was true. Ipi's cannon never fired again![102]

Frank makes a telling observation about fighting in Waziristan, as true today as then:

> [We] confronted the unpleasant truth about the task before us, that is of unreconnoitred country about which nobody seemed to know anything, not even our commanders, and that it was going to be one of those hardly won, difficult to force, infantry jobs, winkling out little pockets of resistance and enemy pickets, in terrain which told heavily in favour of the defenders.[103]

And he was under no illusions about the fate that awaited any soldier who fell into enemy hands:

> If you got captured, you were not only killed in a lively and imaginative manner, you were carved up and quartered and had your cock cut off and stuffed in your mouth, for good measure.[104]

---

101 Today in north-west Pakistan, close to the border with Afghanistan.
102 *Officer Boy*, p. 175.
103 *Officer Boy*, p. 193.
104 *Officer Boy*, p. 145.

A few days later Frank found himself on the front line in a rocky defile by a tributary of the Tochi River giving close artillery support in an attack on a Pathan stronghold by Gurkhas, and he saw for the first time the reality of war on the ground:

> There is something indefinably majestic in watching a detachment of infantry setting out to capture an objective. It is one of those rare sights which in the modern world are at a premium, like the glimpse of hounds in full cry, with breast-high scent, roaring down a slope, or the glorious departure of sailing ships.[105]

Soon after, and while advancing as the operation's forward-post-observation officer, Frank came under enemy fire and had his first experience of death on the battlefield:

> Our pickets had been impetuously stabbed, most of them had been knifed in the spleen from the back, and from some of their wounds, extruding the gap of the knife-cuts, ballooned a lobe of their liver ...We had emerged into the clarity of sunlight and the freer atmosphere of this miniature upland enclosure to be greeted by that rudest of all shocks to those not inured to war, namely a realisation of a slaughter having taken place and human blood having being spilt, among scenes of exalted natural grandeur.[106]

The battle ended with Frank's unit bringing up their gun and Frank efficiently and coolly directing fire at a strategic Pathan redoubt – the Tower of Mianzali – and destroying it.

He concludes:

> One has to admit, after all, they do make a solider of you on the North-West Frontier. And what does it matter if, for the sake of realism, a few sepoys or some benighted Pathans get bumped off in the process?[107]

---

105 *Officer Boy*, p. 186.
106 *Officer Boy*, p. 199.
107 *Officer Boy*, p. 207.

But for all that, *Officer Boy* is not just a soldier's tale; it is also a delicate record of a young man seeking and finding his pleasure – of physical encounters in a sensuous and libidinous land. It is a fitting prelude to what came next.

SIX
LOVE AFFAIR WITH THE CHINDITS

FRANK LEFT HIS MOUNTAIN BATTERY IN MARCH 1942 – many of those who stayed with his unit later perished in the Battle of Kohima[108] – and he was sent on a Camouflage Course to the Army School at Kirkee near Poona. Frank excelled there and was promoted to the rank of Captain, and after completing the course, he was invited to stay on as an instructor, lecturing on the arts of concealment and deception in the field to young Indian cadets in the Urdu language. This was the first such vernacular course in the Indian army, and a harbinger of the way the army would develop after independence. Camouflage seems oddly appropriate for a man who was himself to appear in so many different guises; and fittingly it was in Kirkee that Frank started to explore a new dimension, which over time would lead him to assume a new identity. By now fluent in both Urdu and Hindi, he had begun to read widely from ancient Hindu and Buddhist religious texts and took up Hatha Yoga – the physical exercise practised by yogis before meditation:

My researches at the Camouflage School among Hindu and Buddhist systems alike indicated to me that my entirely European-based education

---

108 Fought around the town of Kohima in north-east India from April to June 1944, the Battle of Kohima was a turning point which thwarted the Japanese plan to invade India.

71

was dangerously out of proportion and imbalanced. My European-orien-
tated philosophical system was in ruins.[109]

But he also thirsted for action, and, largely as a result of his own
clever scheming, in June the following year (1943) he wangled a transfer
to 111 Brigade, which was to become part of General Orde Wingate's
crack force of Chindits.[110] Based on information that he gathered
through his social network, Frank wrote a report for the Army's High
Command outlining his plan to take on the Japanese in Burma with
unconventional warfare — the first time that he put his pen to work
for him. As a result, Frank was seconded to Brigade Headquarters as
Staff Officer, Grade III (Camouflage) with the rank of Staff Captain,
and thus embarked on one of the defining experiences of his life.

By that time, General Wingate had achieved fame leading a Long
Range Penetration expedition behind Japanese lines deep inside Burma
and demonstrating that the British — reeling from a string of humiliating
defeats across Asia — could indeed fight the Japanese in the jungle. The
military achievements of the Chindits in their first sally into Burma
remain questionable — Wingate lost one third of his men — but the propaganda effect was electrifying. Winston Churchill, an ardent proponent
of commando operations, recognised this, and was all the more prepared
to overlook Wingate's very evident eccentricities. For instance, the
Chindit leader often wore an alarm clock around his wrist, which
would go off at times, and a raw onion on a string around his neck,
which he would occasionally bite into as a snack. He liked eating boiled
python. He would also go about without clothing. Lord Moran,
Churchill's personal physician wrote in his diaries that Wingate 'seemed
to me hardly sane — in medical jargon a borderline case'.

Frank talked of his 'love affair with the Chindits', and for rest of

---

109 An abandoned draft of an account of his time at Kirkee and subsequent attachment to the
Chindits (Random House archives).
110 There is disagreement about how the Chindits acquired their *nomme de guerre*. Some believe
it is from a corruption of the name for the mythical Burmese lion, the *chinthe*, others that
it was after a figure of Hindu mythology, others after the Burmese word for griffin.

his life he was obsessed, overwhelmed and traumatised by his experiences fighting with this unorthodox force behind enemy lines. He saw himself essentially as an amateur among hardened professionals, but he acquitted himself bravely and shared all the ghastliness of the five-month campaign. He also behaved in an unorthodox way: he fell in love with one of his Gurkha riflemen. Frank told his Chindit story in a book which he started 25 years after the war and which, though re-written, remained unpublished when he died.[111] The account of his service with 111 Brigade is at times lyrical, and it records Frank's love affair with his orderly, but it is factual and brutally honest. Its most obvious omission is the story, told by others, of Frank's own courage, cheerfulness, and readiness to face the enemy.

Their mission was an unenviable one:

111 Brigade's role had been presented to me in the light of a suicide mission. The object of training was to have us ready for action by November 1943. We were then to march unobtrusively through the Japanese front lines and, by avoiding engagements, penetrate into the heart of enemy-occupied Burma. There we were to blow up bridges, demolish railway stations, liquidate ammunition trains, ambush commissariat columns, in such a way that we would create maximum confusion.[112]

Frank reported for duty at the Brigade's jungle training camp near Lalitpur in Central India. The Brigade had little use for him as a camouflage expert, but they took him on initially as the Animal Transport Officer and then permanently as Orderly Officer commanding Brigade Headquarters defence platoons. He was given command of two platoons, each of 50 Gurkha riflemen, and it was leading them that Frank went to war in Burma. They were mostly little more than boys, but they were brave soldiers. One of them, Dal Bahadur, who was probably only 16

---

111 *Prisoners of Hope* was the title Frank gave to his account of his time with the Chindits, published as *Chindit Affair* (Pen & Sword, 2011). The original typescript is in the possession of Dan Sansom of Coggeshall.

112 *Chindit Affair*, p. 1.

at the time, became Frank's orderly, and Frank fell in love with him.

Frank served under Major Jack Masters, an extraordinarily able and aggressive officer with a brilliant but chequered career and a searing intellect, who was to be in the thick of some of the bloodiest fighting. After the war, as John Masters, he became a best-selling author, writing more than 20 novels, including *Bhowani Junction*, and a number of autobiographical works of which one of the most celebrated is *The Road Past Mandalay* – which includes his own account of his Chindit campaign.

Born in Calcutta in 1914 and schooled at Wellington College and trained at Sandhurst, Masters came from a long line of Indian Army officers and public servants; and, although he did not know it until much later in his life, he was part Indian. Following service on the North-West Frontier, he saw action as a young adjutant with his Gurkha regiment, the 4th Prince of Wales, in three countries in the early stages of the Second World War – in Syria, Iraq and Iran – and he was then posted to Staff College at Quetta, where he fell in love with Barbara Rose, the wife of one of his fellow officers. To have become involved in a divorce in the socially up-tight British Raj would have meant Masters resigning his commission. The couple took furtive holidays together, and finally Barbara left her husband and bore Masters a child out of wedlock, all stirring minor scandal. It was when she was pregnant with their child that Masters was posted as Major to 111 Brigade, where Frank describes him as follows:

> Already, for so young a man, deep speculation and profound thought (for it never occurred to me at the time that his haggard look might have some-thing to do with unhappiness) had furrowed his brow and gouged out the eye-holes. From their sockets, challengingly alternating with currents between placidity and ferocity, a pair of opaque, sepia brown eyes gave little away. Currents of placidity and ferocity alternated. Emotive yet inno-cent, his expression evoked the patient ox rather than the volatile satyr – and yet there was something too of the centaur (I am thinking of Cheiron).

Masters looked at the world with a satirical eye, and yet saw it also as his oyster.[113]

Regarding his handlebar moustaches, which developed into unshorn handlebars, Frank found Masters 'inflexibly unhandsome ... He was, with the solitary exception of General Wingate, the most uncompromisingly inelegant regular officer I have ever met.'[114]

The Brigadier, Joe Lentaigne, was 'like a great, gaunt, belligerent, battered vulture':

> He talked with a slight lisp on account of his front teeth having been bashed out while he was leading his battalion during the retreat from Burma. He was full of coltish, middle-aged fun in a galumphing, carthorse kind of way, although neither was he without subtlety. Periodically he would allow himself to surrender to an infectious, boyish sort of high spirits which he was not too pompous to translate into juvenile exploits, for he loved dashing around in jeeps and terrorising junior officers into accepting hair-raising joy rides.[115]

As the Orderly Officer charged with protecting and looking after Brigade Headquarters, Frank's experiences with the Chindits were centred on the Brigade Major, Jack Masters, who was ultimately to be set an impossible mission. Wingate's original plan was to insert his specially trained Brigades into Upper Burma and to harass Japanese communications and threaten the rear of their army by waging guerrilla war. The bulk of his Chindit forces were flown into Burma in early March 1944 in an American-led air armada that was code-named Operation Thursday. But Wingate was killed in a plane crash on 24 March shortly after the start of operations – some continue to believe that it was not an accident – and soon afterwards his plan was abandoned for something far more ambitious. The American Commander in China and Second-

---

113 *Chindit Affair*, p. 6.
114 *Chindit Affair*, p. 7.
115 *Chindit Affair*, p. 10.

in-Command in South-East Asia, General Joseph 'Vinegar Joe' Stilwell, who now effectively took overall command of the Chindits, wanted more help on the ground to support his thrust into Burma from neighbouring China. Stilwell ordered the seizure of a strong-point near the Burma Road, and the lightly armed Chindits were therefore redeployed from what they were originally equipped and trained for – hit and run operations – to dig in and engage with the enemy, far from the front, without big guns and relying entirely on air support. Masters, promoted in the field to command the Brigade in place of Brigadier Joe Lentaigne who was flown out to replace Wingate, was ordered to occupy and hold a strategic area, perversely code-named Blackpool, a low spur rising above the paddies and jungle near Mogaung in northern Burma. It was no holiday. For 17 days and nights, and during the onset of heavy monsoon rains, the Japanese repeatedly attacked and shelled the block, killing two hundred of the defenders, and gradually reducing the redoubt to a sea of bloody mud. When he finally gave the dazed command to withdraw, Masters had also to order the shooting of 19 stretcher-cases too badly wounded to be moved.

They got away from Blackpool into the jungle hills because the Japanese did not pursue them; but that was not the end of the campaign. Masters regrouped his battle-shocked men and was then ordered to take another strategic position in northern Burma, a hill commanding the road and rail approaches to the town of Mogaung, which was known as Point 2171 – an action in which more of his men were killed and wounded.

By the time they quit Burma at the end of July, Masters's original force of 2,200 had been decimated by death, wounding, capture, malnutrition, malaria, dysentery, general sickness, desertion and madness to just 118 fit men: eight British officers, a score of British soldiers and 90 Gurkhas. They had endured and survived five months of the utmost hardship, each losing between 30 and 40 pounds; Frank was one of those eight officers – one of the last men standing in 111 Brigade.

Frank's odyssey with the Chindits began in a somewhat comic fashion, and almost ended before it had really started. He was injured shortly after joining the Brigade: a field radio, tossed from the back of an angry mule, dropped onto his right arm and the wound turned gangrenous. Frank kept himself going for a few weeks during training exercises in the jungle-clad Vindhya Hills on illicit barbiturate pain-killers, but when the wound did not heal he was carted off to hospital where he narrowly escaped having his arm amputated. He was patched up and sent back to the Brigade in time to march to war. Masters, who wrote well of Frank, said he only took him into Burma because he showed guts over his injury. He had told Frank that he would have to make himself useful and prove himself; and in the event Frank won his spurs with the Chindits grappling with a runaway mule.

Frank seems to have impressed both his fellow officers and his men. Richard Rhodes James, the Cipher officer who was with Frank at Brigade HQ through most of the campaign, saw him as a highly unusual and exceptionally entertaining soldier. In *Chindit*, his account of the campaign, Rhodes James wrote: [116]

Perhaps for our future history the most significant event during our month's stay at Gona was the arrival of Frankie Baines.

He came to us for attachment as GIII Camouflage for no particular reason, and so firmly did he attach himself to us that we eventually managed to smuggle him into Burma when no one was looking. He took a delight in running down his own job. 'I came from the camouflage pool,' he would say, 'where the sedge is withered and no birds sing.' His life was a defiance of all convention, from the time that he ran away to sea to the time, when in need of a cheap leave, he dressed up as an Indian and travelled third class to Darjeeling. His Urdu was superb and he almost got away with it. He could pour out words of great eloquence for hours on end ... But he

---

116 Published by John Murray in 1980, *Chindit* is one of only three accounts of the campaign written by officers of 111 Brigade, the others being by Masters and Frank.

was hampered in his speech by no inhibitions, and his frankness about everything, especially his own defects, was at times embarrassing.

He was perhaps the greatest contributor to our fund of story tellers, and even the Brigadier had on occasions to take second place to his rich yarns. A sailor's life does not appear to add refinement, and some of his tales of foreign ports had to be reserved for special occasions when the drink was flowing freely. His outrageous and spontaneous comments were an easy target and Jack Masters, when feeling provocative, used to arouse him to fierce protests over some very trifling matters. Life without Frankie would have been a much duller thing.[117]

The Brigade celebrated Christmas Day 1943 at their training camp with a show put on by a troupe of ENSA entertainers, and with a visit by General Wingate, of whom Frank writes perceptively:

The impression he created was both considerably less than, and at the same time more – infinitely more – than his myth. Initially, I felt inclined to give way to disillusionment. The wildest stories about his looks and his deportment were current. Consequently I felt cheated when he appeared clean-shaven, without his missionary topee, and with no visible sign of the razor-slash across his throat as proof of the assertion that he was an attempted suicide ...

His expression was of a deliberately assumed sternness and implacability which did not ring quite true. Through it, however, two trapped eyes, like holes burnt in a piece of snow, peered with the beseeching intensity of a tortured animal.[118]

Wingate had indeed tried to take his own life by slashing his throat in a Cairo hotel in 1941 after his successful campaign against the Italians in Abyssinia had been criticised. He was a complex and uncon-

---

117 *Chindit*, pp. 23-4.
118 *Chindit Affair*, p. 45.

ventional man, who commanded both intense loyalty and intense loathing. During a parade inspection, he frightened some of the men by telling them bluntly that they should not expect to return. On the eve of their departure, he exhorted his men with an Order of the Day that quoted from Zachariah: 'Betake ye to the stronghold, ye prisoners of hope.'

Frank saw Wingate as a 'myth-maker and magician', but he could not help admiring him:

> By comparison with him, all other commanders appeared as complacent and commonplace as a row of carrots, that is to say, utterly flavourless and without savour ... Wingate was simply more monstrous, as well as a more successful commander, than the rest.[119]

In January 1944, Frank embarked with his men on the long train journey from Central India to Silchar on the Burmese border, where they prepared for war. Rhodes James takes up the story:

> We cropped our hair, actuated I think by the desire for cleanliness and a sense of separation from the past. Frankie Baines, true to his nature, went the whole tonsorial hog and had his head completely shaved, allowing only a small tuft of hair to remain. He had long given up all pretence of being a camouflage officer and had taken over command of the two Gurkha defence platoons, the little men regarding him with awe and wonderment as a sahib who conformed to none of their preconceptions. To the British officers, until they got to know him, he was equally an enigma and he remained unique.[120]

Masters certainly saw his Brigade Orderly Officer as an enigma – at least at the outset – and like a good tactician he probed for Frank's weakness. Who did Frank think he was? In *The Road Past Mandalay*, he introduces Frank as 'an artillery man, and distinctly odd; he wears

---

119 Unpublished account of Chindit service (Random House archives).
120 *Chindit*, p. 36.

a huge opal ring on one finger, later shaves his head in order to look and think like a Gurkha, or perhaps a Burmese – he is not sure.'[121]

Wingate and the top brass made a final inspection of the force, and in early March 1944 111 Brigade – complete with mules and armaments – was flown from Imphal into Burma in a huge airborne armada, codenamed Operation Thursday. Frank landed in enemy territory with his men on the wings of a Dakota snuggled up to his orderly Dal Bahadur together with three mules, tethered in their makeshift stalls in the forward section. He writes of two facets of war:

> Not only did it prove possible to transport 8,000 men and several thousand mules to a spot some 200 miles inside Burma by a sort of magic carpet technique, without the Japanese becoming aware of it – it also proved a poetic experience.[122]

But Frank was not only going to war in a poetic mood; he was also falling in love:

> Take a plane-load of young soldiers. Fly them away on a suicide mission, their destination unfamiliar to them. Melt two of them together emotionally.[123]

III Brigade landed at an improvised airfield codenamed Chowringhee (Calcutta's most fashionable street), east of the Irrawaddy River, which they now had to cross in order to proceed with their military objectives. From here on, and for the next five months, everywhere the Brigades went was by foot and everything they needed in between air drops had to be carried with them.

The river crossing was not a success. The men and their equipment got over on rafts and rubber dinghies, but the majority of the mules simply refused to budge. Frank points out the significance of this:

121 *The Road Past Mandalay* (Michael Joseph, 1961), p. 138.
122 *Chindit Affair*, p. 77.
123 *Chindit Affair*, p. 84.

The immediate prospect was bleak. A column without its transport was inoperable. It meant it would be without its three inch mortars, its heavy machine guns, its reserves of ammunition, its explosives, its demolition set, its medical supplies and its radio transmitters, all of which depended on mules.[124]

More supplies were flown or parachuted in as the campaign progressed – air drops from India were the Brigade's lifeline – but the loss of so many transport mules at the outset was a big blow.

Not long after the Irrawaddy was crossed came a far bigger blow. News arrived of General Wingate's death in a plane crash, and plans had to be changed.[125] Masters was put in charge of the Brigade in place of Lentaigne, and new orders ensued. The build-up to the disastrous operation at Blackpool began. The Brigade switched to the offensive with a series of ambushes and attacks, and Frank was sent on a number of missions by Masters – each one progressively more perilous.

'Baines looks weird,' Masters wrote, 'his shaven head shining and his huge ring gleaming. He'll frighten the Nips out of their wits.'[126]

Frank and his men consistently held their own. 'Frankie Baines's rear section engaged what turned out to be six Japs and killed three of them,' Rhodes James writes about a skirmish near the main north-south road.[127]

In his first operation, Frank was despatched to take out a Japanese fuel dump and food depot in a Burmese village, and he was ordered to bring back a prisoner.

'Frankie Baines and a platoon of Gurkhas went off,' Rhodes James writes of the event, 'Frankie getting a big cheer from us, a camouflage officer going into action. One Jap was found, who scuttled away. The gallant Frankie fired on him, but he escaped.'[128]

---

124 *Chindit Affair*, p. 99.
125 Orde Wingate was killed in a plane crash in north-east India with nine others on 24 March 1944, and some people continue to believe that it was not an accident.
126 *The Road Past Mandalay*, p. 197.
127 *Chindit*, p. 102.
128 *Chindit*, p. 105.

Frank maintained, at least later in life, that he let the Japanese soldier go, and that after he had fired his rounds at him, the helpless soldier, still standing, gave a bow and ran off into the jungle.

Masters recounts sending Frank into action when they surprised a group of Japanese soldiers standing near some huts directly in front of them:

> I realised that the four soldiers were Japanese. They were staring at me. I moved behind a tree, called my nearest officer, Baines, pointed out the Japanese and told him to kill them. When he had done that he was to keep the huts under observation until the rear of the force got well past the spot. Baines, too, stared at the Japanese. 'My God, so they are,' he said. The Japanese kept staring. 'Get going!' I snapped. The Brigade Defence Platoon ran down the ridge, firing. Two Japanese ran away, two were killed. They were all armed. Ten minutes later, we crossed the road, unmolested.[129]

Frank endured, and chronicled, the full book of horrors and hardships of the campaign – long days of footslogging with 50-pound loads in searing heat, clawing paths uphill through dense bamboo forest and teak jungle, walking along narrow ridges, wading through rivers, being swamped by monsoon rains, sleeping out or 'harbouring' for the night in rough bivouacs, contending with mud and rotting feet, living under the constant threat of Japanese sniper bullets and mortar fire, coping with blood-sucking leeches, ticks, gnats, horseflies and malarial-carrying mosquitoes, being cut by bamboo spikes and pampas grass, and surviving with dysentery on K-rations and a daily round of thirst, hunger, fear and fatigue. Frank had his own personal nasty little experiences: he came across the remains of a Japanese cannibal meal; he found the corpse of a British soldier sucked dry by leeches and another impaled by bamboo; and he wandered into burnt-out villages which even the dogs had abandoned. He heard the wounded dying, watched men going mad with cerebral malaria, and took part in the court martial

---

129 *The Road Past Mandalay*, pp. 212-13.

and execution of a hapless Burmese traitor. He was reticent only about his own discomforts, but Rhodes James took note:

> Frankie Baines came in one day with fifty leeches on him, and with his usual gusto he told me exactly what he felt like. The ground, he said, had moved with leeches, and in the area where he had camped they were inescapable.[130]

A few days later, he saw that Frank was in a 'bad way':

> His struggle with the leeches left many ugly sores on his legs, which started to fester, and he walked around wreathed in bandages. His high spirits were by no means curbed by these trials; in fact he used to explain with peculiar heartiness how awful he felt.[131]

Even deep inside enemy country, where silence during the long day's march was the norm, there were occasional let-ups when Masters decided that that they were far enough away from the Japanese to light fires and issue rum.

Always up for a party or for a bit of fun, Frank danced and sang for his men on one such night off:

> I wandered off to the Gurkhas with Frankie Baines. The rum was flowing freely and the little men were beginning their peculiar chants ... We found a primitive delight dancing and singing by the light of the blazing fire, losing for a moment our fears and forebodings for the future.[132]

Meanwhile, in the thick of the jungle and in and out of skirmishes, Frank pursued his affections for his Gurkha orderly Dal Bahadur.

Their love affair was consummated in a jungle bivouac near a hillside pass above Mokso Sakan, which Frank had been ordered to secure and hold 'to the last man' in order to maintain a safe passage

130 *Chindit*, p. 178.
131 *Chindit*, p. 183.
132 *Chindit*, p. 111.

from the shores of Indawgyi Lake to the site selected for the defensive block the Brigade would lay down at Blackpool. They had covered 10 miles through rough jungle from Brigade Headquarters on their way to the pass, and after the camp fires had been put out and sentries posted for the night, Frank shared his blanket with Dal Bahadur:

We were lying breast to breast. Our shirts were open and our trousers unbuttoned … he yielded to my silent importunity without demur. [133]

Frank was left with a strange mixture of elation and introspection and was emboldened for the morrow's task – taking and occupying the pass:

I was feeling particularly well. What had been wrong with me was only too apparent. Now that I had fulfilled my function as lover, I had merely to fulfil it as soldier. This I felt superlatively able to do. I was so full of fire and fine spirit that it never occurred to me that the role of soldier, so similar to the role of lover, can be distasteful. Of course, I know that such moods vary considerably. At that moment, however, I am sure I would have bayoneted an enemy without compunction, and certainly would not have connived at his escape, as I had done with that Jap officer.[134]

Frank's men took the pass the following day after a skirmish with some Japanese soldiers:

'Look to your front, Tej Bahadur,' I upbraided him irritably, 'and attend to your business. Now let 'em have it!'

Dimly, figures could be seen running and dodging between the trees. I had hardly given Tej Bahadur the order when Thaman Bahadur opened up from behind me with everything he'd got. My own party at the bottom of the hill followed almost simultaneously. Our fire was delivered from

---

133 *Chindit Affair*, p. 142.
134 *Chindit Affair*, p. 144.

the whole of our armament: two Bren guns (Tej Bahadur was firing his from the hip) plus a fine selection of small arms. It had the requisite effect.

The enemy disengaged promptly. He brought into action his grenade launcher (always the sign of a withdrawal) and under the cover of its bombardment, retired to a cautionary distance, leaving me technically in possession. I had fulfilled my orders. I had not only seized the head of the pass; I had also seized the initiative. It now merely remained to see whether I could keep it.[135]

Rhodes James gave his own account of the engagement:

Frankie went on ahead with his platoon to guard the pass until we were through. We heard noises of firing and wondered if we would have a safe passage over the top ... Frankie was roaring about after suspected Japs and disappeared south along the ridge; there was sound of much firing and news came of a fierce little engagement.[136]

In the event, Frank and his men held this lonely but strategically important position for 28 days. The Brigade marched through on its way to meet its doom at Blackpool. The Japanese were ever present and there was another terrific engagement but the only time that his men were seriously challenged was when an elephant broke through their defensive perimeter. The terrain was their biggest threat. As the battle raged over the hills beyond in Blackpool, conditions in Frank's redoubt deteriorated and the monsoon broke. It rained and rained, and they ran out of food. One of his riflemen died.

Left behind to hold the pass, Frank missed out on Blackpool – a decision he vehemently protested about. But it was part of the overall plan: Masters had stationed a strong rearguard on the other side of the pass, by the shore of Indawgyi Lake. Rhodes James comments:

---

135 *Chindit Affair*, p. 146.
136 *Chindit*, p. 121.

He was very annoyed at this and said so emphatically, until Jack Masters had to ask him to desist. Poor Frankie, he was longing for this opportunity to fight and make good. Perhaps later he was not so very sorry at what he missed.[137]

That may well have been so. Frank was there when Masters and his defeated men, emaciated and exhausted, trudged back over the pass after they had been pounded into retreat from Blackpool:

Parties of wounded men, in twos and threes, were struggling up it, their eyes glazed with exhaustion, while the leaden hue of their faces, dull like some lustreless metal and as blue as cobalt, betokened many hours of wakeful nights. They exemplified the frightful effects which a decisive defeat can have on an army, for these stricken wretches, reeling from fatigue, shock and humiliation, belonged to no recognisable unit and owed allegiance – temporarily – to nobody. They were intent solely upon saving themselves and their mates, and if any attempt had been made to rally them with the familiar slogans, they would have turned on the individual attempting it and torn him to shreds.

But this was merely the advance party – a faintly adumbrated foreshadowing of what was to follow. There were simply the walking wounded, those who could fend for themselves. Some of them had uniforms hanging in tatters, ripped from their backs by shell-splinters and exposing ghastly, shrapnel-shredded wounds. Others, except for the parachute-cloth or segment of torn blanket which covered their genitals, were naked. Their unresilient flesh was mercilessly exposed to the teeming rain.

Next came a party of mules. They had managed to get some of the more seriously wounded men astride them bareback, and to support them there with some success. The men walked, one either side, to prop them up. At just the place on the path, however, where I had encountered them, some

---

137 *Chindit*, p. 121.

jutting rocks and a sharp, precipitous ascent made a successful negotiation very problematical. The leading mule gathered her legs together for a jump, thought better of it, stumbled, and in striving to regain her balance, struck her rump against a rock. She lurched drunkenly off the path and, in recovering herself, threw the man off her back. He fell in the mud with a sickening thump. The expressions on the faces of people who are old, sick or injured, and on account of their disability are subjected to galling indignities, are often strikingly pathetic. I remember particularly the expression on this man's face of outraged innocence. He looked like a very old baby who has been rudely precipitated from his pram. We all rushed to pick him up, but it was plain that he was dead.

I did not want to witness the look of baffled fury, mortification and perplexity which invaded the face of his friend – who had been supporting him – but I could not avoid it. He simply sat down on the edge of the path and surrendered helplessly to a fit of sobbing and to a wringing of his hands.

I moved on down the hill into the thick of it – where the hundred and fifty or so casualties the doctors had managed to evacuate were being borne on improvised stretchers by the West Africans.

Here, the sheer carnage caused by intensive shelling was painfully apparent. It was particularly evident, too, how the fog of war had confused the combatants.[138]

The Brigade recouped and regrouped at Indawgyi Lake, and the wounded and sick were evacuated on Sunderland flying-boats. New orders were given; they marched north, Frank initially taking up the rear with orders to rally and collect the stragglers. Then offensive operations resumed:

All protests notwithstanding, Stilwell had his way. We were ordered to

---

138 *Chindit Affair*, p. 164.

descend towards the plain and put in a frontal attack ... Given the mental
and physical state of the troops as I have described them, it was universally
conceded that our orders were tantamount to condemning the lot of us
to death.[139]

They advanced through the jungle fighting, with Frank and his men
on perilous patrols. The objective was Point 2171 and the valley below.
Frank was in the field when Captain Jim Blaker was killed storming
it. (He won a posthumous Victoria Cross.) During a fierce Japanese
onslaught, in which Brigade Headquarters was shelled, Frank stood
helplessly by as one of his favourite riflemen died and his orderly was
blown up.

'Just like Blackpool,' Masters writes. 'Baines's orderly, Dal Bahadur,
hit. Left side of chest stripped, exposing lung. Right wrist smashed.'[140]
In the midst of it all, Frank found God:

I caught a glimpse of blue sky. The revelation only lasted a few minutes,
but in that interval God was present. Despite the deceptive appearance of
things, I was assured that everything was divine.

I glanced about me. At my feet, the mud was dark and bloodstained. At
a little distance my men were examining the corpse of Tej Bahadur. Further
away, Dal Bahadur lay wounded. Yet the message was unmistakable. God
was tangibly present. God was present, not as an abstraction or a concept,
not as a philosophical statement, not as a metaphysical speculation, not
as an old man in a white sheet sitting on a cloud, God was present in everything around me – in the howling Gurkhas, some of whom the medics had
succeeded in collecting and who were now neighing like horses.[141]

A few moments later, one of Frank's soldiers told him to look at
his trousers:

---

139 *Chindit Affair*, p. 188.
140 *The Road Past Mandalay*, p. 273.
141 *Chindit Affair*, p. 211.

I glanced down and behind. To my amazement, the seat and legs of my trousers were in shreds. They had been torn in tatters by shell splinters. Yet I was unscathed.[142]

Frank helped to save Dal Bahadur on the battlefield; the medics staunched the gaping wound on his punctured lung. Masters summoned Frank to express his sympathy and to issue Frank with half a bottle of rum. The Brigade consolidated its newly won position, buried its dead, and dug in. They were subjected to heavy shelling, night and day.

Dal Bahadur recovered, but Frank spent the next few days in desperate straits, living like the rest of them under sustained bombardment. He had a narrow escape when he ran headlong into a Japanese patrol while moving through a teak forest. Frank was spared because he was not carrying a weapon:

I had quite ceased to carry a weapon, and went about completely unarmed. This could hardly have failed to attract attention.

It was the only symbol, however, which I could think of to emphasize that I bore no animosity towards anybody – least of all towards the Japanese. As a matter of fact, we had long since arrived at that point where the only people any of us felt like murdering were our own generals.[143]

In mid-July orders finally came to abandon Point 2171 and to withdraw:

I had been aware for some time that Jack Masters was locked in an unprecedented struggle with his higher commanders. It revolved around the bitter controversy then raging about whether or not the Brigade was physically fit and whether we all ought to be flown out. Stilwell still insisted that we were in perfectly good shape and were simply not doing our duty.[144]

---

142 *Chindit Affair*, p. 212.
143 *Chindit Affair*, p. 221.
144 *Chindit Affair*, p. 226.

They were in a desperate situation, facing the prospect of having to fight their way out, carrying 60 stretcher cases. Frank led the retreat, pushing out ahead, keen to get Dal Bahadur and the other wounded back to a medical evacuation station, and all the while hanging on himself in increasing mental anguish and physical discomfort.

But Frank was still soldiering – doing his duty as the Brigade made its way out of Burma through the last pockets of Japanese positions to the safety of liberated territory and the British lines. Rhodes James writes:

> Frankie Baines went on ahead to clear the way and reported back shortly afterwards looking very fierce with a grenade in each hand. There were Japs ahead. As they had not made their presence felt and would probably be in small numbers we took no notice as the wild-eyed Frankie, still firmly clutching the grenades, made his way forward again.[145]

They finally flew out of Burma after five hard months. Rhodes James reflects:

> Jack Masters, Briggo, Frankie, Mac;[146] we had seen so much together which had changed our lives and which no one else would quite understand. For the moment, we were content to be alive and eager to be at rest.

'How much he (Frank) coloured our lives,' Rhodes James wrote at the end of his book, 'and how much he strove to find a meaning to his own.'[147]

Frank ended the war in Rangoon. The Chindits were disbanded. He was suffering from mild amoebic dysentery when he left them. The commendation he received from Jack Masters was brief, but then Masters

---

145 *Chindit*, p. 193.
146 Major Jim Macpherson and Briggs, the signal officer.
147 *Chindit*, p. 206.

was always a man of few words:[148]

'Owing to the exigencies of the campaign, Captain Baines was not able to do much camouflage. In action, however, he did well.' Signed J. Masters, Commander.[149]

Rhodes James says the commendation was well deserved.[150]

Still going strong in 2010 at the age of 87, Rhodes James, who went on after the war to become a respected and much loved housemaster at Haileybury College, recalls Frank as a very special person. He says he had never met anyone quite like him, and that having Frank there gave an extra thread to their lives. Brigade Headquarters was a small unit, so everybody was noticed, and there was a spontaneity about Frank which added liveliness to everything. He was the only person at Brigade Headquarters who was in charge of troops, and he seemed to enjoy it – and did well.

Rhodes James's view is that Frank's account of his time with the Chindits, while very personal, was largely accurate. He doesn't, however, accept Frank's description of the operation as a 'suicide mission', preferring to call it plain 'hair-raising'. He says that Frank's account is very vivid, and very much at the sharp end, although Frank did not accompany them to Blackpool.

Rhodes James was himself in the thick of it at Blackpool, and he squarely blames the American commander in China, General Stilwell, for the disaster, saying that he was determined to run the Chindits into the ground, which he did. One battalion, the 1st Cameronians Scottish Rifles, even went on strike. They were the star battalion, but they had had enough. They simply refused to fight – which, when behind enemy lines, made for an awkward position.

All those years later, Rhodes James is still amazed that so many of them came back, saying that he sometimes thinks it was a miracle that

---

148 Frank brought back an unusual trophy from Rangoon, a privately printed first edition of *A Vision* signed by W.B. Yeats. The book had evidently spent the war, or the duration of the Japanese occupation, buried, and it was dug up again and put on sale when the British reoccupied the city. (In possession of the author, with an explanatory dedication from Frank.)

149 *Chindit Affair*, p. 234.

150 Interview with the author in 2009 at Rhodes James's home in Cambridge.

any of them got out of Blackpool. However the Japanese had had enough. The Chindits had suffered appalling causalities, but the Japanese had also had a terrible battering, and they just let the Chindits go.

Masters, who died in 1983 after a successful second career as an author living in America, paid a crowning tribute in his book *The Road Past Mandalay* to all those who served under him:

> The difference between our war and normal war was simply extraordinary – the absence of supply lines, the knowledge that if you are sick or wounded your future is incalculable, looking always in all directions, always under-nourished, always extremely vulnerable to certain types of enemy action – the cumulative effect bears down on even the hardiest.[151]

Frank too knew that he had had to rise to challenges such as few men ever face:

> A little of the furore and the excitement rubbed off on me too, if not the glory, and it was, after all, my finest hour – if we amateurs may be permitted to have one.[152]

---

151 *The Road Past Mandalay*, p. 287.
152 Unpublished first draft of *Chindit Affair* (Random House archives).

SEVEN

HINDU MONK

FRANK WAS DEMOBILISED IN 1946 AND HE RETURNED home on a troop ship to Liverpool to see his mother in Coggeshall. After five years in Asia and his gruesome experiences of war, he was decidedly ill at ease in peace-time England.

A cousin, Bob Oldham, came down from Warwickshire to see him in Essex and found him in a very bad state. He was asleep in the middle of the day at a farmhouse near Braintree, in bed with someone and clearly the worse for wear. Frank asked Oldham to pop down to the local pub and order him a bottle of whisky, telling him that he could put it onto his tab. But the landlord said Frank's credit was no good. So Oldham bought him the whisky from his own pocket and took it back to him. Oldham never saw Frank again.[153]

Frank's own account confirms that he found peacetime life in England demanding:

Being completely without academic distinctions or technical skills, it was difficult to know what to do.

I couldn't use a typewriter or drive a car. But I could ride a horse and fire a gun! They didn't seem the sort of qualification that would get me very far in a commonplace world of post-war realities.

---

153 Bob Oldham, son of Walter Edwin Oldham, one of Rhoda's younger brothers, interviewed by the author in 2009.

Moreover, I felt totally emasculated. The experiences of first-time love, plus fear, lust and sensuality seemed to have reduced me to a jelly. What I needed was to find some sort of hole or corner which I could climb into while I reconstituted my ego. There were also other considerations. However trifling they were, they made a deep impression on me in my deplorable condition.

Standing outside our house in Coggeshall during my demobilisation leave, I was admiring the roses which Mother had planted against the railings under the study window that looks down the street. She had planted them the year before in celebration of V.E. Day. It was now June 1946, and they were in full flower and leaf. Suddenly a man came up behind me. I didn't know him, but: 'We've finished with your sort of people,' he whispered malevolently. 'We don't want anything more to do with you. You can get out.'

He obviously knew me. As an expression of the native's sentiment towards one of their returning sons, it did not seem to offer much encouragement to stay in England.

Another consideration was: I had got religion!

I had got it, not as a born again Christian or some sort of crazy church-going fundamentalist, but in the sense of pledging myself almost unwittingly and without conscious volition to ... devote my life to God ... After all, I had seen God up there, in the jungle clearing, when Dal Bahadur lay wounded to death and bleeding, with Tej Bahadur stretched dead at my feet.[154]

Frank decided to return to India and become a Hindu monk. In fact, he had already been thinking about such a path for quite a long

---

154 Chapter 1 (and the only surviving chapter) of an unpublished draft of what was intended to be a book about his experiences at the Mirtola Ashram (in possession of Dan Sansom of Coggeshall).

time; but the unpleasant encounter in Coggeshall appears to have been the final catalyst:

> Standing outside our house in Coggeshall, and boiling with indignation at that impudent fellow's coming up to me, I had already made up my mind. Sri Krishna Prem had agreed to accept me into his community and I eagerly anticipated becoming a major spiritual light.

Frank was writing about Ronald Nixon, a former English World War I fighter pilot and a former university professor who was now a Hindu monk, Sri Krishna Prem, and head of an Ashram in the Himalayan foothills in the remote North Indian village of Mirtola.

Nixon's story is itself remarkable. After surviving a near-death experience in an air battle with the British Royal Flying Corps during the 1914-18 war, he went on to study at Cambridge University, where he grew increasingly fascinated with Eastern religions. He came to India in 1921 as a lecturer at the English Department in the newly opened Lucknow University. There he lodged with the Vice-Chancellor, Dr Chakravarti, fell under the spiritual guidance of his wife, Monika Chakravarti, and gradually embraced Hinduism. Monika left Lucknow, moved to the hills and took the Vaishanav vows of *sannvasa* (renunciation). She adopted the name Sri Yashoda Ma. Nixon followed her shortly afterwards, and he, too, took his Vaishanav vows and assumed the new name of Sri Krishna Prem.

Together they set up the Radha-Krishna temple and established a thriving international community at Mirtola. Among their first disciples were Moti Rani (Yashoda Ma's youngest daughter) and Major Robert Dudley Alexander, who took early retirement from his post as the Principal of Lucknow Medical College especially to join the Ashram. Over the years, the Ashram evolved a unique philosophy, blending Eastern mysticism with Western thought, and it attracted a significant following, among them diplomats, politicians and writers. Distinguished 'alumni' include Dr Karan Singh, a former government minister and Indian ambassador to the United States, who is also the Maharaja of Jammu and Kashmir; American businessman and Theosophy teacher Seymour B Ginsburg; and Scottish travel writer Bill Aitken.

Sri Krishna Prem (the former Ronald Nixon) took over the Ashram following Yashoda's death in 1944 and he ran it until he died there in 1965. Fluent in Hindi and Bengali, he wrote a number of books on Yoga and prayer. *The Yoga of Kathopanishad* was the beacon that attracted Frank to Mirtola. Prem was sometimes described as the 'last English Saint', and it was he who was in charge when Frank offered himself to the community in 1946.

Frank described the strange coincidences that drew him to Mirtola and inspired him to believe, 'however naive and ridiculous', that he had a vocation for a spiritual life as a Hindu monk:

The first circumstance goes back to when I joined 111 Brigade, and was sent to hospital in Lucknow with a lacerated arm. There was a legend going around the wards about one of Lucknow's most talented physicians, a gifted consultant named Dr Alexander, who had abandoned his career and gone off to practise austerities according to the Hindu tradition in the Himalayas.

The second circumstance also refers to the same period. I bought a book.

The pain of my gangrenous arm was so agonising and I became so bored and restless by confinement in hospital, that I begged the doctors to strap up my arm, give me a packet of pain-killers, and let me loose in the bazaar. They agreed. I made straight for a bookstall. There I bought a volume entitled *The Yoga of Kathopanishad* by somebody calling himself Sri Krishna Prem. It was full of tantalising glimpses and seductive insights, some thwarting and some titillating, about the spiritual life. It contained some really fascinating comparisons between the ancient Greek, Christian and Hindu traditions. It became virtually my *vade mecum* and bible.[155]

---

155 First published in India and brought out in England in 1955.

Prem's teaching appealed to Frank's hunger for the mystical and the unexplained, and set him on the path of escape from his Western Christian upbringing. He would never turn back.

'Neither religion, nor life itself is, has been or ever will be a matter of reason alone,' Krishna Prem wrote in *The Yoga of Kathopanishad*. 'Religion springs from the depth of the psyche and its rational elements are only part of its total content. Not only the "rationalist", but also the protestant type of reformer is apt to make this mistake and, in rationalising religion, to render it sterile.'[156]

The Yoga of Kathopanishad is an exposition of the ancient road that leads from death to immortality, and it seeks to demonstrate that the road is not confined to any one religious tradition. But it makes clear that in order to gain enlightenment, a person must undergo a 'mystic death' and renounce the world.

'This is the same eternal wisdom,' wrote Prem, 'the wisdom that teaches us that if we would find our true life we must first lose the false one that is lived in the sunlight of the world.'[157]

It was in pursuit of this wisdom that Frank attempted a life of self-abnegation in the Himalayan foothills:

After my wound had burst and began to heal, I was transferred to Ranikhet hospital in the hills, for a skin-graft. There I learnt of the strange community, some Hindu and some Europeans, leading a monastic life in the remote backwoods beyond Almora.

I did not at the time put these three elements together. They were brought into association by a much later concurrence.

After the Chindit operation, one of my frequent physical breakdowns landed me up in hospital in Shillong. It was a healthy station in the Khasi Hills, the headquarters of the Provincial Government, consequently comparatively civilised. One afternoon I fell asleep while reading (Krishna

---

156 *The Yoga of Kathopanishad*, p. 17.
157 *The Yoga of Kathopanishad*, p. 21.

Prem's) *The Yoga of Bhagavat Gita*.[158] It lay open in my hands. I awoke to find an elegant English lady standing over me. She apologised for disturbing me and we embarked on a polite, meaningless, vaguely witty conversation which might have been scripted by Oscar Wilde.

As our acquaintanceship ripened – a matter of nothing more than ten minutes – I was visited by the most striking flash of intuition. I divined, quintessentially out of the blue, that she must be the wife of the Chief Secretary, a very important Indian Civil Service official, who virtually ran the Assam Government. I challenged her with it and, and she assented. I supposed it wasn't really so surprising. There was something in her manner which was incontrovertibly unassailable. Nevertheless our encounter displayed a quite prescient incidence of foreknowledge. She was engaged in one of those missions of mercy which such ladies were expected to undertake, of visiting the wounded, many of whom were sent to Shillong to recuperate, on account of its salubrious climate.

I apprehended in her demeanor, however, something which was not purely social or official.

Finally she came out with it.

She indicated the *Bhagavat Gita* and asked me diffidently if I was interested in Hinduism.

Well, sort of yes!

'My brother,' she began, as if confessing to a shameful secret.

And for the second time during that interview – actually within seconds of the first time – I was possessed by the complete certainty of an insight. And of course she confirmed it. I was correct.

---

158 Published by John Watkins in London in 1938.

Her brother was Dr Alexander. The Ashram, or hermitage, to which he had retired, was that locality beyond Almora which I had heard of when in Ranikhet. And Sri Krishna Prem, the author of that book, *The Yoga of Kathopanishad*, which had so influenced me, actually an Englishman by the name of Ronald Nixon, was the veritable source and inspiration of all these indications, the head of the Ashram and Dr Alexander's friend (they had been to Oxford together) and guru!

So all these circumstances came together in one fell swoop! Is it surprising that I felt there was some occult influence at work here, that I was being guided in a pre-ordained direction, towards an inexorable consummation?

The speed and flawlessness of the fitting-together of all these pieces of the jig-saw puzzle left me quite breathless.

I persuaded the lady to give me a letter of introduction to her brother, and I kept this by me when I returned to duty.

Frank duly wrote to Dr Alexander and arranged to visit the Ashram before taking a ship from Bombay back to England for demobilisation:

Now I descended from the mail train at Lucknow, and bade farewell to Dal Bahadur. I was to take the small, metre-gauge railway to Kathgodam, the railway whence departed all the buses for all of the hill country of Naini Tal, Ranikhet and Almora. It was a route I had travelled several times before, so I was fairly familiar with it. The first occasion was, of course, when I was sent up to Ranikhet hospital for a skin graft. The countryside was so beautiful, however, that I returned there whenever I could, snatching periods of short leave between intervals of duty. I used to stay in the Dak Bungalow at Almora, a pleasant, primitive hill-town with past glorious frontier associations, an interesting bazaar, and a little fortress which had about 1830 formed the western outpost of the Gurkha kingdom of Nepal.

During these furloughs, I had already tried several times to reach Sri Krishna Prem's Ashram at Mirtola, but my attempts were constantly frustrated. Always, on the eve of setting out, I was either recalled to duty by an emergency signal from my operating headquarters, or I fell ill.

This would be the last opportunity, and all the more compelling for the mysterious circumstances which had led up to it, for me to make the acquaintance of these singular personages and to lay – for yes, this was my intention – my life at their feet!

Our initial confrontation, however, had not been all that encouraging. I had made the 20 mile trek to Mirtola in heavy army boots. It was autumn and the track was hot and dusty. From Almora it is only a gentle climb from 5,000 feet to about 7,000 feet. My first landfall was the Post Office and general shop. From there I was directed along a forest path, under ragged evergreen oak trees, whence the land fell sharply away to the right in open, grassy terraces (the original fortified demesne of the temple) to pine forests, beyond which were distant views over undulating hills towards Almora to the south. To my left a hill rose steeply, heavily afforested with oak.

It was a delightful place, situated at that exact height where the native pine forests of the lower slopes gave place to high altitude oak forests, with yellow horse-chestnut trees flaming among the evergreens. And even as I walked, some several hundred feet above the pines, their heady, turpentine tang rose up like an enveloping blanket.

I passed a row of pretty, tumbledown cottages (they turned out to be the cow-house and servants' quarters) with a roofed verandah above and below, then a small but more pretentious house unsuccessfully imitating the same style. It was standing rather awkwardly in the centre of a stone-paved terrace. In spite of obvious attempts to conform characteristically, it looked self-conscious and stiffly out-of-place. The path then divided between high, grassy banks, skirted a little wooded ravine, and came out on a miniature platform. The plateau was neatly hemmed in by hills whose trees and shrubs all bent down towards it nicely. In the centre was a temple sporting a short, blunt *shikara*[159] (the nearest equivalent is spire), washed-over with cement and crowned by a gilded finial. It was encircled by a wooden-constructed corrugated-iron-roofed verandah on the first floor, supported from below on wooden posts, the woodwork painted the unflattering colour of red oxide, which had been turned into a sort of purply brown by the weather. The plateau was actually divided into two parts on two different levels, something to do with the foundations and construction, one surmised, of the temple in the first place. There was a small isolated shrine in the middle of the upper part, with a cement path which connected directly from it to the principal door of the temple – on account of the different levels, actually on the first floor – over a concrete bridge. Behind the shrine, and slightly elevated on the hillside, was another (this time in minimally more congruous harmony but still not *right*) quite agreeable house, bowered in trees, with a glazed in upper verandah which was reflecting the evening light.

On the plateau, and to the front and sides of the temple, there were vestigial traces that someone had tried to construct a garden. The humped outlines of geometrical flower beds, in token whereof one or two scrawny rose bushes clung dejectedly, looked like the archaeological excavations of some residual city.

I was a bit taken aback. The aggregate presented an appearance of dereliction that was totally unaesthetic. I had imagined, in my innocence, that an inner devotion to the spiritual life would have transferred itself to the environment. This seemed not to be the case. A faint whiffle of anxiety surfaced within me, which I immediately suppressed. The word 'temple' implies, to a European psyche, visions of Dorian elegance and Lacedae-

---

159 Literally a mountain peak, this is the term used for a rising tower in the Hindu temple architecture of north India.

monian excellence. Perhaps I had been misled by my Hellenistic illusions. But as if to palliate the something less than perfection of this spot, I noted that a riot of self-seeded annuals from an original sowing had established themselves naturally. With their thin, feathery foliage and simplistically-coloured, star-like flowers, they weltered over everything. They created a confusion of cosmos (the botanical, not the macrocosmic sort) through which the globular blooms of the gorgeous French marigolds glowed exaggeratedly golden like yellow and orange suns through misty cloud. Doubtless, Nature was redressing the balance!

Treading delicately, like Agog (1 Samuel, 15:32), I entered this suppositional paradise as cautiously as an interloper, my big army boots going clump, clump on the cement. Complete silence. The absence of reaction was like a positive assertion of the place's indifference. I marched up and down several times in order to draw attention to my presence. Nothing happened, so I descended to the lower level and went round to the back. Here, a flight of stone stairs led circularly upwards. The steps – their solid substantiality cut out of the living rock – gave encouragement to my evaporating confidence, for they added a touch of authenticity to a scene that was increasingly looking unmeretricious and trashy. I was standing indecisively in front of these, debating whether to mount into the higher regions, when a disturbance along the upper verandah indicated that someone was coming.

God knows what I expected! My febrile imagination had led me to anticipate something really arresting. But Sri Krishna Prem, for it was he, proved to be remarkably unremarkable. I was deeply disappointed. He was an ordinary- looking man from whom my objectifying fantasy had required an impossible ideality.

After we had greeted each other, there was an embarrassed silence. He glanced at my boots with an air of extreme apprehension. Mercifully, I was aware of the Hindu prohibition about wearing leather, as well as of not entering a house with your shoes on, so I unlaced them and, for good measure, peeled off my socks as well. My red, perspiring feet looked even worse than I had expected. Ghopal da (as I learned to call him – *da* being an abbreviation of dada, elder brother in Bengali) glanced at them more apprehensively than at my boots.

He was a tall man, with the cultivated professional stoop (half-cringe) of the specialist expert in holiness and humility, and he too had huge (except mine weren't really so large) red, but in addition positively disfigured by calluses, feet. He was a long-head, very definitely brachycephalic, bald, with cropped grey hair at back and sides, a reddish complexion, and a tiny spume of frothy bubbles which gathered at the corners of his mouth when he spoke. He was about 43 and no beauty! He took me upstairs onto the upper verandah (glassed-in) where a cosy corner in the prevailing unsociability had been staked out with tables, chairs and cushions.

Tea was served in decent, bell-metal glasses, and Dr Alexander joined us. I was conducted to the guest house, which was the pretentious building I had passed earlier, placed in the centre of its stone-paved terrace. There supper was brought to me (two fat *parottas* – unleavened wheat cakes baked on a flat-iron with clarified butter – and a glass of hot, sweet milk), and I was provided with a small oil-lamp.

My sleeping quarters were lined with a very catholic collection of books. I selected Jane Harrison's *Prologomena to the Greek Religion*[160] and retired to bed. It was cold, lonely and utterly inhospitable.

But evidently, I had made a good impression. Going up the steps that evening, I had even offered to take off my leather belt. I was so conscious to do the right thing that I would have discarded my trousers! My readiness to conform in this way seemed to have predisposed them in my favour.

---

160 Jane Ellen Harrison (1850-1928) a British classical scholar, linguist and feminist who specialised in Greek mythology and Greek religion.

For there were *three*! At breakfast the following morning, much to my aston-
ishment, a woman appeared. Moti was charming, charismatic, civilised,
sophisticated, well educated, as well as fair, fat, and one year younger than
me, but actually born on the same day, a circumstance which inevitably established a secret bond between us which continued more or less uninterruptedly
right up to the day of my departure thence some four years later.[161]

It immediately became evident, of course, that I would never have been
allowed to meet her had I not somehow passed a subtle test. The four of
us soon began to get on famously.

The upshot was: that I was accepted, and after returning to England for
demobilisation and paying my duty to my mother, I would come back to
India, take an initiation in Hinduism, to be enrolled into their happy band.

Frank was not the only ex-serviceman to make his way to Mirtola
after the War. A Scottish aircraft engineer, Alexander Phipps, arrived
there in 1946 and he stayed on. Phipps converted and became Sri Madhava Ashish, and he in turn took charge of the community and, like
his predecessors, became a much revered Guru. Ashish was also a prac-
tical man and he did a great deal to help the local hillside communities
improve their farming techniques, and he was widely mourned when
he died in 1997.

Life at the Ashram was not easy. Those who accepted the full vows
had to renounce meat, fish and hot water, and they seldom ate any
warm food. They meditated round the clock in a perpetual struggle
to control physical desires and channel their emotions – although not
always in perfect harmony, and not always with the desired effect.

As far as possible the Mirtola Ashram was self-supporting, growing
wheat, barley, rye, sweet-corn and some fruit. The farm produced milk,
butter and ghee. The cow-shed facing south had wire-meshing put up
in the 1970s to keep out leopards.

---

161 Moti was Yashoda Ma's youngest daughter.

Frank was one of just five people there, and it was in such surroundings that he was to spend three years of his life. He writes:

In spite of my enthusiasm I did indeed have a good many reservations.
These were to accumulate and gain force over the years, and were eventually
to wreck my commitment.

Dev Ashish, in charge of the Ashram in 2010, said the years at Mirtola were a difficult time for Frank. In many respects Frank turned out
to be a square peg in a round hole: he talked volubly, remained actively
homosexual and seemed at times to get on better with the animals than
with his fellow monks. Ultimately he fell out with the other Briton who
joined with him, Alexander Phipps, who was to become Madhava
Ashish.

Writing 40 years afterwards, Phipps left his own account of the
period. It gives an insight into how hard life was at the Ashram and
also reveals the sort of petty human squabbles that can prey on even
the most holy places:[162]

In 1946 a new era started in the Ashram which was to last five years,
ending with Moti's death.

It began with the visit of Frank, a young English Captain of the British
army who had been with the Chindit expeditions (sic) in Burma. Conditions
had been so tough for them that, according to him, they all had to go into
hospital on their return. There Frank had met Bob's sister who was married
to the then Governor of Assam and was doing her duty by visiting the men
in hospital and offering them books to read. One of those books was
Krishna Prem's *The Yoga of the Kathopanishad*, which thrilled Frank. So
when he was transferred to the military hospital at Ranikhet for conva-
lescence he made it a point to walk over to Mirtola and meet Krishna Prem
and, incidentally, Moti.

---

162 Chapter 12 and part of Chapter 13 of MS provided by Dev Ashish from Mirtola which
record the period when Frank was at the Ashram.

He seems immediately to have envisaged the Ashram as his next step in life, and even thought that he might be Krishna Prem's successor if he played his cards right.

Frank's father was of Irish extraction,[163] and Frank must have kissed the Blarney stone, for he could talk and charm the hind leg off a donkey. He soon saw that Moti was susceptible and that if he was to get in at all, it would be through Moti's influence, for Krishna Prem was much more difficult to impress. Moti was attracted but not bowled over. However, she pushed Krishna Prem into accepting Frank as a new member of the Ashram by saying that if he did not take on anyone because they did not measure up to his standards, then he would never get anyone. Krishna Prem reluctantly agreed, and Frank went off to England to get himself demobilised and then return.

Phipps, who was demobilised in August 1946, came to the Ashram shortly before Frank returned from England. They were joined by a third novice, a very good-looking young Bengali who had enlisted in the RAF during the war:

We were all given initiation and given new names. I came first because I had settled in first and was given the name Dev Ashish.[164] Frank came next and was called Govinda Priya. And Nilomani, the Bengali boy, was called Keshab Priya. Moti promptly called me Ashish, so the name stuck. Keshab's name also stuck. But Frank for most of us remained Frank.

Krishna Prem was still living an austere and orthodox life, rising early to perform the temple *puja*,[165] which lasted up to three hours, and then doing his morning *sandhya*,[166] which might go on till ten am. After a short break for tea, he would then have to start the temple cooking which went on

---

163 This is incorrect.
164 When Phipps was given his *Sannyas* in 1947 he dropped Dev and became Sri Madhava Ashish.
165 *Puja* is a ritual Hindu act of reverence and prayer.
166 Meditation.

till twelve when *bhoga*[167] was offered in the temple and then taken down to the newly built *Samadhi*[168] temple of Yashoda Ma. I suspect that Moti put pressure on him to change his timings because nothing could move in the place until he was ready, and the rest of us were not yet capable of such intensity. Besides, the orthodoxy excluded us from both the temple and the kitchen.

One of the many hardships we had to get used to was the cold water bath which continued right up into December. When it was thought cold enough for us to start having a wood fire in our rooms at night, we were issued with a large brass or copper water jar *(ghara)* which one stood in the fireplace and, if one managed things properly, got enough hot water for a really good bath.

Life at Mirtola wasn't all prayer and fasting. Almora, a short drive or a few hours' walk down the hills, was a thriving little mountain city perched on a spur, with houses built of dry stone with wooden balconies. It was a commercial centre, a bazaar for the mountain people, and also home to an array of artists and interesting people, some of whom lived on what later became known as 'Cranks' Ridge', which overlooks the gleaming white Himalayan wall that separates this Hindu valley from Buddhist Tibet, the ice-covered 25,000-foot mountain range of the Nanda Devi, the Nanda Kot and the Trishul. One of the most colourful residents at the time was the American artist Earl Brewster, who had been a close friend of the English writer D.H. Lawrence, and had lived and worked in France and Italy, spending a long time in both Capri and Sicily. Usually dressed in a white suit and sporting a white Beret, Earl was locally regarded as a *Rishi*.[169] The town asked him to raise the Indian flag on Independence Day. Phipps and Frank got to know him very well.[170]

---

167 Offerings of food.
168 State of spiritual contemplation.
169 A poet-sage or 'seer'.
170 Earl Henry Brewster (1878-1957).

Other 'odd' residents included a Dane who liked to dress up as a shabby monk and a German Buddhist monk who assumed the name Anagarika Govinda and took a wife. A former British Secret Service agent also lived there together with an adopted son, a former Tibetan monk called Ram Jor, a gifted artist who painted magical-looking landscapes which were much admired. A few years later, Frank was to write about the sad end to Ram Jor's artistic career.

Phipps continues:

Moti was given *Sannyas*[171] in November some time before we were given initiation. I helped her pack up parcels of her expensive *saris* to send to her friends. In an Ashram of *sadhus*[172] clad in ochre or white, Moti's brilliant colours had led Krishna Prem to call her 'Tuppence' from the English phrase 'penny plain and tuppence coloured'. The village people all called her *didi*, elder sister, while the rest of us said Motidi, which has the same elder sister connotation.

Both as a sequence to her Sannyas and to see how I would adapt to a totally Indian setting, Moti decided to go to Brindaban[173] in the winter with Krishna Prem and me. My favoured status in such matters did not endear me to the others, particularly to Bob who had been in the Ashram for eight years but never taken out on a trip, and Frank whose position as blue-eyed boy I had usurped.

The journey down to Brindaban was Moti's first appearance in public as a *Sannyasin* with shaven head and ochre-coloured clothes. Likewise, it was my first public appearance in Indian dress. Krishna Prem must have found us very trying, because our social behaviour was not yet patterned on the norm for sadhus. From now on for quite some time I felt peculiarly helpless, for I was forbidden from behaving in the English mode as a *Sahib*,

---

171 Status as a 'renunciate'.
172 Holy monks.
173 Traditional birthplace of Lord Krishna, south of Delhi.

and had not yet learned how to behave as an Indian. Krishna Prem was obviously unhappy at having to cater for such a dimwit.

Phipps writes openly about the tensions inside the close-knit community, and about Moti's seemingly irrational temper:

> There was an occasion in 1949 when Krishna Prem was so shaken by the attack Moti was making on him that he began to doubt her sanity, for she was raving. I found myself arguing forcefully that she was an exceptional person and was trying, through this behaviour, to achieve changes in him. She was by no means mad. Thus I was handing back to him the very same teaching he had given me two years earlier.

> Moti's dedication to the Spirit was so total that she allowed herself to be used by the powers behind her to achieve effects quickly that might otherwise have taken lifetimes. Although there was that astounding detachment one finds in rare people of this sort, which allows a raging fury to turn to utter calm in an instant when the occasion demands, this did not mean that it was all a pretence and that she did not suffer. She suffered both in her feelings and in the effects these outbursts had on her sick body. And this real suffering was again used, because one could not but feel responsible for what she was undergoing.

But there were also other underlying tensions and some apparent skulduggery, which the community believed emanated from Frank and which ultimately led to his departure. Somewhere along the line, too, a belief took hold that Frank was psychic. Frank, himself, seems have believed this. Phipps continues the story:

> 1947 was the year for the three newcomers to do a lot of adjusting. Frank and I in particular were undergoing a massive reorganisation of our cultural values and standards, besides the changes required of our behavioural con-

ditioning. I was fortunate in having faced the problem of instinctive resistance to a complete change in diet while I was at Raman Ashram[174] in 1944, so that the Ashram's totally vegetarian diet cooked in Bengali style suited me well. The only trouble I ran into with food was that I was eating too much. This dropped off as soon as Krishna Prem pointed out to me that the psyche was trying to make up in quantity for what it was missing in terms of what it was accustomed to.

A short while after our return from Brindaban, I found a strange bundle under my pillow in the little downstairs room in which I was staying. It was daytime, and I had certainly not slept with it there. My room was never locked and anyone could go in during the daytime. But there was something unpleasant about it and I went straight off and told Moti. She told me to bring it to her and, having seen it, to call the servant who was at that time employed to look after Krishna Prem's room and to see to the needs of visitors. Moti challenged him with knowledge of the bundle. He denied it, but looked sheepish and took the bundle away. Moti pointed out that, had it not been his, he would never have touched it, for it was plainly placed there with magical intentions.

Some time passed. Moti told me to move upstairs and sleep in Krishna Prem's room and to take over much of the work that the servant previously did. I was hoping for opportunity to talk to Krishna Prem about some of the personal problems that were bugging me, but when I tried to start, he shut me up with: 'Oh yes. I believe people do have problems.' It was probably the best thing for me at the time, and it was certainly very different from the intense analysis we engaged in later.

Now I got a bad attack of amoebic dysentery. Unlike the majority of my English colleagues at work, I had never suffered from dysentery. I had noticed that the less they liked India, the more severe the attacks seemed to be. I had seemed to be immune, but that was no longer the case. Bob

---

174 In Tamil Nadu State, southern India.

tried all his medicines with no effect. Homoeopathic medicine was tried without effect. I got worse and had to spend most of the day lying down. For whatever reason, the thought never crossed my mind that I should go and get treatment in the town.

Then one morning I woke feeling that I was well again, and my body showed me that my feeling was right. When I told Moti she looked hard at me and gave a humph. The improvement lasted for three days and then the whole thing started again, making me very depressed, for I thought it was over. It went on for a few days and again suddenly stopped with an immediate feeling of well-being.

The previous day I had noticed Moti and Krishna Prem talking quietly together and had known, in the way one does know, that they were talking about me. So I now tackled Moti, for it was becoming clear that the improvement in my health was connected with something they were doing. She told me that on the occasion of the first improvement she had closed me against influences that she thought might be making me ill. My improvement proved her point, but it needed doing every day, and she was too ill to do it. So she had asked Krishna Prem to take it on.

The next thing that happened was that Frank developed a fissure in his anus – an extremely painful complaint – and Bob was rushing him off to Almora in a Dandy to be operated on by a doctor friend.

That night Krishna Prem told me what he had done. To begin with he not only closed me, but also sent the influence, ill will, or whatever it was, back to its source, for he wanted to be quite sure from where it was coming. When he saw what suffering it was causing, he continued to protect me but stopped sending it back.

Phipps indicates that they believed that the source of this evil spirit was Frank!

Perhaps nothing was said to Frank about it, and it is hard for me to understand the reasons. Furthermore, I was not the sort of tough young man who would propose fighting it out. The only thing that fits is that when Frank finally left two years later, Moti began by turning him out because of what he was doing, but then allowed him to return, and only then turned the pressure onto him so that he eventually took himself off. The servant he had involved in his attack on me left almost immediately of his own accord and died within a year. He lived in a village close to the local cremation ground, and it was supposed that it was from there that he brought earth to put under my pillow.

I was in the habit of meditating or, more truly, trying to meditate in Krishna Prem's room which was directly above the kitchen where Krishna Prem would be cooking the evening offering for the temple. Frank was allowed to sit in the anteroom to the kitchen and to talk to him. If meditation went well one could ignore the conversation, otherwise one was compelled to hear.

One conversation that stayed in my memory was Frank talking about his psychic powers and Krishna Prem saying that they might develop. Some time later a Bengali visitor was staying in a room that could be entered by a door that opened into the temple anteroom. Frank was paying an evening visit to this friend, and I was doing the evening *puja*, and again could not avoid hearing Frank loudly declaring that Krishna Prem had told him that he should develop his psychic powers and then move on to other places. It seemed not what Krishna Prem had actually said.

In 1947, the year of the partition riots, Krishna Prem took Moti to Delhi for medical treatment. I had to take on the temple *puja*, while Keshab took on the kitchen. I was in the unenviable position of being put in charge of a place I had no idea how to run, so I was constantly treading on everyone's corns out of sheer stupidity. Adding to the general difficulties were detailed instructions of how to give special care to Yashoda Ma's dog, Sonny, how to care for Alu who had developed a cancerous growth and was being well looked after by Bob, and how to care for a wretched horse with a broken leg which some muleteer had callously left on the Ashram boundary. When the horse strayed so far from the stable in the old Post Office building that it could not get back, Frank heroically stayed out at night with a bonfire to scare off leopards – and had the animal fall down the hill and into his fire. I organised a gang to carry it back, doing more damage to the broken leg, and wondering whether leaving it to a leopard might not have been kinder. But the rules were so strict that we were not allowed to kill so much as a fly. I had become expert in catching flies in my hand and releasing them out of the window to save Moti from their harassing presence.

On the morning of the day we knew Moti was to have an operation, Frank appeared in front of the temple where I was engaged in the *puja*. 'Moti's all right,' he said grimly. Both Alu and the horse had died in the night. What sort of occult exchange of subtle forces was going on one could only guess at. But both those animals in some sense owed their lives to Moti, and they were perhaps allowed to give up their lives for her. Indeed, on her return Moti told us she had seen Alu come into her hospital room that morning. With badly damaged kidneys Moti was a high risk patient, but she came through it well.

As time went on we got to know more about Frank and his unusual life. His father was an architect in charge of ancient monuments in England, including St Paul's Cathedral and St James's Palace, while his mother was a Cornish farmer's daughter. Frank did not know where he belonged. As a British officer staying in the Grand Hotel in Calcutta, he would be drinking tea with the bearers in their cubby hole. At the Ashram he would read poetry to Moti, discuss mysticism with Krishna Prem, and have a homosexual affair with the cowboy at the farm. However, he also volunteered to go out with the cows and buffaloes daily when they went to the forest for grazing, playing the flute to them and having the huge old buffalo lie down and put her head in his lap.

As a boy he had run away from school to go to sea, but had been found by his parents and then put onto one of the old square-rigged four masters which continued to carry Australian grain to England until World War II and trained many young men. He had then worked as a sailor on merchant ships, travelling all over the world. Then he had applied for and been accepted on the Shackleton expedition to the South Pole just before the outbreak of World War II and had even drawn his equipment, but did not join at the last moment. Finally he got a Commission in the army and came to India and the Chindits.

There are several misinterpretations of the facts here – Ernest Shackleton died in 1922 when Frank was just seven years old – but Frank had indeed signed up for an Antarctic expedition on the Discovery II in 1935.

What stands out from this account, however, is not so much the factual details about Frank's past as the observation that he did not know where he belonged. This was true. He had run away from school, run away to sea, deserted ship, crossed the lines as an army officer, and taken refuge in a monastery. He had never quite fitted in; and now he was about to be forced out of the Ashram.

Frank evidently grew increasingly jealous of Phipps and moreover had begun to lead a distinctly un-monastic life. His departure in 1950 was a traumatic affair for such a close-knit and apparently highly-strung community. Phipps wrote about 'an eventful six months' which began when Prem and Moti were away. It ended with Moti, Frank's original ally, turning on him:

> It started with the discovery that Frank had quarrelled with Bob and, in revenge, had fed false reports to Bob, who was in charge, so that Bob would dismiss the farm employees who were loyal to the Ashram and promote Frank's own favourites. The cowboy with whom Frank was having a homosexual affair was now the head *mali*, and what little milk there was being taken up to Frank's cottage for their enjoyment.

Of course there was one hell of a row, and Frank was turned out. But before he had time to leave Almora, Moti had second thoughts. By her reasoning, Frank had come for the inner work, and she had no right to drive him away. So she sent him a message that he could return if he wished. Krishna Prem laid out the Tarot pack and said it was absolutely clear that he would not return, and he said he would despair of me if I could not see the truth of this reading in his layout. After what he had done to me, I loathed Frank and feared him, and I was absolutely certain that he would return, Tarot or no Tarot. He returned, and I got no pleasure at all from being proved right.

However, whereas Krishna Prem and I had been the only targets of her anger, Frank was now included. It was not long before he was being lambasted in a manner I was all too familiar with. After a particularly bad outburst from Moti in front of us all Frank left the room. I grabbed one of Moti's cigarettes and ran after him, sensing that this might be more than he could take. He was now a companion in misery and I wanted to help.

We squatted together on the verandah, sharing the cigarette. He gave a mirthless laugh, and my intuition told me that he was seeing the grim humour in receiving sympathy from the very person he had tried to get rid of. 'I demand better treatment than this,' he said – a phrase that remained with me as representing a total rejection of all that the inner work is about.

Nothing I could say made any difference. The next day he told Moti he was leaving. 'Then take your bloody boy with you,' was her response. This time he was leaving by his own choice, and Moti had no second thoughts. 'There, but for the grace of God, go I,' was my unspoken feeling. Seeing Frank suffer under Moti's whiplash had somehow changed my feelings both for him and for the punishment. What had been unadulterated hell was now modified by a sense of meaning.

EIGHT
FAREWELL TO DAL BAHADUR

NOT MANY MONTHS AFTER LEAVING THE ASHRAM, Frank decided to visit Dal Bahadur. It was a poignant reunion and he wrote about it a way that leaves no doubt that this young man was indeed the love of his life.[175]

***

My final meeting with Dal Bahadur was profoundly sad. It occurred in December 1951, as I was contemplating leaving India for ever.[176]

Although I had continued to get news about him through the good offices of a friend, I had preferred to keep my enquiries a secret and remain in the background. I thought that he should have the opportunity to get shot of me and develop without interference along lines of his own.

I had not seen him since we said goodbye on Lucknow station in December 1944, but, of course, I knew his address. It was: Village Lamma Gaon Busti, Post Office Phulbazaar, District Darjeeling, North Bengal.

---

175 This is the final chapter of *Chindit Affair*.
176 In the event, Frank did not leave India until early 1956, and even then that was not for ever.

And I went there.

I had been to Darjeeling several times before but on this occasion the landscape looked particularly magnificent. As the little puff-puff came to the top of the hill at Kurseong, where the Hindu monastery is, it was evening. The setting sun was shining full on Kanchenjunga, ruddy as an apricot, and the mountain stood up before me tall and powerful, obscuring half the panorama with its bulk. Then the train ran slowly down the incline and came to rest.

On the following morning I started out on my investigations. Finding the actual whereabouts on the ground of Dal Bahadur's address turned out to be comparatively easy. When I enquired at the General Post Office where the Sub-Post Office of Phulbazaar was, an obliging counter clerk accompanied me outside onto the street and showed me. It was right down in the bottom of the valley, six thousand feet below.

'And Lamma Gaon Busti?' I enquired hopefully. 'Where is that?'

My informant pointed to practically dead opposite. It was, as the crow flew, only about five miles distant across the intervening valley. To get there, however, I would have to descend six thousand feet to the valley floor, cross the river by rope bridge, and then climb back up another ten thousand feet.

As I did not have much time at my disposal, I started out right away.

Phulbazaar proved comparatively easy of access. The walk there, through fruiting orange and tangerine groves and sometimes between terraces of tea-garden cultivation, was entirely delightful. A heady scent of citrus fruit was in the air and the turpentine tang from the pine plantations and the forests of cryptomeria was almost overwhelming. As I descended deeper into the valley, it got hotter.

I arrived just before mid-day at the little cluster of wooden houses, with their balconies from which flowered a riot of geraniums. I stopped at a tea-house to refresh myself, and then went along to the village store, which served as the Post Office, in order to pursue my enquiries.

This time I actually mentioned Dal Bahadur by name. As I knew not only his caste designation, namely Chettri, but also his patronymic, namely son of Tensing Bahadur, I was reasonably certain of getting fairly near my target. I succeeded beyond my wildest expectations.

My questions as to Dal Bahadur's whereabouts and the best way of getting to Lamma Gaon Busti were greeted with a curious sense of expectancy. I was told readily enough what to do and which was the easiest path to follow, yet I was left with the strange feeling that they knew all about me. Quite soon the entire community seemed to have foregathered and to be regarding me with what was plainly considerable respect.

As I was unaware of having done anything to deserve such V.I.P. treatment, I began to feel very uncomfortable.

I was asked if I would like to rest. A chair was produced and I was practically forced to take a seat. Then there appeared before me the village elder. This gentleman, being endowed with the communal authority, came to the point at once.

'Are you,' he asked politely, 'Dal Bahadur's sahib?'

'Well ... er ... yes,' I assented. 'As a matter of fact I am.'

'Are you,' continued the old man relentlessly, 'the officer who gave him the beautiful inscribed cigarette case?'

'Er ... yes!' And fancy him knowing *that*!

'Are you,' he continued with mounting enthusiasm, 'the same officer who gave him the priceless gold amulet inscribed with the sacred letter "Om" and containing a miniature copy of the Lord Krishna's song called Bhagavad Gita [powerful magic]?'

'Yes!'

'Then, sir,' chanted the old man, by this time positively lyrical – and the whole community standing behind him seemed to concur – 'you are truly welcome!'

They all bowed down before me in an elaborate prostration.

Absolutely horrified, I sprang to my feet. It was too late. I was already launched into a full civic reception. A garland of French marigolds was produced, and from somewhere behind my left elbow somebody thrust into my hand another glass of sweet tea.

'You saved his life!' said the old man, coming up and whispering into my ear affectionately. 'He told us himself. You saved his life!'

Such was the welcome. I believe I might have stayed in that place for the rest of my life. I think I would have been happy there.

Somehow, however, I managed to struggle away. I crossed the river torrent by the rickety string bridge which was strung across it, and the whole village waved me goodbye.

The ensuing climb up the hillside in the heat of the day cost me an enormous effort. The sun blazed down unremittingly and, being out of condition, I poured with sweat. I was relieved, however, by my every so often encountering a Gurkha villager who greeted me with the most dazzling smile as well as a profound obeisance, indicating that my reputation and the news of my presence had in some mysterious way gone before.

At about nine thousand feet, with the sun striking behind Tiger Hill above the cantonment of Darjeeling to the west, and the mist on top of my mountain getting lower and lower, I began to have doubts as to whether I should make it before night. A bitter cold had descended.

Suddenly, above me, I spied a little procession. Made up of youths and maidens, it was like something which you would not be surprised to have found in Ancient Greece.

It was him all right. I would recognise that figure anywhere.

We met in the middle of an open hillside that was quite bare of cultivation. It had started to rain. And in the rain, on that bare hillside, we embraced.

He had become subtly older and wiser. In fact he had grown up and become a man. Yet I knew that he was the same.

He didn't say anything. He simply took me by the arm and led me forward. Indeed, as it transpired afterwards, he had prepared a stunning reception. He had despatched messengers to bring elegant dancing-boys to entertain me from far and near.

We sat under a thatched awning outside a sort of hut. His own house had been destroyed in the recent Darjeeling earthquake and there was nowhere else to receive me. It turned out to be the local shop and to belong to him. I was glad to learn that he had always been a rich man and owned such important property.

When we sat down, I was able, for the first time, to steal a close but covert glance at him.

He had aged considerably. That is to say, although still young and handsome, he was no longer a boy. A dashing, Kshatriya-style moustache sprouted from his upper lip in silken splendour, and he looked like the young Buddha of the Gandharan sculptures.

Huge bonfires were lit. The whole village came up to be presented to me and then sat round me in a circle. Several beautiful boys appeared, bearing gigantic earthenware pitchers of wine, for Dal Bahadur well knew my tastes. In the background, the women-folk began preparing the rice. We were all so tensed up by the solemnity of the occasion that none of us needed much persuasion to eat and drink.

Throughout the whole of that misty night, Dal Bahadur and I sat cross-legged together, leaning shoulder to shoulder. Quite early on in the proceedings his mother had come up and covered us with a single blanket. It was like a sort of wedding symbol. Under cover of it our arms entwined.

Within the circle of the firelight the dancing-boys twisted, stamped and pirouetted; the drums and *tablas* sobbed; the viols moaned.

Gradually the spectators got more and more drunk and finally flopped on the ground, fast asleep. Towards dawn, the dancers and the instrument players departed for their homes. The fires died down. Dal Bahadur and I remained wide awake. While the crickets chirped and rustled in the great bundles of paddy-straw, we talked of the past.

And later we returned to the present – and he revealed to me that he had developed phthisis in his infected lung, and was not expected to live much longer.

Before the sun was up, while daylight was yet seeping through the cloud-base, I left.

He was very stoical. Yet we wept and wept.

We wept for our lost youth and for our dear departed – which was *us* when we were young. And we wept because he was ill, and was feeling feeble and faint-hearted, and must prematurely die. We wept because I was leaving India for ever and because our passion was spent. And we wept because, although we loved each other, we were no longer in love.

During the whole of the long trek back to Darjeeling I did not encounter a single soul. Phulbazaar, when I passed through it, was deserted and gloomy. The river beneath the string bridge roared menacingly. I felt as if I were fleeing the wrath to come. The gorge had become a torrent for dead souls. Even the geraniums had withdrawn behind closed shutters.

But the landscape was a blur to me, for I was much preoccupied with my own sad thoughts; and I knew for a certainty that, far behind me in Lamma Gaon Busti, Dal Bahadur was preoccupied with his.

I never saw or heard of him again.

* * *

What Frank omitted to say, however, is that he never forgot Dal Bahadur. He would have many more lovers over the years, but none in his mind ever quite matched up to this first love. Many years later, he was to recreate his passion for the young Gurkha in literature, reliving the drama and spectacle of his lover lying wounded in the chest, and late in his life he would still hear inside his head Dal Bahadur's cries for help.

NINE
ON THE MAKE IN CALCUTTA

IN THE EVENT FRANK STAYED IN INDIA FOR another five years, and for most of that time he was in and around Calcutta.

By his own account, he was not in a good state when he arrived there. 'I was shaken and terrified,' he wrote later. 'They'd shaved my hair and you could still see where I had a caste mark.'[177]

Matthew Screaton, a friend from Coggeshall, recalled that Frank said he had initially fallen on hard times in Calcutta and that he had been rescued from the gutter by Mother Teresa's Missionaries of Charity. This could well have been true, and he did eventually live and mix with people who knew Mother Teresa well.

Dev Ashish said that on leaving Mirtola, Frank took a job at an architect's office run by a family friend – not unlikely, given his father's distinguished career. His former colleagues from Mirtola kept in touch, and there was a disturbing postscript to his monastic life. Alexander Phipps tells the story:

Many things were to happen before Krishna Prem, Moti and I were to go to Calcutta and get news of what Frank was doing there. At this point in the story one thing can be mentioned. We knew that Frank had got work

---

177 The biographical briefing note prepared by his publishers Eyre & Spottiswoode in 1971 (Random House archives).

in an English firm owned by a friend of his, and we discovered that some of our Bengali friends were working in the same firm. When one of these Bengali friends came to call on Krishna Prem he noticed that the friend was wearing a protective talisman. This seemingly superstitious behaviour was entirely out of character, for he was very much the intellectual type. So Krishna Prem teasingly asked him how he could be wearing this, and the friend rather shyly confessed that many people in his office had found it necessary to protect themselves against Frank's ill will. No hint had been given to anybody about the causes of my illness, or even that I had been ill.

Calcutta, the principal city and commercial hub of Bengal and the former capital of the British Raj and the once headquarters of the East India Company, was an exciting, even racy place in the 1950s. For the few rich Indians and the remaining Europeans it had everything to offer – from polo playing and horse racing to belly dancing and brothels where hemp was smoked. A port city on the Hoogly River, it was open to the outside world: London, which had once been a six-week sea journey, was now only 32 hours away by airplane. India was in the heady early days of independence, but social life was still largely dominated by the ways of the old British Empire and the substantial club-obsessed European community. But this was of course the shrinking oasis of a charmed existence amidst the chaos and poverty of the world's most destitute and crowded city.

Frank was aged 35 when he arrived in Calcutta. He was fluent in Urdu and Hindi, fully at home with living in India and, despite the scars of his war, still in his prime. He left only a sketchy account of his time there, and never wrote directly about it, but he made his mark in Calcutta in several quite unexpected ways.

He set up his own business in the Kidderpore Docks repairing and making tea chests. He traded as: Baines, Repairs to Tea Chests.

Calcutta was then at the heart of the world's tea trade. Tea from the Assam plantations was shipped from the wharves on the River

Hoogly in vast quantities, and all of it in wooden chests. Frank's officer training and his education at Oundle, where basic engineering and carpentry were an obligatory part of the school curriculum, came into play.

Philip Crosland, a former senior editor and general manager of the leading Calcutta newspaper, *The Statesman*, and possibly the last expatriate alive in 2010 who remembered Frank during his time in Calcutta, says that Frank did very well out of his tea chest business. The tea industry in Calcutta was very short of packing cases at the time. Frank went down to the docks and saw all the empty cases, cases that had been kicked about and broken up, and realised that they could be salvaged. He employed a gang of men to repair the cases and sold them to the tea industry. Crosland says he had no idea what those cases were made of and what they contained before they fell into Frank's hands, but he is sure that Frank made a lot of money from this business.[178]

Frank briefly described his business in a form he completed for the army in 1953 to register as a reserve officer. He was: 'Sole proprietor trading in Baines, Repairs to Tea Chests, engaged in contract work for managing and repairing damaged chests of tea in Kidderpore Docks, Calcutta, contract work for managing and supervising tea warehouses in Kidderpore, contract work for loading and unloading of lorries, wagons, barges and the stacking of tea chests.'[179]

Frank also referred to another equally unexpected aspect of his life in India – he was a part-time farmer. His subsidiary occupation, he wrote, was commercial farming and running an orchard on 50 acres near Calcutta.

Crosland, who was born in England and was just three years younger than Frank, remembered him above all as a great talker, who could expatiate on any subject. For much of his time in Calcutta Frank lived with Desmond Doig, a former Gurkha soldier and also homosexual, but Crosland comments that that kind of thing was never discussed in those days.

178 Interview with the author in London in December 2009.
179 Army Personnel Records.

Doig was a fine writer and an amateur but highly gifted painter; and he was a regular contributor and illustrator for *The Statesman*, which he had joined after the war as a recruit in the advertising department. Adventurous and outgoing, he was also a creative artist who took a keen interest in architecture and landscape – a man of action and an aesthete, very much in Frank's mould. In later years, Doig went on expeditions with Edmund Hilary searching for Yetis, producing with him in 1962 a classic book, *High in the Thin Cold Air*. He also wrote an early account of Mother Teresa in 1976 and published a book of his drawings of Calcutta. Doig remained in Calcutta until 1975, and for the last 10 years there he edited a hugely influential and trend-setting magazine, the *Junior Statesman*. The magazine was cult reading for young India and a training ground for some of India's best journalists, including Shashi Tharoor who became deputy foreign minister. When the *Junior Statesman* was closed down in 1975, Doig moved to Kathmandu, where he died in 1983.

Crosland says that Doig was responsible for the best part of half the newspaper. As well as his reporting, he was a tremendous illustrator, although hopelessly unreliable at meeting deadlines. It was through Doig that Crosland got to know Frank. Frank and Doig shared a duplex flat with a magnificent roof garden in a terraced house in the Hastings Alipore district of southern Calcutta, between the Maidan Park and the Hoogly River. Dubbed the Pleasure Dome, it became a legendary place of culture and a menagerie, and played host to an astonishing array of artists – from the American dancer Martha Graham to the young British composer Benjamin Britten.[180]

Doig described the premises in his memoirs *Look Back in Wonder*:[181]

I do it much discredit to call it a flat. It was a fantasy – two layers of Marwari Moghul architecture that sat atop a fairly ordinary building, presently rented to a telephone company. A portly Nepalese durwan (door-

---

180 In interview with the author in London in December 2009.
181 Privately printed in Kathmandu.

keeper) lazing at the gate said it was empty because no one wanted it. The landlord, allegedly, had nothing to do with it other than collect rents, because, when built during World War II, some British soldiers who occupied it made a habit of holding barbeques in sort of haveli (inner courtyard) on the roof. Foreign sahibs, mems particularly, thought it to be too oriental, as did local sahibs and mems, but for different reasons.

Having climbed a stairway through telephone offices one emerged on a marble terrace, the haveli on the right, with two small suites of rooms ahead and behind. Up another stairway tricked out in wrought iron Krishnas playing his flute, were kitchen, pantry and servants quarters. Most impressive was the deck space. As I looked over it with the Nepalese durwan, I imagined meals on the terrace in season; parties on three levels with some attraction emerging from the haveli. The rooms were more than a trifle small and one of the loos was quaintly built on an ascending plinth so one could be genuinely enthroned. But I loved it.

On one side, the mock Moghul balustrade supported a view of the immediate garden, the then village look of Hastings and a few high buildings in the distance. On the other, one looked across a rather noisome bustee (slum) which happily rose no higher than one storey so it was possible to romanticize about roof views, when not actually peering into private rooms and court-yards. The snag was the rent. I couldn't possibly meet it alone. But where was the valiant somebody who would see the potential magic in what even I was beginning to realise was kitsch?

I had a rather bohemian friend in a very respectable firm on Park Street who invited me one night to dinner – a miracle. The dinner, cooked by his cordon bleu wife, was fairly miraculous by my usual kati kabab standard, but the miracle I had been invited to was the flowering of a midnight cactus. Several of us watched a rather shaggy khaki coloured bud slowly unfold until it became as large, and even more chastely beautiful as a lotus. Its sickly sweet perfume increased as it opened. Our host told the story of how in its native somewhere, the cactus blossom lured small animals, night birds and insects to their death. They apparently impaled themselves on the cactus thorns.

One of those present was an English house-guest who contrived to steal almost as much attention as the cactus flower by appearing in a saffron lungi (long male skirt) and a string of tulsi beads. His head was shaved. To satisfy immediate curiosity he was introduced as Peter Maine, recently retired from an Ashram in Almora, who intended to settle in Calcutta for a while. Talking in sudden bursts of conversation, his hands helping to articulate his words, Peter Maine had us so in thrall we forgot to watch the slow dying of the miraculous flower.

We met often after that, his lungi exchanged for saffron trousers and bush shirt, his tulsi beads discarded. What amazed even more than the slow unfolding of his adventurous life, was his choice of an occupation. He decided to mend tea chests, so there he was, on the Kidderpore dockside, hammer, nails and steel tape in hand, repairing tea chests that had burst or were showing signs of disintegration. He was joined by one, two, five, a dozen, eventually a small army of expert helpers. He became a businessman, with a small office within sight of the ships and the noise of winches and cranes. He flourished. He took a partner. He sought a flat of his own and decided instantly upon seeing it to share my Hastings extravaganza.

So the Pleasure Dome, as an American friend called it, came into being. Frank settled meditatively into the small suite at the top of the stairs, and I took the opposite, with the elevated loo and kitchen above my head. Frank, with his memories of his stately home in England firmly in mind, had a famous Calcutta furniture maker create all his requirements in the very best teak to designs he himself supplied. The classic lines and proportions, instead of clashing hideously with their uncertain surroundings, blended without fuss, even with my deal tables, rented desk and bed. Such was the magic of the Dome. Seating, in the sitting room of much coloured glass and incredible porcelain tiles, was on the floor, mattresses wrapped about with chaste white to try and dampen the overall ferocity of colour.

I went theatrical with colour. The outer walls of Frank's suite were painted a vivid blue against which iron pillars glowed brightly orange. On my side the walls were warm brown, the pillars turquoise. The Krishna stairway got the full treatment of blue body, green trees, white cows and gilt head-dress. Large terracotta pots made, I believe, for dhobis (for washing clothes), stood between coloured pillars spouting the most colourful plants I could find. Frank remained remarkably calm, even when I started moving in a menagerie of miscellaneous birds, a slow loris, three Assam gibbons, a deer, a sarus crane, two peacocks and twenty pigeons that were soon sixty.

Breakfast on the patio was out of movie land. Pigeons, peacocks, the sarus crane and the deer stood about for handouts, often helping themselves when we weren't looking. The Assamese gibbons were wont to join us, dipping their knuckles into the butter and jam. Parrots chained to large brass hoops screeched for attention. Only the slow loris kept to its own devices, although whatever a slow loris's devices are, I never found out.

When word of the Pleasure Dome got to the Editor of the Paper, G.A. Johnson came calling with the First Lady to see for himself. He even contributed to our collection of the weird and wonderful by carrying behind him, so it would come as a surprise, one of those large models of a spotted deer that used to be fairly common on Calcutta's pavements many moons ago.

Remarkable things happened at the Pleasure Dome. It was as if that architectural meringue, failing in its original duty to delight its creators through no fault of its own, was now embarked upon providing pleasures one would never dream of in other houses. Like Martha Graham and her entire troupe, Uday and Amala Shanakar (husband and wife and pioneers of modern Indian dance) and some of their troupe, the Royal Manipuri dance troupe, a Tibetan folk dance group, Kalamandalam Govindan Kutty and his troupe, and everybody who was anybody coming to a midnight party on New Year's Eve. Frank and I contributed the Dome and invitations. A diplomatic American friend laid on the hooch. A good friend from the USIS (US Information Service) provided the food, including vast Alibaba urns of Firpos tomato soup that nobody drank and was found congealed into an evil smelling jelly a few days later. What a party. Apart from that rich assembly of dancers, there was the famous British composer Benjamin Britten and accompanying tenor Peter Pears, and English stage and screen actress Hermione Baddeley, the brilliant Spanish dancers, El Greco, and a famous French concert pianist whose name escapes me.

All the many levels of the Dome were outlined in hundreds of oil lamps. Martha Graham, familiar as she was to the magic of theatre, was moved almost to tears. When she was introduced to all the dancers present she reclined on cushions in the haveli while the Tibetan folk dancers leaped into life. To the thud of flat, hand-held drums beaten with curved sticks, and the shrill singing of two men and a woman, they leaped and gyrated, often it seemed daring to incline their bodies too steeply to remain on their feet. Some of the young members of Martha Graham's troupe joined the frenzied dancing. When it was done, Govindan Kutty gave one of those satisfying performances of Kathakali that explains the nuance of the dance step by step, mudra by mudra. Once again the Graham dancers, particularly a lithe Negro couple, tried successfully to imitate the steps.

By the time the lovely Manipuri group performed, their tinsel and tiny mirrors reflecting the firelight, everyone seemed to be joining in … Americans trying to learn Kathakali, Kathakali dancers abandoned to the rhythms of Tibetan folk dancing, Tibetan dancers trying the gentle steps of Manipuri, Manipuri attempting the symbolism of American interpretative dancing, Martha Graham swaying and posturing to the strains of a Nepalese folk song.

The pollution over the bustee was a tawny brown, the sky red with dawn when the party fell suddenly apart. The signal was given by a Sikh taxi driver who returning to reality discovered his fare of several hours before.

Even the slow loris had a party. It escaped, by clambering onto the shoulders of an unsuspecting guest, only to be returned in a shoe box a few days later.

Doig met Martha again many years later in New York and she looked at him searchingly and said: 'Desmond, Calcutta, New Year's Eve. That enchanted house, those lovely people.'[182]

Frank became a major item in Doig's life. He introduced him to his circle of friends, a group formed around what was called the 'Saturday Club', which included members such as John Mitchell, a socialite, and a Hungarian doctor, Tibor Lantos. Doig said Frank taught him how to talk. The group also frequented one of Calcutta's most popular expatriate watering holes, Angelo Firpo's Italian restaurant in a beautiful balconied building on Chowringhee Road by the Hoogly River.

Crosland says that Frank was a total misfit in Calcutta, completely out of place in the European community. It wasn't so much that he was gay; it was more that he simply did not belong with those people. The Europeans, for instance, set much store on membership of the Bengal Club, and he simply wasn't interested in that sort of thing. The club situation in Calcutta at that time was silly and snobbish. Frank had his own group of friends and some of them, of course, were gay.

The gay community in Calcutta in the 1950s was pretty discreet. Calcutta, for all its steaming humanity, was not another Tangiers. Nonetheless, some surprising people turned out to be gay, such as Ian Stevens, the courageous editor of *The Statesman* at the time of the 1943 Bengal famine who challenged the Viceroy to come and see for himself the devastating effects of the rice shortages in eastern India.[183]

---

182 *Look Back in Wonder*, pp. 112-16.
183 Millions died as a result of the famine which was brought about by wartime market distortions, poor harvests and hoarding.

But Philip Crosland is convinced that there was no exotic gay under-world. He says that he would have known about it if there had been. The Indians were very Victorian in their attitudes. There was just some occasional whisper among the Europeans about a nest of buggers, and there was one incident when a man from Northern Ireland was caught by a policeman getting up to something in the Maidan. The policeman flagged him down as he drove away, but the man did not stop, and the policeman was run over and killed. But it was all hushed up and the Ulsterman was simply kicked out of the country.

Frank's major legacy in Calcutta is in print. He became an art and drama critic and a columnist for *The Statesman* and he also contributed a number of short stories. Founded in 1875, *The Statesman* is one of India's oldest newspapers. It was, and remains, an up-market paper with a wide circulation, both in Bengal and in Delhi, and it has always prided itself on being fearless in its reporting. Still British-owned in the 1950s, it had enormous influence in both Calcutta and beyond. The newspaper was edited and printed at Statesman House, a marble-lined colonnaded headquarters on Chittaranjan Avenue, and was big enough and rich enough to maintain its own London offices. The paper's Calcutta and Delhi offices were obligatory staging posts for foreign correspondents sent to India to cover the tumultuous stories leading up to and after Independence. Over the years it attracted a succession of English editors and reporters, among them Malcolm Muggeridge and Lord (Sidney) Jacobson; and there is an additional unsung claim to its credit – *The Statesman* launched the writing career of Frank Baines.

Philip Crosland says that *The Statesman* was the seed from which Frank sprang. He came to the paper thanks to Desmond Doig, and did some pieces for it, stories and art criticism. There was one memorable occasion when he reviewed a lady's watercolours. She was a middle-aged European amateur, and of course she should not have been subjected to normal criticism; but Frank gave her the works. This was considered by the Europeans to be a very bad show.

It was in Calcutta that Frank wrote his first book, an autobiography of his childhood. Although centred on Cornwall, it bears the scent of the tropics: the opening paragraph recalls hot, monsoon gales. The book also grew from supportive friends in Calcutta, especially Doig, and from the journalist James Cameron.[184] Many years later Frank acknowledged his debt to Cameron, who was then working for the long vanished *News Chronicle*. A frequent visitor to Calcutta in the 1950s, Cameron left a vivid account of his own personal take on the city in his memoirs *An Indian Summer*:

> Experienced travellers argue and contend over their images of what is best remembered, of beauty or pleasure or tranquillity or fun, but among them is rarely any difference of opinion about what is worst, the most irredeemably horrible, vile, and despairing city in the world; few who know it will dispute that this place is Calcutta. The inhuman cruelty of Calcutta defies the normal language of odium; its total wrongness has become base-measure of injustice ... This place could have been designed as the demonstrable end-product of civic disorganisation ... Nowhere else is there beggary of such a ubiquitous, various and ever-present kind. To a European, and especially to a stranger exposed to it for the first time, this mass industry of organised misery must be a seriously disturbing experience; nothing in his ordinary Western responses equips him to come to terms with it.[185]

Frank, by contrast, had no such qualms. He was never sentimental about India; his early work published in *The Statesman* reflects a deep knowledge of the country, which is carefully and sympathetically observed, but also detached. The emotions he describes are only personal; he does not shed tears for humanity.

---

184 British journalist (1911-1985).
185 *An Indian Summer* (Macmillan, 1974), p. 178.

TEN

NEWSPAPERMAN

The Tank, A SHORT STORY BY FRANK BAINES, appeared in the Sunday
supplement of the Calcutta *Statesman* on 4 July 1954 alongside a
suitably sinister illustration by Desmond Doig, which seemed to have
been inspired by Edvard Munch's *The Scream*. This was Frank's first
by-lined piece in the newspaper; the writer of the opening paragraph
is every bit the son of an architect, and the story as a whole is visually
powerful and highly imaginative. Frank found his style from the outset.

* * *

The house was one of those ramshackle affairs that you find lying
about the outskirts of the city – all peeling plaster and Ionic pillars –
built about a hundred and fifty years ago on the edge of a tank. In it,
declining Moghul and mis-appointed Palladio had combined into a
sort of clumsy grace, to which the damp and decay added a quaint
charm its builders had never designed. For all that its porticos were
afflicted with elephantiasis and its architraves with cramp, it was not
a building you just despise. This alone gives it a certain dignity in my
eyes. And the adjoining tombs were quite fine.

I had arrived in the city suddenly and unexpectedly one day from
Chittagong with neither the money to stay in the most expensive hotels
nor the inclination to accept second best. As it was at the height of the
housing shortage, I determined with ludicrous inconsistency to try for

a flat. With this end in view, I drove straight from the station to my ex-cook's. My cook was in; his wife was having her fourth baby; and he was broke. They seemed pleased to see me. 'I want,' I said, 'a flat.'

'Sahib, I have a place.'

'That's fine. Let's go and see it.' I paid off the taxi and we set out on foot there and then. The whole thing was as if planned. We reached the place in fifteen minutes. Rather a fat and very voluble woman showed me about. She threw open the whole of the ground floor. It looked as if it had seen neither daylight nor a duster for years. It was heavily and ornately furnished. Bats hung from the chandeliers. Forgetting even to enquire if there was a lavatory, I took it for a hundred rupees a month. My cook, his wife, the three children and the unborn baby and myself moved in. I enjoyed comparative quiet for about six months.

I can't remember exactly when I first heard the child crying. I have an idea that it just seeped into my consciousness together with the noises of the other children. As a distinct phenomenon I only became aware of it gradually and after quite some time. A day came, however, when I knew that a child cried nearly every and nearly all night. It didn't disturb me; but I used to wake up and hear it or listen for it. And once, when it was quiet for a longer period than usual, I became positively restless until it started crying again. In this way the com-monplace noise and a certain part of myself developed a nodding acquaintance, became almost friendly, and at last associated. I started listening for the child with an intensity that surprised and slightly terrified me. I ended up by giving to it attention of all my nights. Still, I was only under the impression that I had yielded to a morbid obsession which no doubt the onset of the cold weather would cure me of.

I was not really worried. The thought of leaving my lodging had not even occurred to me, so that I was spared until recently the distress of discovering that I am somehow incapable of taking such a step. I really do believe that the child's sobbing exercises a sort of fascination over me. But it is quite a gentle fascination: I should like to go to it, to help it.

Just as I cannot remember when I first heard the child crying, so I cannot remember when I first took to walking along the edge of the tank. If I did not believe such a thing preposterous, I should be inclined to say that I came to my senses one night while actually doing it. Of course, in retrospect, this is only how it seems. I must have been engaged in thinking deeply about something else when I found myself suddenly and abruptly in the water with the sound of the sobbing coming from directly in front of me. I was only then that I became aware of the ubiquitous quality of the crying, its all-round-ness, or as if it were humming inside my head. My peregrinations of the tank taught me another thing. The child actually cries from the middle of it. There is no doubt about this, because I have walked all round it. This is the only really extraordinary thing about the whole story. Except, of course, my encounter of last night.

I awoke suddenly at three this morning. Moonlight was seeping through the shutters like an intangible fluid. I got up and went out feeling strangely refreshed.

To my surprise I found a man sitting on the steps of the tank leading into the water, and smoking a hookah. I returned for my cigarettes, and with a sense of relief joined him. 'Good morning' and 'Huzoor', we said.

We remained for quite a time silent together, enjoying that remote companionship of strangers who meet by chance in unexpected places and at an odd hour. When I felt that a decent enough interval had elapsed I addressed him in English. He replied to me in a courtly Urdu I had seldom heard in Bengal. I had an idea, however, that he was quite familiar with English.

Subjects of conversation seem peculiarly limited at such an hour. Because of this perhaps, I was indiscreet enough to ask his origin and with a sweep of his hand he indicated the great colonnaded façade behind him. 'I am of the family,' he said, and the domes of the tombs seemed to tremble a little. 'My father was a great man.'

I digressed upon the beauty of the place and sympathised with hard times. He sighed a little; quite slowly we thawed each other's ice.

'Surely,' I said after a minute or so of more animated conversation, 'this house must be historical? And yet I have never heard of it. If you know anything, tell me the story of it in this full-moon night.'

The child was mercifully silent. I was not even thinking of it.

He laughed. 'Things have happened here,' he said gazing rather fixedly at the water in front of him. 'Take this tank,' he paused, and added almost to himself, 'I daresay I was wrong. It was bad.'

Then with a friendly confident air he turned to me. 'The bricks for this house were excavated from this tank. But it was quite empty; and when we had completed everything, it was still dry. We dug and dug, but still no water came. You understand,' and he emphasised the point with his finger, 'it was a disaster. For ourselves,' he shrugged. 'We had wells. But our people.' My imagination conjured a legion of servants in the now waste places. 'Nowhere to bathe,' he continued. 'Our women,' he lowered his lids. 'Our cattle.' I felt the list getting longer and longer, and coughed. With sudden decision he came to the point. 'I bought a boy. Only a very young one,' he said as if sensing my difficulties. 'About two or three. You could still get them. Slave people.'

'But the Government,' I almost choked. 'The administration.' I was considerably shaken.

'Pouff,' he said and it conveyed everything that I didn't want to know. 'We brought him here and put him in the dry bed of the tank. We had a sort of ceremony,' he was not using the technical Urdu term but was paraphrasing for me. 'There were djins,' he said. 'You know djins?'[186]

'Yes,' I said.

They demand sacrifice. They killed the boy ritually with flowers and rice. Almost immediately the water flowed in. It has been like this ever since.' He stopped short again and gazed at it and in that smaller voice of his. 'Perhaps I was wrong,' he said. 'It was bad.' And then more confidently. 'But you have to do something for the common good.'

---

186 Arabic term for supernatural creatures.

A distant cock crew and in the east there was a faint light. A warning rustle stirred the air from the tombs to our right and he glanced towards them. Then, grasping his hookah, he got up to go. 'The child too demands sacrifice.' His teeth flashed at me in the moonlight. 'And sometimes,' he said, 'he cries at night,' and slowly he walked towards the domed mausolea and disappeared in them. And from the tank the boy started his broken sobbing. I was glad it was dawn and would soon be light.

But now it is again night. I sit on the steps of the tank where I sat this morning with the stranger. I am alone. My cook, his wife and the four children have long since fled.

The moonlight glitters upon the water and it is quite implacable. The child is sobbing. I cannot distinguish between the noise of it and the impalpable water that seems to close about my body and to reach up towards my head.

* * *

Frank's next contribution to *The Statesman*, in a special supplement to mark Independence Day on 15 August 1954, was reportage about a rural community worker, and it draws directly on Frank's own experiences cultivating his 50 acres outside Calcutta. *Real Life for the Cultivator and Hope for Mr Ghosh Too* demonstrates a native knowledge of growing crops in Bengal's rich alluvial soil, and Frank's evident enthusiasm for organic farming that he doubtless would have learned from his time at the Ashram. Farming would also have taken Frank back to his childhood – both at Combroke and St Keverne.

Mr Chandi Prasad Ghosh turned up at my place in June last year. He was the new VLW (Multi-Purpose Village Level Worker). In our sub-division the Community Projects had started in 1952 but most of the officers were appointed a year later, and Mr Ghosh was my first contact with it. Rather a heavy propagandist effort in the Press had pre-disposed me unfavourably towards Community Projects and I was a bit suspicious of Mr Ghosh. I felt he had certainly come in some way to curtail my freedom. So I told him straight out most of my agricultural problems in the hope that they would frighten him away and leave me to my difficulties and my freedom. So, of course, after a year of working more or less under Mr Ghosh I'm naturally surprised to find that I've still got my liberty but that my troubles are considerably less.

The VLW turned up again the following day with the answers to my problems all scientifically co-ordinated into a sort of manurial programme, supported by hosts of examples and his own experience in the district. We looked over the place together and he admired my new cement compost-pit. I showed him the sun-hemp. 'Are you growing this for green-manuring or seed?' he asked. 'For manuring,' I said. 'I think you ought to plough in straight away, then. When the flowers form, the plant withdraws nitrogen stored in the root-nodules for depositing in the seed, and the effect on the ground is less.' As he was leaving, he said: 'Anything you think I can do for you, please let me know and I'll do my best.' I thought the whole thing over rather carefully, and then in the evening ploughed in the sun-hemp. I had a bumper crop from the ragged old guava trees in the field during October. I felt much warmer towards Mr Ghosh.

Frank goes on to describe Mr Ghosh's remit – 500 villages spread over 184 square miles, in a remote backwater some 100 miles north of Calcutta – and the extraordinary range of his work. The VLW scheme was introduced across India in the early years of Independence to help rural communities develop and to make their farming more efficient and ultimately boost food production. A good VLW officer would turn his hand to anything – from distributing seeds to pulling teeth. He follows Mr Ghosh around some of the villages, listening to him talking about kitchen gardens and the cultivation of soybeans, and watching him at work with the community:

And here, after riding six miles across country on his bicycle, Mr Ghosh ploughs and plants, extracts teeth, vaccinates children, delivers calves, demonstrates implements, settles disputes and lances boils.

Frank ends the piece on an optimistic note. He quotes Mr Ghosh:

Here we are making a real life for the cultivator. And there is hope for me, too.

In the same Independence Day supplement, Frank published a short story which is intensely autobiographical. It was 20 years since his father had died under a mountain of debt, and *Except the Lord Keep the House* – an exhortation from the Psalms – is a story about a father, a rich Calcutta merchant, who has lost everything and kills himself:

My father came back home on Thursday, driving through the rain in a closed carriage. Khanti Babu had visited my mother the evening before and had been with her several hours, but it was not until morning that I heard the Bank had crashed …

As I went in my father was going upstairs, his back unbowed. I saw him dismiss with a gesture he servants, before the door of his room. I only saw the tall doors flung open and then closed. After about 15 minutes I heard the shot.

The fictional son in Frank's story goes through his father's papers – the assets and debts – just as his own father's disastrous affairs were wound up after his sudden death:

I ran through the list of properties, bonds, investments, and then through the debts. I made a rough assessment. Things looked pretty bad.

There was nothing left and Frank's 'son' is forced to sell the grand house, which had been the family home since the time of Warren Hastings. Twenty years on, Frank was still yearning for Trenoweth. The rest of the story revolves around the sadness of leaving the house, with even Lakshmi, the Hindu Goddess of wealth and prosperity, weeping for its loss.

The Metamorphosis of Mr Sen, another short story by Frank in *The Sunday Statesman* in October 1954, touches an altogether lighter mood:

> The strange disappearance some four years ago of Mr Utpal Sen and his wife from their compartment on the Madras Mail caused quite a stir. Mr Sen's files at the Finance Ministry were carefully scrutinised and Mrs Sen's private life was laid bare. All to no avail. Mr Sen's files were perfectly in order and Mrs Sen apparently never had lovers. The enquiry eventually lapsed through want of evidence and nothing more was heard of the matter until about a year ago when Mr Sen suddenly turned up and succeeded in establishing his identity beyond any doubt.
>
> Mr Sen's story was so extraordinary, however, that his brother-in-law, who was enjoying the administration of Mr Sen's property and was consequently disinclined to receive Mr Sen back, moved to have him committed for lunacy.

The reader is instantly drawn into Mr Sen's fate; Frank could spin a good tale, and, inevitably, there is an unexpected twist – Mr and Mrs Sen wake up in a snowy landscape in Imperial Russia on a train bound for Moscow.

Frank also contributed art reviews and articles on diverse subjects, such as *Pictures under the Skin,* a history of tattooing, and *Aspects of British Architecture.*

Reviewing Bertram Hume's *Form and Reform in Architecture,* Frank is on home or at least in familiar territory, and there are strong echoes of his father:

One cannot but admire the subtlety with which he leads the reader inexperienced in handling architectural theory to assent to more and more startling principles totally at variance with ordinary man-in-the-street opinion, until one really does begin to see the whole process of architectural design in a cogent, lucid manner, as something with an organic life with meaning its own, not just as a matter of drain pipes and gables, glimpsed through the distorting lens of a frosted glass window.

In another powerfully written piece in *The Sunday Statesman* on 11 July 1954, Frank argues the case for Indian sculptors. It was called *Let us See the Work of Indian Sculptors in Public Places*:

In Indian cities public sculpture takes the form of eminent city fathers chilled for all time in smooth marble, viceroys, governors and royalty contriving to look dignified in stone and famous generals dramatically riding to new conquests in heavy bronze. Occasionally, cherubs and nymphs disport themselves on infrequent fountains and gargoyles peer at one from old buildings, but by and large there is little if any creative art of the sculptor to be seen in public places.

Frank laments the fact that India's great legacy of creative sculpture had been repressed during British rule in favour of civic sculpture and, drawing on his experiences of England, he says there should be room in public places for both classical and contemporary Indian designs:

We hear that the city fathers of a certain well-known city in England have protested violently against the gift of a Henry Moore intended for erection within the limits of their jurisdiction. Yet I remember a Moore looking remarkably at ease and easy to appreciate in the corner of Battersea Gardens, where a classical statue would have passed almost unnoticed … Barbara Hepworth's poetic monoliths looked as well standing on the hard pavements of London's South Bank exhibition as they did in the rustic surrounds of Battersea Park. I believe a group of Hepworth sculpture set up in any open space anywhere would have the same awesome near-religious feel as the ancient monoliths at Stonehenge.[187]

With his slightly devilish humour, Frank acknowledges that city authorities were generally wary of erecting sculptures in public places because, like buses and trams, they were frequently attacked during civic unrest. 'It's easy to imagine what would be done with a small *Woman in Toilet*,' he says.

But his message is a sincere plea for public commissions for India's emerging generation of new sculptors – such as Prodosh Dasgupta, Roy Chowdury, Ravinder Reddy and others who later became well known:

> Government, city planners and architects should remember the now forgotten Indian sculptor, who, long underground because of the unconducive atmosphere of the past several hundred years, is eager to emerge and restore to his country the great tradition of sculpture it boasted when artists were encouraged to perpetuate their creative energy in metal and stone.

In another memorable piece in the Sunday edition on 22 August 1954, Frank writes about the artist Ram Jor. Frank would have first heard about Ram Jor in Almora; his story is tantalising and ultimately sad. Ram Jor was born by the high Tibetan lake of Koko Noor (known in China today as Qinghai Lake) and at the age of five he was dedicated to the local Buddhist monastery by his parents and trained as a junior artist. However he abandoned monastic life before he had even learned how to use colours. Ram Jor made his way to India and was later taken up by an Englishman, a former Secret Agent who was living in Almora. His English benefactor encouraged him to resume painting, and the result was an instant success. His first exhibition of naive and magical-looking landscapes in Calcutta in 1945 was a sell-out. Frank writes of Ram Jor as follows:

---

187 The reference to the Moore and Hepworth sculptures implies that Frank had seen them in situ and that he had therefore travelled back to England to see his mother sometime in the early 1950s, although there is no record of any such trip.

His work has been likened to Chagall, Rousseau and Matisse, and all these contentions bear a certain truth. For despite the fact that Ram Jor had never heard of these artists, nor of the school of modern French painting, he is modern with a surprising sureness of touch, a splendid eye for composition and a sincere regard for purity and truth. His is a living art, an art with its roots firmly set in tradition but with a mind free to interpret the visions of a modern world in a spontaneous and original manner.

Ram Jor has reversed the usual process of success. Successful in the first outpouring of his brilliance, he is unknown today.

For explanation we must return once more to the great lake of Koko Noor, and the child who imbibed absolute truth and absolute sincerity on its shore. Left suddenly alone when his English Guru returned to England, the liberated voices and visions of the man Ram Jor were in an instant homeless, for in their stead had collected the fears, doubts and uncertainties he had until that moment never known. Life was suddenly without purpose.

Abandoned and without his mentor, Ram Jor opened a teashop, and he tells Frank that it is now too late to take up painting again. This remark challenges Frank and prompts him to dwell on death and immortality in highly lyrical passages that underline a deep inner spirituality and transcend a simple review by *The Statesman's* Art Critic:

Yet strangely men are seldom afraid to die. A child is taught that he may already have died several times, and that the next death might merge him with the Absolute. The terrifying aspect of his gods is as exciting as it is fearful. A child of vision can conjure them up at will, lurking in caves, behind rocks, in trees, in the sky, in animals, in people and in the ever-changing mood of the lake. Time is of little consequence; there may be a thousand lives yet to live. A rock can be the reincarnation of a sinful life, a soaring bird a soul on its way to eternity. A child born within sight of

Koko Noor can travel to the ends of the earth, hide himself in foreign cities and embrace alien ways, but he can never escape the presence of his gods; neither can he hope to forget the ever-present problem posed by death. In a tea shop surrounded by the bustle of civilisation and twenty years removed from Koko Noor, Ram Jor sees visions unclouded by time, visions peopled by strange animals and beings created in the images of his gods. The landscapes they prowl are tinted by the omnipresent, dark, foreboding, familiar and yet remote. On paper they are portraits of a distilled essence. The essence of Tibet.

But is it too late for Ram Jor? When the storms scream across Koko Noor and prayer flags tear and blow away in the wind, do not people in their homes fear perhaps that this is the night of the final reckoning, when the dead and living shall gather together and be judged by all the vast concourse of the gods and their Shaktis; and is there not always the next morning with its visions of an unimagined peace and its promise of a more bountiful day?

ELEVEN
MIRROR, MIRROR

WHO WROTE SHAKESPEARE, ASKS A SPOKESMAN OF THE British Council, and divides up the answer between the Earl of Derby and Bacon?

As a matter of fact, I wrote Shakespeare. I wrote the whole of Shakespeare in three days, fourteen hours, fifteen minutes while hanging upside down from a fan in the luggage compartment of a slow train to Delhi.

Frank staked his claim to being the great English bard in one of his first columns for *The Statesman*, which appeared from May 1955 under the title *Mirror, Mirror*. Signed by Merlin, the column appeared mainly on the front and back pages, side-by-side with serious national and international news stories. *Mirror, Mirror* was anything but serious; and yet it hit some deadly truths:

This leaves open the question of who wrote me. A fellow scribe claims he did, but I don't see how this was possible since I wrote him. We are fighting it out at the Badminton club at 6.30 tomorrow without seconds. This opens up a larger question of the pursuit of literature. Now that the twilight of the gods has deepened into night vulgar people hunt literature with headlights in jeeps. This has led to literature becoming more and more protected, not to say hedged about. This is a good thing and one of the blessings of the Welfare State. I am probably the last of the hyenas to render the night hideous with his mournful cry.

Mirror, Mirror was a startling departure for this serious broadsheet, and a big gamble for its editor, G.A. Johnson. Frank was let loose, often on the front page, to take pot shots at the newly created India, fulminate against its socialist and welfare policies, lampoon Prime Minister Jawaharlal Nehru and other politicians, poke fun at local dignitaries, and generally to be Frank. He cajoled, he moralised, he mocked, he teased, he bristled, he bridled and he entertained. He was also highly productive, writing almost a column a day for nearly two months, often covering a range of different topics each time; and he seems to have enjoyed and relished every minute of it.

Merlin first appears in print on 11 May 1955, when he takes a swipe at India's attempt to emulate Soviet-style economic development – 'the inflexible determination to march on, shoulder to shoulder, against the mad, capitalistic-monopolistic jackals forging the steel bonds of indomitable endeavour upon the anvil of cooperative agronomic feasibility'.

Done with agronomic-economic experts, Merlin turns to fish:

People who are partial to prawns had better look out. Specimens are now on the markets which are computed to be 145 million years old. They possess a cleansing, palatable flavour and are best eaten with a dish of Chinese eggs. The particular variety is Blenkinsopia Chopra. (This was a reference to a local personage; there are many such in the column.)

Merlin expounds on the characteristics of ancient prawns, and then continues:

More recently a Coelacanth was discovered in the plumbing of the New Secretariat when a Deputy Minister went to wash his hands ... This is the first occasion when a Coelacanth has met a Deputy Minister. In an exclusive interview, he surmised that the Deputy Minister must belong to a type at least 200 million years old, probably a survivor from pre-Dravidian India. He expressed great surprise to find such a well nourished specimen in such perfect health. The skin was sleek and glossy, the eye shifty and the handclasp moist and slack.

In following days, Merlin has another go at the 'Welfare Heaven' – this time over the state of the railways – and he also vents Galactic spleen at Air India in a piece that anticipates Douglas Adams's 1978 *Hitchhiker's Guide to the Galaxy*:

Air India Interspatial's Martian Princess throbbed on the skids. We mounted the launching platform and filed into the rocket through the tubular vents. Above me the tritanium ducts keened faintly in the jube-light. The globulators sizzled and a terse glug from the jinkhorn turbulated the flax. I heard the whine of the streptomatic ports and their closing click. Jube-lights were winking on the axial-frame and I knew the torsion rings were opening. Quite soon we would be off.

Space-hostess Grexa Hkleg came down the self operating lift-way … Swallowing my intromission pills I relaxed on the gimballed space-foam pad and waited for induced intromission.

When I awoke, we were clear of the bathosphere gliding towards Moon. Grexa Hkleg was serving Air India Interspatial's Tourte de Bombard au Mars in ray-proof cosmophane. I dialled 'Service' and ordered an Ortolan '97.[188]

Suddenly the rexine screen before the pilot-tube flashed off. I knew it was an emergency. My Ortolan '97 was in the service-feeder, but I ignored it. Space-officer Trab came through the depersonalised screen wearing ray-mask and carrying a transmogrifier. 'We've unfortunately left the pilot behind,' he said over the intercom amplifiers. 'Completely forgot him. Little oversights of this sort sometimes do happen on Air India Interspatial.'

---

188 The ortolan is a tiny song-bird that was long considered the pinnacle of gastronomic delight by the French. It is now a protected species after being hunted almost out of existence.

Merlin has his home country in his sights on 16 May:

If there is anything I like better than a good funeral, it's a good election, so I have naturally been thrilling to the news from Sleepy Hollow (an insignificant little island off the north coast of Europe) where 'Don' Attlee and 'Rocky' Eden are grappling in a death-grip from which practically every hold has been barred except the big-brotherly embrace and the love-tap.

The following day, Merlin takes his first swipe at the United States:

Considerable anxiety is being expressed here lest the Shrimatis of India imitate the Begums of Pakistan and form themselves into an organisation like the Daughters of the American Revolution. This possibility is considered to be a most unfortunate aspect of American Aid. Modern American Woman, probably the most frightening aspect of femininity since the Amazons, has struck terror into the heart of every nation that has met it.

Merlin also introduces his readers to a major political leader – Sri Hamhandra Mullet, his cartoon name for a West Bengal political leader – but he starts off gently with him, and reserves his most caustic comments for the newly constructed building in Delhi that houses the Indian Council of World Affairs – 'a neat jumble of architectural styles painted to resemble mousse of ham … crowned by a small wart'.

He chides Nehru the following day for wielding a small baton to drive back a crowd of welcoming Indians as he stepped off a plane at Rangoon, and pokes fun at one of his anti-capitalist speeches and has another laugh at the Welfare State – 'which will now have the goodness to come into being at the behest of the Congress'. But in a spoof on the poet Thomas Gray's *Elegy Written in a Country Churchyard*, the day's tears are shed for Calcutta's old buses:

Your prayers are solicited on behalf of Displaced Buses who are having difficulty in rehabilitating themselves in West Bengal. Lowing herds of homeless buses wind slowly o'er the lea and No 79K homeward plods his weary way, leaving the route to the double-decker of the nationalised Transport Service. No more for them the blazing neon signs shall burn or busy housewife ply her evening care, no children run to lisp the old bus's return, or climb upon his seats the envied tootle on the horn to share.

The self-inflicted austerities of Indian politicians catch Merlin's attention on 20 May:

I notice that Mr Takhtmal Jain, Chief Minister of Madhya-bharat, will use only two of the three rooms in his official residence. The remaining portion to be converted into a Circuit House. High dignitaries will use it during visits to Indore.[189]

Mr Jain has ordered the removal of luxurious articles like sofas, cushioned chairs and costly carpets. There will be no curtains on windows or doors.

A communiqué issued two days later from the Ministry of Salt-licks, Commerce and Industry emphasises that there is absolutely nothing in all this for Mr Jain to congratulate himself on. Sri Hamhandra Mullet, when he becomes Chief Minister, intends to camp out on the lawn in a shanty made of bird cages and old Chianti bottles. He will order all the doors and windows of Government House to be ripped out and distributed to the poor for fuel. The official residence will be converted into a Cats' Home. Every amenity conducive to the comfort of cats will be removed. Shri Mullet won't mind. Since he has decided to mortify himself for a bit, everyone else might as well be made to feel it.

Following on the heels of Mullet's manifesto comes one from the office

---

189 The State of Madhya Bharat was incorporated into Madhya Pradesh in 1956.

of Acharya Attabhoy Bhoobi. Bhoobi declares that when he becomes Chief Minister he will live on the branches of a tree on the Calcutta Maidan, wear a garland of soda-water-bottle tops and eat nothing but curried golf balls. He will levitate to and from his office.

Finally Shri Sombernath Bhupati declares that when he becomes Chief Minister he does not intend to live at all, but will be transmogrified at dawn on Ekadashi[190] accompanied by a distant bumble of blurb.

Merlin has a classical knowledge teaser on 24 May – 'for all you people who think you are better educated than I am'. He asks the Classical Boys who have been to Oxford whether Plato refers to the City of the Golden Gates as being the principal city of Atlantis?

But apart from his by now routine broadsides at local politicians, his primary target is the absurd egalitarian propaganda of the new Indian State:

Psychologists working along novel lines have discovered that incalculable damage is done to the human psyche by reason of its having to suffer various forms and humiliation and frustration.

In line with this, railway authorities have decided to alter the designations of compartments to first, super-first, and super-duper first, to prevent anyone having to suffer the odium of travelling third.

It is the turn of education in the new Nationally Planned India on 25 May:

It's perfectly obvious that at this critical stage of National Planning we must pack our universities as tightly as a panel of South African Supreme Court judges ... The Education Industry has the most productive teaching shops and instruction factories in Asia and it is the only one in which mass

190 Ekadashi is a Hindu holy day.

production and assembly line methods have been really successful ... we are churning out matriculates, B.A.s and M.A.s in unprecedented profusion. And as a consequence the market price of a B.A. has fallen to Rs 100 or below, and matriculates are selling on every street corner for from Rs 40 to Rs 60.

Merlin ends the day by reporting that the Indian Army is proposing to replace P.T. with Russian Ballet:

An issue of classic-sided ballet shoes in three pastel-shaded colours has already begun and Madame Vana Mahastsova has been borrowed from the Bolshoi theatre for the kick-off ... Colonels are busy being measured for their ballet skirts.

The proclivity of Indian politicians, and for that matter most Indians, to make long speeches is Merlin's primary target on 27 May:

A bulletin issued from the residence of Acharya Attabhoy Bhoobi says the Acharya has been smitten with pomphols. Sir Smatterin O'Medicine, who is not in attendance, describes pomphols as a fibrous growth which if not attended to eventually strangles the patient. His condition is then deplorable.

Developing from a morbid sensitivity to spiritulation, the subject takes himself very seriously. Thereafter the humour religiossifies accompanied by marked intolerance. At this stage a number of dangerous phobias develop and occasionally the patient is very intractable.

Tertiary stages of the disease show symptoms of self-identification with an increase in the proselytising proclivity. If he subject is educated he may burst into print. At this stage the disease is highly infectious and should be isolated. If this is not done, symptoms multiply due to infections from the olfactory trap or contagion from a rash of print.

Sir Smatterin O'Medicine adds that the disease is endemic to India and we are suffering a particularly painful endemic at the present moment ... Treatment. Continued douches of cold water taken with several grains of salt.

The same day he takes aim at a new law in the State of Madhya Bharat, which will require everyone to do at least five days manual labour every year:

I seem to remember a couple of guys called Hitler and Mussolini explaining that the gas-chamber and the rubber-truncheon were intended to create public opinion in favour of the Pure Aryan Race. But that was totalitarian and wicked. Although the idea of the Pure Aryan Race seemed quite a good one to its sponsors at the time it is now recognised as ridiculous. In this enlightened age of politics and trade it has been replaced by Apartheid as being more logical and consistent.

But for really enlightened legislation we return back home. All men between the ages of twenty-one and fifty residing in any panchayat area of Madhya Bharat will be required to do five days manual labour a year towards development projects.

After informing his readers on 28 May that he is seriously considering having himself deified, Merlin turns the tables and sends himself up:

I certainly don't consider that I am writing all this blurb by chance. I am doing it by the will of God – and my god at that. And of course it is perfectly evident that my god is different, and immeasurably superior to yours – somebody who went to the very best public schools and who moves in the most exalted social circles.

Frank, by now with the self-appointed title of Merlin Meglomaniacus I, continues in the same vein, and with some honest insights about

himself he steers the column round to his serious gripe of the day:
You probably think I am terribly well-educated and between you and me
I am not displeased with myself. But the awful truth is that I've never
passed an exam in my life. The reason was that we were so stinking rich
in my younger days that I didn't have to.

I have always laboured under this insuperable advantage all my life, and
every time I tried to get down among the roots I have been yanked up again.

Consequently I have absolutely no sympathy with the orthodoxly educated
and the very word curls my lip with disdain and sets the stomach heaving.

He then goes on to complain bitterly that graduate and matriculate
clerks in Bombay's Cotton Textile Mills are getting a pay rise while
non-matriculates of the same grade are not.

On 30 May, Merlin is warning Indian visitors to England not to
go north, which like India he says has been overrun by Scots. He quotes
from James Cameron's newspaper:

The *News Chronicle* of London has said that the true backward races of
the modern world are the white people who seek to keep the coloured man
in perpetual servitude.

This has raised to fever heat the whole question of the backward races of
Lancashire where people are still hopelessly addicted to cotton gin. My
special correspondent just returned had some terrifying experiences with
wild white women in clogs and kerchiefs.

These people live in a sort of troglodyte existence between piles of satanic
mills all tumbled about as if in an earthquake. They speak a peculiarly
stilted dialect derived from Cimmerian and worship Ultima Thule, a goddess
with a face like a horse who walks on high heels. They wear socks in bed.

They work in an industry run on lines derived from the Pharaohs ... This part of the country used to be inhabited by picturesque people clad in a sporran and girt about with a sassenach. But now, of course, it has been captured by the unspeakable Scot − as indeed has much of India.

Young Indians going overseas should be warned against venturing north of Regent's Park under any circumstances.

On 1 June, Merlin is complaining about the heat in Calcutta, but his real targets are the heavy-handedness of big government and the hypocrisy of the world's emerging class of post-colonial dictators:

This hot weather has been indescribably boring; there hasn't been a decent riot for months. People are getting soft.

Merlin declares that he intends to stir things up by publishing a series of inflammatory revelations about vice and crime and generally promoting mayhem with a succession of increasingly spectacular acts of defiance:

If the masses rally to my cause, as I have absolutely no doubt they will, being completely gormless and gullible, I shall levy a subscription of one anna from all of them to be devoted to the survivors of my atrocities and pack 'em off to the front where I shall direct operations from a commandeered villa in a suitable hill-station.

Whether the war goes well or ill doesn't really matter. As one of the leaders, I shall be assured of a prominent place at the peace conference and live in the best international hotels in order to promote expulsions of population by agreement. I shall insist that everyone has the right to go into exile unmolested and of course unhampered by overmuch worldly goods. This will prove that I am ready to co-operate.

As a last gesture before allowing myself to be persuaded not to retire I shall draw up and sign my Convention for the Protection of Human Rights and Fundamental Freedoms. This will guarantee every natural and legal person enjoyment of his possessions except in the public interest, and subject to the conditions provided for by my laws and by the general principles of international law laid down by people like me or where the right of the State impinges in any way or where the Enforcement Branch deems necessary to control the use of property or in the general interest or to secure payment of taxes or other contributions or penalties. Or for any other reason. This should allow me a pretty free hand to expropriate whatever I please in case of an emergency or when I feel like it.

I am confident that there will be thousands of ways of persuading myself that I am entitled to some or all of the other person's possessions and I intend to see that there will never be a shortage of flatterers, politicians or agitators to back me up. And there will be thousands of ways of securing the transfer. Discriminatory taxation, nationalisation, inflation, price restrictions, ceilings on holdings or wages. These devices have already been made legal, and I don't need to bother any more about moral sanctions. This makes the whole process quite respectable, not to say bourgeois, and the word looting need never be mentioned.

Having secured the right of self-determination I might as well use it. What would have been the purpose of all my struggles unless they included the power to dispossess aboriginals and foreigners alike and establish me and my new regime and our adherents on a solid footing.

Merlin punches a hole in another sacred cow on 2 June; he takes exception to a report that the followers of Vinoba Bhave, an apostle of non-violence and one of the spiritual fathers of modern India, has described their activities as 'looting with love'. They were at the time following him on his 13-year walk around India collecting land from

landowners to redistribute it to the poor. Merlin is not impressed:[191]
To be looted with love is one of the most refined sensations. It's all designed along the best psycho-analytical principles to bring about 'transference'. I am reminded of the smiler with the knife ... Personally I have absolutely no affection for cold steel. On about the only occasion when I was confronted by a defenceless man while I had in my hand a spent rifle and a bayonet I ran away screaming. My intended victim looked considerably surprised. But if he would have submitted as readily to being smothered in my great big motherly embrace as he was prepared to receive my bayonet in his guts I should not have batted an eyelid.[192]

Merlin envisages deputy magistrates pardoning criminals who display a degree of kindness:

These refinements are all part of the latter-day development of non-violence. They demonstrate the road along which a noble philosophy, if carried to its logical conclusion, will carry you. They might surprise the founder, but so would the latter day developments of Islam, Buddhism or Christianity. It's inspiring to know that in the hands of apt disciples the sky's the limit beyond which one cannot go. This is known in scientific circles as crossing the frontiers of thought. We are delighted to feel that India is rushing towards them.

Still vexed, Merlin returns to this obsession with love in his column on 4 June:

Oh for a breath of good clean hate to dissipate the foetid air in this infernal charnel house of impeccable motives. What's got into everybody? Why are we all being sucked into this octopus-egg of love? Whence this preponderance of the mawkish in sentiment and the mealy of mouth?

---

191 Vinoba Bhave (1895-1992), an advocate of non-violence, is considered one of the spiritual fathers of modern India.
192 This is a reference to his close encounter with a Japanese officer during the Chindit operations.

His spleen is evidently up; Merlin also ridicules concerns about children being run down in traffic in Darjeeling – 'as if anyone cared for horrid children':

They are always dashing about under motor car wheels in their beastly high spirits. India's overpopulated.

Merlin laments the passing of the tram in Calcutta and reports on the interment of the city's last tram tracks. He then turns on just about every Indian in sight:

Look here! I am just about sick of your perpetual belly-aching. Can't you ever do anything for yourselves? I know the government stinks and for why? Because you're just a lot of pongy blugards as well. Haven't you realised yet the truth in the adage that a nation gets the government it deserves. Well if you are so beastly dissatisfied, jolly well go and do something about it.

Who made you the chosen people? Do you suppose that just because you've got five thousand years of progressively disintegrating civilisation behind you, you are therefore entitled to sit on your bum and moan, moan, moan? Are you mentally so completely stultified, petrified, as to think you cannot just relax and get it done for you, you ossified idiots?

I'm telling you, freedom means perpetual watchfulness and if you're not prepared to take that much trouble you won't have it very long ...

If your spiritual heritage is half what you're always telling me it is, let's see it in action. That is assuming it to be something of the heart and feelings and the flesh and bone and not a series of repetitive formulas learnt by rote and gabbled off in a dark corner like the gobbling of a turkey-cock.

Taking all your colossal pretensions for granted, then get up off your knees.

Awake, arise, or be forever fallen. This means YOU!
By 8 June, Merlin has switched his focus to food and government
central planning – in his mind all the same thing:

I have invented my new Dinxie-Winxie Breakfast food for all Indians. It
is something pretty big. Low-cost, high-falutin, anti-corruptive, corrugated,
shock-proof, and duo-adrenalin, it is part of my Five More Fatuous Years
Plan.

I have long thought that rice and atta, not to speak of meat and two veg,
are far too good to give the poor, apart from being highly expensive. What
we need is a cheap, nasty, ersatz, substitute food to keep down their energy
and prevent them from protesting.

Fed to children in forced concentrates under the Compulsory Projects
scheme, it will have all the advantages of hitting 'em below the belt.

And meanwhile:

The Indian Standards Institution has issued a tentative specification for
table fans. This is about the only tentative thing the government have ever
done so far. They generally blunder about like a bull in a china shop, rush
in where angels fear to tread, cry over spilt milk, close the stable door after
the horse has fled, put the cart before the horse, fish in troubled waters,
count their chickens before they are hatched, look gift horses in the mouth,
cry stinking fish and all the rest.

Merlin, the ex-soldier, takes on the Indian Army, or the National
Defence Academy, in his column on 9 June. He sees the army going soft:

Power of Love will be one of the principal subjects, and attention will be
devoted towards looting with love, turning the other cheek, loving those
that hate you, etc, etc. It will be based on the master-disciple relationship,

cottagy-còttagy industries, community meditation and respect for dumb blondes. Every National Defence Academy girl will be instructed to say boo to a goose.

A new tank, called 'Community Project' will be rolled out:

The tank is fitted with an amplifier for relaying to the enemy the peace speeches of Shri Hamhandra Mullet. If this fails it will emit a stream of hot air right in the face of its enemies. Then it will take to its heels and scamper for safety.

Demonstrating his worldwide remit, Merlin notes that a British official had inadvertently addressed a letter to a Mau Mau rebel leader as 'Prime Minister', and that the Argentine Senate had unanimously passed a bill giving full provincial status to the Falkland Islands, and he then turns to the subject of working practices in India:

Don't get unduly worked up about any orders you may receive. Just perform your work as you feel like. You may have Saturdays and Sundays off with full pay, also all Hindu, Muslim and Christian holidays together with any other benefits your union is able to collect. I advise forming this immediately. The baby? Keep it locked up in the kennel.

Mountaineers are next up, more specifically women climbers:

I understand that the Central Government is considering the banning of mountain climbing. It is thought that the modern mountaineering girl is bringing the ancient sport into disrepute.

Meanwhile, the Abominable Woman writes a series of informative little articles for me on how to make up at 20,000 feet. She says a hint of mascarenas at the corners of the eyes gives that teeny additional sparkle which is so important for every well groomed girl on the nursery slopes. I always use *Poudre Glamoreuse de Haute Himalayas*. It comes in 60lb tins and makes such a convenient load for those dear companionable little men, the Sherpas.

Lipstick. Use a deep-gashed orangey-red. It comes out wonderfully in those photographs of you leaning up against a cwm or crevasse.

Accessories. Snarshall and Melgrove[193] are selling the niftiest ice-axe in rain-washed colours to match your hair. And don't miss the diamante and rhine-stone oxygen mask at Negretti and Zambra's.[194] It's a must if you are to look your best in the evening.

And on 11 June, it's the weather:

The monsoon is reported to be feeble. It would have been too much to have expected it not to reflect the general malaise. I saw a debilitated little rain shower dragging its painful way across the city the other day. Nobody even bothered to take shelter.

And alas, also, for poor penniless politicians! Have we reached the age yet of maximum disenchantment. Well, I have but I gather it will take you some time longer.

Merlin goes to war with the United States on 14 June. He is incensed by a State Senate bill in Florida which forbids public-school teachers and professors and State-supported universities to discuss, on pain of dismissal, a long list of subjects:

Communism, Nazism, socialism, collectivism, planned economy, one-world government, or similar Anti-American doctrines, theories about the field of business other than the theory of free enterprise, or any other theory

---

193 Marshall & Snelgrove was a fashionable garment and textile retailer, now taken over by Debenhams.
194 Negretti & Zambra, famous instrument makers, founded in 1850.

that would undermine or destroy the fundamentals of any religious faith, including the Christian faith.

Dear Americans, we all like you ever so much, reely we do! But ... ! I know there would have been no victory without you in the last war, and that there will be no victory without you in the next. But ... !

I know that you are financing the free world, and out of the goodness of your heart will probably continue to do so, almost ad lib. But ... ! But why don't you give me a little more encouragement in liking you? I want to, but ... !

Forgive me my old fashioned and conservative estimate of the meaning of freedom. But, dear Americans, this sort of thing hurts. Yours more in sorrow that in anger, etc!

On 20 June Merlin writes:

Our pose for today will be one of resignation and world weariness. Life is not only an illusion, it's a bore.

He returns to America; he has been told that he will become terribly popular if he goes on attacking the United States. But Merlin has second thoughts:

I may someday have to seek political asylum there and don't want to queer my pitch. When freedom in Europe goes, as it will, America will be among the few places left for me to run to.

Not to be bowed, however, he then goes on to denounce the widespread use of phone tapping in the United States.

On 22 June, Merlin takes up the idea of converting some of India's castles into hotels.

Castles, I'm afraid, do things to me which the ordinary dark bungalow doesn't, and I am perfectly prepared to live in squalor so long as I have a few crenellations for company, one or two-barbicans, a moat, a portcullis, and, of course, thou beside me in the wilderness. I have always wanted to drive two chariots abreast, preferably along a rampart opening on the foam of perilous seas, in faery lands forlorn.

My original suggestion was for a like idea here. Some of the strongholds of Northern and Western India would prove quite irresistible. A friend pooh-poohed it. He immediately started talking of bathrooms and plumbing but this merely confirms him as a hopeless pedestrian. The idea of a tourist as a man madly rushing from bathroom to bathroom is out of date. Tourists come to gain insight, to study ethnology, in search of the quaint, to expect discomfort. All of these we have in good measure. I am quite an interesting ethnic group in myself. Herded into a fort, slapped in irons, condemned to death, reprieved, made Commander-in-Chief, granted a jagirdari,[195] intrigued against, poisoned and finally murdered, every tourist should be allowed to depart with a castle as a souvenir to raise Cain in his home town and keep memory green. It would be big. It would be different. It's our life. It's what we are used to. Anybody can produce an enormous hotel packed with drain-pipes and sanitary fittings. And how dull too. Give 'em battlements and a hint of menace, the back stair and privy way, small airless rooms, and the intricately conceived device, and plenty of machico-lations to eat, a palanquin, a terrapin, and a railway guide. Give 'em garlic, give 'em glue. It doesn't matter; but do it with imagination.

Merlin didn't know it, but his column was coming to a close. Fit-tingly, in his penultimate outing on 27 June, he pleads for tolerance and liberalism:

---

195 A feudal system of political and revenue administration.

No one has ever questioned that the abuse of alcohol is ungentlemanly, chota log, and degrading. But so also is the abuse of political power and money, nuclear fusion, the right of assembly and open speech, the freedom of the press, the inalienable heritage of air-conditioners and electric cookers – everything. The operative expression is 'abuse of' and not the quality in question. Vulgar people succeed in abusing anything, not excluding the virtues; men of stature raised even the debased to their own level. They ennoble it. Emphasis must be on the sort of people, not the sort of thing.

Search you own heart chum.

I can go on *ad nauseam* like this. It's perfectly obvious that by legislatively banning something you don't abolish it. You merely make it a furtive, hidden secret, shameful thing. In fact you become a sort of political ostrich, intoxicated with ideological panaceas that are all very well in their way, but which should be drunk heavily diluted with a soda of commonsense. Intellectual intoxication is more deadly and more dangerous.

If any of you are worried about your morals, look to them. Each to your own. Forbear to pry into my dustbin. I am perfectly aware that it stinks. Personally I have too much trouble keeping Merlin to the straight and narrow to have an awful lot of time left over for preaching to my neighbour.

Search your hearts and look to your own.

Frank's journalism in Calcutta came to an abrupt halt; the newspaper made no mention about what had happened to Merlin. Suddenly he wasn't there and a few months later – in March 1956 – Frank made a hasty departure from India; he fled the taxman.

Philip Crosland says that Frank had some difficulty getting out. In those days when you were leaving you had to have an exit visa showing that you had paid your taxes, and of course Frank had never paid any tax and they were onto him. He got on a plane to Dhaka in what was then East Pakistan, but he had to do a bit of artful dodging when his flight back to London touched down in India.

After Frank had gone, the tax authorities came looking for him at *The Statesman* offices. The editor, G.A. Johnson, who had helped Frank with his flight out, had to feign ignorance of his whereabouts.

The next time Frank refused to pay his taxes it would cost him more dearly.

TWELVE
WRITER

COMPARED TO INDIA, THE ENGLAND FRANK RETURNED TO in the mid 1950s was a gray and sullen land. It was still scarred by the war and overshadowed by its recent memories. Winston Churchill left office for the last time only in 1955. A cold war between the Western democracies and the Communist states of the East was enveloping the world in a new ideological struggle. Britain was losing its Empire, and Egypt seized the Suez Canal in 1956, forcing a temporary return to petrol rationing. John Osborne's play *Look Back in Anger* made its debut in London.

Coggeshall, where Frank's mother had by now been living for almost 20 years, was little changed from war-time. With a population of around 2,000, it was still predominantly a rural town – a community that largely depended for its livelihood on local farming and agricultural industry, such as the seed merchants E W King and John K King. It is today a dormitory town for office workers in the City of London and elsewhere and has more than 5,000 inhabitants, but commuting to London in the 1950s was almost unthinkable. The buildings on Church Street and East Street and Market Hill were not painted in bright colours as they are today, and many were in a bad state of repair. The town's fire-engine was housed in Market Hill and there was still a large house on what is now the Doubleday shopping precinct. There was a town tailor and a baker and there were three butchers and some 15 pubs. Only one of the town's now widespread new housing developments, at Monksdown Road, had started.

Although Frank would continue to travel and live on and off in London, for the next 10 years The Cedars at Coggeshall would be his principal home, and in the somewhat dreary surroundings of this small town in North Essex, Frank stood out like a exotic potentate from a far-off land. Moreover, he had paid for a teenage Indian boy called Gopal to accompany him to England, and he paraded him through Coggeshall, dressed in his Hindu robes, causing quite a stir among the natives.[196]

Jill Baines, Frank's cousin by marriage, recalls that Frank brought the boy to stay with them. Frank was in his Indian robes, and in bare feet, and she remembers Gopal as 'a beautiful boy' – and that sadly he went back to India and died of TB.[197]

Possibly under pressure from his mother, Frank made some attempt at getting a serious job. Writing from *The Statesman's* London offices in Whitehall, he registered for employment with the Officers' Association.[198] But he had returned to England focused, indeed fixated, on becoming a serious writer, and he seems to have quickly gone off the idea of pursuing a serious career. Instead he took a series of labouring jobs, which left him free to write in his spare time. Labouring, he said, was a good life for a writer. For a while he was in Glasgow, where he worked for a steel company and lived in digs, and this proved productive; he wrote his second book there. He then moved back to the South and took up residence in various London flats, first in No 9 Charlwood Street in Chelsea and then in East Dulwich, at No 44 Champion Hill.

Frank's connections with *The Statesman* and India opened doors in London, and led to some interesting relationships with writers and would-be writers. One of these was the novelist Simon Raven.

Raven and Frank shared not only homosexuality and quite possibly a brief relationship; they also had in common a similar gilded upbringing, short careers in the army, and India. After National Service in the Parachute Regiment, Raven transferred to India for officer training in Bangalore.

---

196 Mark Marchant, Coggeshall antique and picture dealer, and Stanley Haines, ex-Chairman of the PCC, interviewed by the author in 2009.
197 Interview with the author in 2009.
198 Letter dated 28 March 1956, Army Personnel Records.

Like Frank, Raven turned a deaf ear to outrage, saying: 'I've always written for a small audience consisting of people like myself who are well-educated, worldly, sceptical, snobbish (meaning that they rank good taste over bad).'[199]

Twelve years younger than Frank, Raven made his literary debut at about the same time as Frank with *Feathers of Death* in 1959. This was the story of a homosexual romance in the Army and doubtless made Frank determine that he, too, would one day tell the real story about male love on the battlefield.

Frank also got to know, very fleetingly, the novelist Colin Wilson, author of *The Outsider*. This time it was the Cornish connection; Wilson, who then lived in Cornwall, stayed a night at Frank's flat in Denmark Hill and some years later he wrote a kind note to Frank's publishers saying how much he admired his writing.

During the early years back in England, Frank also developed a close relationship with Angela Pain, the daughter of the broadcaster and playwright Nesta Pain. Angela lived in Chelsea in London with her mother, and she had a weekend cottage in the village of Good Easter in North Essex, 15 miles from Coggeshall, and Frank used to stay there. Angela was dark-haired and pretty. She had a First Class degree from Oxford, where she had read English at St Hilda's College, and was something of a blue-stocking. She worked in publishing and in 1951 contributed menus to a book written by her mother – *Science and Slimming* – which the publishers Secker & Warburg claimed on the dust-jacket would put paid to myths about slimming.

In exploding a number of the most treasured fallacies about slimming, she [Nesta Pain] points out that a five-mile walk will only cancel out the effects of one pint of beer, and that toast is nearly four times as fattening as potatoes. At the same time, she stresses the excellent effects of a diet designed on scientific lines.

There is a hint that Frank's relationship with Angela Pain may have

---

199 *Daily Telegraph* Obituary, 15 May 2001.

evolved into a heterosexual affair; she was 11 years younger than Frank and in 1958 he wrote about his 'homosexual period' as if it were in the past.[200]

In any case, Angela figured prominently in Frank's life, even spending time with him in Italy, until sometime in the 1970s when they had a major row and she left to farm sheep in Wales. Frank owes Angela, who died unmarried in 2000, one major debt – she also encouraged him in his writing.

Frank had returned from Calcutta with the first draft of his autobiography; and he had quickly begun work on his second volume and at the same time set out to find a literary agent. The Indian connection once again came into play. The journalist James Cameron, who had known Frank in Calcutta, recommended him to another old India hand, and so Frank was taken on by a young writer who had been in the Indian army during World War II and had served as a logistics officer in the campaign to reconquer Burma from the Japanese. This was Paul Scott, the future author of *The Raj Quartet*, a four-part novel which explores the tensions in India in the final years of British rule and which was turned into an award winning television series in 1984 as *The Jewel in the Crown*. In the 1950s, Scott was working for the literary agency Pearn, Pollinger and Higham – one of the most successful in London. Scott became Frank's literary agent in the summer of 1956 on the basis of his first two draft volumes of autobiography; and Frank was already talking about a third.[201]

David Higham left the agency in 1958 to set up his own firm, and he took Frank and Scott with him, and their relationship was to last until 1960, when Scott himself left to become a full time writer. It was Scott, who had suffered a near record 17 rejections before his first novel *Johnny Sahib* was published in 1952, who found Frank his first publisher, and he wrote to Frank to congratulate him.[202]

---

200 *Look Towards the Sea*, p. 101: 'Besides, I was in my homosexual period.'
201 Letter to Paul Scott, 21 August 1956, in which Frank sends some biographical information and writes about plans for his third book (Random House archives).
202 Frank refers to the letter from Paul Scott in a letter to his publishers dated 21 September 1970 (Random House archives).

Frank's first book, *Look Towards the Sea*, was published by Eyre & Spottiswoode in February 1958. Frank was very fortunate in his relationships at Eyre & Spottiswoode. The then editorial director, Maurice Temple-Smith, looked after him personally; he believed in Frank and in effect launched his literary career. A graduate of Peterhouse, Cambridge, who had trained as an RAF pilot towards the end of the war but without seeing active service, Temple-Smith invested a great deal of time and effort in his new young writer.

Temple-Smith describes Frank as full of energy, with a sparkle always in his eyes. He says that he got one of his most trusted readers to look at the manuscript. He gave a very good report on it, and Temple-Smith then went through it himself, recognising at once that underneath it had originality and vitality, but that it needed a great deal of work. Frank always said that it was easy to get a book published: all you had to do was deliver a bundle of typed papers and out came a book, but this was far from the case with *Look Towards the Sea*, which (like all Frank's books) in fact required a lot of editing.[203]

Frank also fell under the wings of John Bright-Holmes, who was Eyre & Spottiwoode's publicity director. A gentle giant – he was six foot, four inches – Bright-Holmes had entered publishing after Wellington College, National Service and Cambridge, where he had studied Modern Languages, and he would eventually become Frank's second editor.

Frank was working as a navvy at Victoria Station when *Look Towards the Sea* came out. In correspondence with Scott he gave his address as c/o Continental Services, 123 Victoria Street. Bright-Holmes was quick to exploit this heaven-sent PR opportunity. Frank, their new writer, was 'discovered' down a hole on Platform 8.

Nancy Spain, a star columnist for the *Daily Express*, actually interviewed him down his hole, and she wrote a gushing report on 15 February 1958 under the headline: 'How to survive the shock of success – the man I found on the Golden Arrow platform is getting slightly

---

203 Interviewed by the author in 2010.

worried'. Her story was accompanied by a photo of Frank, with his knowing, slightly slanted smile and his golden wavy hair ruffled and dipping onto his forehead, over the caption: 'Frank Baines, Man of the Moment':[204]

> I went along to Victoria Station to see the man working in the hole on the platform where the Golden Arrow comes in (the deluxe overnight boat train which then linked London and Paris).

> This was 42-year-old Frank Baines, dungaree-clad labouring black-pawed author of *Look Towards the Sea*.

> He is the man of the moment. He has written a book destined for the same sort of success as Axel Munthe's *Story of San Michele*.

> Frank Baines's book is an alarming and beautifully written true story all about his own life from childhood to adolescence. He loved Cornwall; he had an odd, rewarding relationship with his father who was Sir Frank Baynes KCVO. (You will notice the difference in spelling. 'Young' Frank prefers to spell his name with an 'i'.)

> He disliked middle class life in Clapham. Yet he adores London.

> 'It's a mature, wonderful, cultured, sophisticated place. Cockneys know how to mind their own business. Why, if you dropped down in the street they'd probably let you lie there for hours. I respect that.'

> By the time Frank was telling me this we were drinking coffee and milk in a call-in for car men near Victoria. He was gesturing all around him in the air with a foot-long bamboo cigarette holder, something like the one that Princess Margaret uses.

---

204 Nancy Spain, British journalist and broadcaster (1917-1964).

'I am unemployable,' he said. 'That is why I am working as a labourer foreman trainee for £15 a week. No one else will have me. Also, I am inclined to run away, you know, when I don't like things. I am already shaking with terror at the thought of the BBC and all that.'[205]

So far, Frank has run away from Oundle where he was at school and loathed it, and to sea in a Finnish ocean-going sailing vessel. And I suppose, like all of us he has perpetually run away from himself.

He served under John Masters (author of *Bhowani Junction*) in the war and says that Masters writes all his books and carries out his literary plans like a military strategy.

Very different from Baines. Baines was so exhausted after being a Chindit that he spent several months in a Hindu monastery in the Himalayas.

'I know I look as if I were leading a mad kind of poetical existence,' said Baines. 'But I am not an angry young man. I mean I love going to the vicarage tea parties and living with my mother and so on. It's just that this is literally the only way I can make money to live.

'As a matter of fact, the idea of being a successful author appals me. It isn't really me at all.'

He rolled himself another cigarette stuffing it into his holder with his black fingers. Somehow the cigarette paper stayed clean. I was amazed.

'I have my lodgings,' said he. 'My last job was in Glasgow. My new book is still there being typed. I got £200 advance on this one. I thought it was princely.'

We talked about writing and success, and the weird behaviour of people

---

205 The BBC interview was not preserved in the National Sound Archives.

on trains. More particularly on the Crewe platform.

'They all go mad when they get to Crewe,' said Baines. 'I've seen them jump out of trains and buy strange pies and eggs and sandwiches and things they don't want at all really. They even buy books. Someone ought to write about it.'

I have never met an author I like so well. He seemed modest, truthful and kind.

So if you happen to be travelling from Victoria this morning, do look out when the train pulls away.

You may see a tufted shock of yellowish hair sticking out of a hole on the platform by the first lot of signals. That will be Frank Baines, wondering how he will survive the shock of success.[206]

The Sunday Times on 16 February also ran a picture of the newly-discovered author digging a hole on the Continental Platform at Victoria Station. 'I am not an eccentric, but labouring is a good life for a writer, and where else could I earn sixteen quid a week?' the caption quoted Frank.

The book's front cover was designed by the artist and print maker Julian Trevelyan,[207] who was also an inspiring teacher of students such as David Hockney, Ron Kitaj and Norman Ackroyd.

Frank, a new and unknown author, had got off to a brilliant start. He gilded the lily by writing the publisher's blurb himself:

One of the consolations available to the man who has his book published is that he learns the answer to that great secret: Who writes the blurb? Well apparently the author does ... This book is written not for your enter-

---

206 © Express Newspapers 15 February 1958.
207 Trevelyan (1910-1988), a surrealist artist, was living in Hammersmith at the time and teaching at the Chelsea Art School.

tainment, and certainly not for your instruction, but for your pleasure. Librarians may like to note that it can be kept on the shelf labelled 'autobiography'; the common reader will, I hope, read it through and judge it for himself.

In addition to making a news story as the product of a writing navvy, Frank's book was greeted by reviewers with widespread critical acclaim, particularly by those who saw in it some sort of renaissance of Cornish writing. Frank's description of Cornwall, and the account of his Cornish childhood, captured the public's imagination.

Historian and Fellow of All Souls A. L. Rowse, a professional Cornishman and himself homosexual, lavished praise on Frank in *The Sunday Times*:

This is the most remarkable Cornish autobiography I have read, and it is by a non-Cornishman. That is the less surprising when one reflects that some of the best things written about Cornwall have been by outsiders: nothing is more true to Cornish life than D.H. Lawrence's story *The Tinners' Arms*.

Most of Mr Baines's childhood, and all that he values of his life, was passed in the Parish of St Keverne, near the Lizard. It is very queer, and almost inexpressible, how strong is the pull that Cornwall can exert upon people. But this odd fish, sometime a merchant seaman, comes as near as anybody ever has to expressing it; for he has an extraordinary sense of atmosphere and the innate gift to render it in words. No wonder the Book Society welcomed this newcomer with a recommendation.

So like an outsider in Cornwall, Frank Baines saw most of the game, and appreciated its finer points, the place and the people themselves. There were the rivalries and differences among the little coves in his territory, Porthallow, Porthoustock, Coverack. It is as good as Greece. There were characters, like George the farmer-fisherman, with whom he spent blissful days at sea fishing off the Manacles:

'He was my greatest childhood confidant, and was also a friend of my father. They are buried next to each other at the north-eastern angle of the churchyard where you look across Trenoweth lands to Falmouth. From my father's grave you can see our drive gates with their stone eagles under the sycamore trees, and the marled road between the blue hydrangeas and the ash avenue, and the house white between the elms and the blue sea.'

The high point of George's life was when he skippered the Porthoustock life-boat that terrible night when the liner *Mohecan* went in on the Manacles and broke up; and I have never read anything more exciting than George's own story as he told it to the boy. I have always wanted to know about the wreck of the *Mohecan*, which thrilled and mystified my childhood as it did Frank Baines's. It is so mysterious how the great ship came to be so badly off her course. All her officers were lost; her log-book disappeared; the last we hear of her captain is shouting through a megaphone into the night, 'This is the *Mohecan*. I have 500 passengers on board – What shall I do? What shall I do?' He was drowned with 300 more that wild night. None of the other life-boats could even get launched.[208]

Mr Baines's picture of the Cornish society of his youth is no less authentic: one recognises the characters. There are the recognisable Williams clan – one of whom dominated the parish from the plantations of Lanarth – a breed, in that generation, knotty and gnarled, who contrived to be both breezy and stuffy, and all of them wonderful gardeners. It was in gardening that the passions of the Cornish gentry were unloosed, their envy, loves and hates stimulated. All is fair in love and war – the guards that had to be posted, the sharp look-out kept from shrubberies when they visited their neighbours and took their opportunity to snip a cutting or pluck up a root!

---

208 The *Mohegan*, which Frank spells as *Mohecan*, was shipwrecked on the Manacles Rocks in 1898 with the loss of 106 lives; mystery still surrounds the event, and all her officers, including her captain, disappeared.

All is not so simple as it seems with Mr Baines. With the second half of the book – an artful and effective literary device – one reaches the other half of his almost schizophrenic life, that lived the rest of the year in London, middle class, cramped, squalid, with its inner instability. The money ran out: Trenoweth had to be sold – the childhood paradise for ever lost.[209]

The Times Literary Supplement, then an important arbiter of success, was also impressed:

This is indeed an unexpected book by an author who has had a strange life. He illuminates it, now, as it were, by tossing flares, now by the clear affectionate light of a boy's memory.

The poet Edwin Muir called the book 'most unusual and exciting,' while the historian Sir Arthur Bryant described Frank as an 'inspired and evocative writer'.

'It is art that places *Look Towards The Sea* on an altogether different and higher plane,' wrote Walter Allen in the *New Statesman*.

George Malcolm Thomson, writing in the *Evening Standard*, said that 'Baines sees with the eye of a poet'.

'The most entertaining autobiography to appear for a good long time,' said *Time and Tide*.

'Mr Baines writes, as he lives, with tremendous laughing gusto,' *The West Briton* observed.

'Sharp, racily set down, often wonderfully funny,' wrote the *Glasgow Herald*. 'He records his inner life with great descriptive power ... He has made an astonishing beginning.'

The only negative note was struck in Calcutta, where Chancal Sarkar, using the non de plume Waqnis, wrote a rather patronising piece about Frank in *The Statesman* in his weekly column called *Speaking Generally*.

Sunanda Datta-Ray, a former colleague who was now working at

---

the London offices of *The Statesman*, recalls that Frank dropped in one afternoon. He remembers Frank's craggy features and the fact that he wore Carnaby Street attire before anybody had heard of Carnaby Street. Miss Rice, the London office's elderly spinster manager, loved him.[210]

The first edition quickly sold out, and by the end of the year *Look Towards the Sea* was a best-selling Quality Book Club title.

It is an imaginative work – creative, novelistic biography – and a brilliant recreation of a child's world, and of the world seen through a child's eyes. The Cornish chapters are cast with a Celtic and almost magical spell – stones that move in the night, mysterious people, the Holy Grail, tunnels and caves, and the rugged cliffs and lonely moors. There are marvellous characters, fishermen and farmers, and local bigwigs and their garden parties, and there is the memorable description, as told to a child, of the wreck of the *Mohegan* on the Manacles mentioned above. A lot of the boy's story is centred on Trenoweth which was the family home for five years. Frank's Cornwall is embellished but real.

Frank, however, warns the reader not to take his autobiography at face value, and the narrative takes off into a bit of harmless fiction when he turns to his mother's family. He transforms Warwickshire into a P.G. Wodehouse corner of England, and gives the real locations new names. He writes that his mother was a Dingley who came from Crampton, near Stanford; they would arrive there by train (in a third-class carriage) and alight at the nearby station of Bramble. Looming over Crampton was none other than Lord Senn'art, who lived at the big house in a Capability Brown park; the house was called Senn'art Crampton. The Dingleys, however, could claim some sort of precedence over the Senn'arts; they had been in Crampton for centuries, and certainly long before Lord Senn'art. Frank writes of Crampton as the family's ancestral village.

The Dingleys are the Oldhams, and Crampton is Combroke, Stanford is Stratford-on-Avon and Bramble is Kineton. Senn'art Crampton

---

210 Interview with the author in 2009.

is the Robert Adam designed Compton Verney, in which Richard Greville Verney, 19th Baron Willoughby de Broke, lived until he was reduced to penury in 1921.[211] Apart from these invented topographical and family names, the rest of Frank's description of his maternal Warwickshire roots is broadly grounded in fact. He mentions, for example, that his grandfather was a carpenter who became a farmer after founding his fortune on the profits from an apple orchard and a sow – all true. As in Cornwall, he engages with the countryside: it's still the mystical relationship of a child but it is now more disturbing:

> The gods of my native place are terrible and I have to spend much of my energies fighting off the most improper suggestions ... This is me, primitive and atavistic, lurking among the oaks along Fosse Road.[212] [The Fosse Way, now the B4455, runs by the side of Combroke.]

Douglas Oldham, the son of Walter Edwin Oldham, one of Rhoda's younger brothers, says Frank didn't get things quite right, but it was definitely all Combroke, and he could relate to Frank's descriptions.[213]

Frank's mother was still very much alive at the time – she had five years to live – and it would appear that Frank intentionally disguised her country-girl background to avoid upsetting her. Oldham says that just about every Oldham he mentions was still alive, and he thinks that Frank genuinely didn't want to cause anyone any offence.

But Frank was clearly also having some sort of joke – a display, perhaps, of the same devilish humour with which his father described himself as motor oil salesman on his marriage certificate. The choice of the name Crampton was probably no accident. Frank's father and mother were registered as living in Crampton Street, in South London, when they married in 1914.

Look Towards the Sea also blurs the identities of various aunts, real and imaginary, who lived in London, but it takes the reader on

---

211 He wrote a nostalgic account of his last years in the house, *The Passing Years*, and died in 1923.
212 *Look Towards the Sea*, p. 151.
213 Interviewed by the author in 2010.

entertaining jaunts to visit them in Chelsea, Poplar and the Elephant and Castle, and gives a child's insights into family feuds and squabbles, including a major bust-up between his parents over Auntie Em, who was Rhoda's elder sister Gertrude and with whom Sir Frank appears to have had a brief affair.[214] Frank also writes about one of his mother's younger sisters, Auntie Bee (Violet), giving birth to a black child, Zöe, and how he initially refused to kiss the baby.[215] Violet was married at the time to a local white man; Zöe's father was a black Canadian soldier. It was wartime.[216]

Frank boasts of his early conquests with girls at school, and his crushes on matrons. One night at the opera in London in the company of his father and mother he plays a heroic role by shouting from the stalls to 'save' Carmen from being stabbed. His father emerges as a somewhat distant figure, more a visiting VIP than a paternal figure. He writes warmly of his prep school in East Anglia and far less enthusiastically about his four years at Oundle where he is caught making advances to a younger boy – 'one had to, life was so boring'.[217] His escape from Oundle, in the company of a school friend, is gripping stuff, worthy of Richard Hannay.[218]

Frank was working for Mowlem Construction Company at Victoria Station, and the publicity surrounding the launch of his first book came to the attention of his employers. It was not every day that they had a writer digging for them. Mowlem, which was engaged in a project to extend the platforms they had originally built at the station, were so impressed to have an author on the payroll that they commissioned him to write a company history. There was already a hidden family link, which may explain both why Frank was employed by

---

214 'Say, Auntie Em is a naughty girl!', *Look Towards the Sea*, p. 131.
215 *Look Towards the Sea*, pp. 155-8.
216 Violet left England for Canada (her passage paid for by Rhoda) and she had further children – all white – and died there aged 102 in 1999. Her daughter Zöe became a foster-mother of many children, and she died in 2005 in Alberta, where she is buried in the Cathedral.
217 *Look Towards the Sea*, p. 211.
218 Richard Hannay was the hero of John Buchan's adventure novel, *The Thirty-Nine Steps* (1915).

them and why they invited him to write their history. Mowlem had constructed Sir Frank Baines's Thames House and its neighbour Imperial Chemical House, a colossal undertaking from which all parties profited handsomely.

Founded in 1822 by John Mowlem, the son of a Dorset quarryman, Mowlem was one of England's oldest building firms. The company had a colourful history, and it provided rich pickings for a writer, especially for one trained to look at buildings through the eyes of an architect: Mowlem had constructed a number of London's iconic buildings – Billingsgate Fish Market, Smithfield Meat Market, the Great Eastern Hotel, Liverpool Street Station and Victoria Station among them. The company was taken over by Carillion plc in 2006 and no one there knows what became of Frank's history – *The Life of John Mowlem* – but there is a record that he delivered the completed typescript to them.[219]

Jeremy Hill, a former City fund manager living in Essex, recalls meeting Frank at the time when he was engaged in the Mowlem project, remembering above all his flamboyance,[220] and writes about him as follows:

I met Frank on a Blackwell's bus sometime towards the end of 1958. I was cramming for a scholarship to Oxford, and, having spent the week-end at home, caught the bus back to London more or less outside our house where the Greenstead Green road meets what was then called the A604. The occupants of the bus were something less than glamorous – except one, upon whom the attention of the entire busload was focussed. Racily dressed, extremely camp and wielding a whale-bone stick, this character held forth nineteen to the dozen more or less the whole way to King's Cross (where all bus journeys in those days ended). Whoever he was, he seemed to know everybody and everybody definitely knew him. Enter Frank Baines.

---

219 1960 correspondence regarding Frank's *Life of John Mowlem* (originally entitled *The Firm's History*). Frank sent the typescript and photographs to Paul Scott who sent them to K.R. Burt of John Mowlem & Co (Random House archives).
220 A written recollection by Jeremy Hill, 2009.

I made that bus journey every Sunday night for about three months and I was soon on the same familiar terms with him as the rest of the passengers. He was, I think, engaged in writing his abortive history of Mowlem and as a result was enjoying a period of comparative affluence, while living with his mother in Coggeshall during the week.

Frank was enchanted by the idea of meeting a real live Etonian on a Blackwell's bus. It enabled him to construct all sorts of fantasies about the exotic life I ought to lead, and these were reinforced by the prospect – in Frank's mind, the certainty – of my going on to Oxford, an event that was at best highly uncertain. Frank persuaded himself that Oxford was mine more or less by divine right.

For the impending exam I was required, inter alia, to take some sort of general paper and my tutor set me one of those absurd essays the title of which was something like: 'The Three Most Epoch-Making Inventions in History'. I could only think of two and Frank persuaded me that the third was the invention of the flush lavatory. I duly incorporated this into my rather turgid essay, and my tutor was deeply unimpressed.

Look Towards the Sea had been published some months before, in February 1958. Frank salutes our bus journeys in the dedication he inscribed for me:

'Jeremy, you did express what was, I suspect, a fairly formal desire to read this book. Now you must suffer the consequences of showing the slightest consideration towards authors and people of that ilk – namely being deluged with their blasted works on the slightest pretext. For all that please accept this book as a sign of my gratitude for your company during the dreary, dreary hours of that bus!'

The only other event I remember from that time was an evening organised by Frank at the Hippodrome in Leicester Square. The idea was that it was to be outrageous, dancing girls all over the place and lots of champagne. John Mitchell, Frank's great friend who was said by Frank to be 'frightfully rich' and usually lived up to his reputation, was roped in to help with the bill and one or two others whom I forget. The dancing girls turned out to be predictably English and uninspired; there was much playing of the Italian song *volare* and I got very drunk.

At some stage Frank came with me to Blue Bridge House near Halstead where my family lived. I had anticipated and hoped perhaps, that my parents, who were of the conservative variety, would be scandalised by this wild eccentric. But on the contrary he laid on all the charm and they were delighted with him, although I don't remember repeating the experiment.

At the time Frank was finishing his second book, which he had started in Glasgow, and his pen seems to have flowed as effortlessly as his ebullient speech. The book is based on Frank's voyage to Australia on the four-masted Finnish barque the *Lawhill*, and his publishers were pleased with the draft of what was initially called *Deep Water*, which they received in April 1958.

'We all like *Deep Water* very much,' wrote Bright-Holmes, 'and I am relieved and delighted that Frank has brought it off a second time. I was a little nervous in case he proved to one of those naturally gifted writers who are inhibited by becoming regular professionals. But not a bit of it – I think that he has done a marvellous job.'

The book was eventually entitled *In Deep*, and it came out in 1959.

Frank said that he wrote it partly as a riposte to Eric Newby's hugely successful *The Last Grain Race*, which was first published in 1956. Newby had also sailed to Australia on one of Gustaf Erikson's four masters, the *Mohshula*, in 1939 – a voyage that was practically the swansong of big ship commercial sailing. Frank was not impressed by Newby's book, commenting: 'I spent more time at sea than Newby, and I wrote about the sea better than he did.'[221]

---

221 In conversation with the author, 1985.

The two of them were brought together on a BBC broadcast about sailor authors, but the encounter did not go well.

In Deep, also first published by Eyre & Spottiswoode, was again a success; it sold in sufficient numbers to merit a paperback edition with Arrow Books, and it even came out in German under the title *Der Letzte Geschichte einer Langreise*. There were also Swedish and Finnish editions. This time the publishers' blurb was not written by Frank, and it is a valid homage:

> *In Deep* is 'imaginative autobiography', telling the story of a voyage on a four-masted barque bound from London to Australia. It is one of the most extraordinary pieces of writing about the sea that has appeared for a long time. At times it is wildly exciting, at times ribald, at times gentle, violent, nostalgic; everywhere it is full of a sense of excitement and freedom. There is a death, almost a mutiny, and, in the end, a gutsy, drunken uproar in the Australian port at which the ship unloads. But most of all, and at the least unexpected times, there come strange moments of insight when a wave, a cloudscape, the fall of moonlight on a tower of canvas, emerge into pure reality and become symbolic of a deeply felt experience.

> Everywhere this book is the work of a completely fresh mind in direct, sensuous contact with the world around it. It is the kind of book by which reputations are made.

Frank's new book was very well received. Reviewers compared him to Joseph Conrad and John Masefield, and one even coined a new phrase to describe his prose – Bainesian.

'There have been a number of books describing life in the old sailing ships,' wrote Edward Young in *The Sunday Times*, 'but none before this one has been written with such poetic evocation of scenes and emotion, such felicitous selection of detail to bring word pictures into startling focus. This book contains some of the best writing about the sea that we have had for a long time.'

The Times was equally effusive, calling it a 'very remarkable and original book' and praising Frank's 'extraordinary descriptive gifts'. 'The prose is hard, flexible, capable equally of humour and great beauty. It is strong and lyrical, full of flavour and characters, so that the whole book has the tension and unity of a poem. Its genuine excitement is one of discovery rather than of events. *In Deep* contains page after page of controlled lyrical writing of true quality.'

'Readers who were lucky enough to read *Look Towards The Sea* will have been looking for a further instalment from this remarkable character and richly talented writer,' said Roy Perrot in the *Manchester Guardian*. 'Any reader who is ready to let himself get caught up in the exuberant sea-surge of the Bainesian personality will not question the publishers' claim that *In Deep* is one of the most extraordinary pieces of writing about the sea to have appeared for a very long time.'

Walter Allen, in the *News Chronicle*, James Cameron's newspaper, voiced similar praise. 'Frank Baines is a born writer, a natural lord of language,' he said, 'every bit as good as Masefield.'

'Mr Baines writes brilliantly and with the subtlest of perception of what it feels like to be a young man at sea,' said Charles Causley in the *New Statesman*.

The Times Literary Supplement (TLS) suggested that Frank was a true sea poet: 'Now and again perception and expression are matched in one writer capable of adding an enduring stanza to the ocean's poem. Mr Baines does just this. He is unquestionably a brilliant reporter: if, as Whitman believed, poetry is a sharing of significant experience, he is a poet.'

Burns Singer of *The Observer* made a comparison with the great Polish-born writer, Joseph Conrad, describing Frank as a story-teller 'with breath-taking powers', and adding: 'Since Conrad, there have been few writers so wise in the humours of the sea.'

'He captures with considerable effect the wonder and excitement of a lad's first voyage,' wrote Cyril Ray in *The Spectator*. 'A roaring, rowdy recapture of a boy's joy in hardship and danger.'

For the *Daily Telegraph*, Michael Wharton described *In Deep* as a 'visionary dream of the sea, set down with passionate excitement'.

'What an exhilarating gale of a book this is,' said the *Oxford Mail*. 'His prose leaps from the pensive and lyrical to the bawdy and blasphemous, while a sensuous appreciation of the wonders of living informs every page. Mr Baines sweeps us along on the heady crest of his soaring imagination.'

Punch too had a good word for Frank. 'So much gusto and vitality,' wrote David Wainwright. 'It is tremendous stuff.'

This was also heady stuff, and to some extent it did go to Frank's head. For his next book, he would depart altogether from the autobiographical model and rely entirely on his imagination to write a novel. This was not to prove a successful formula.

Frank also became more flamboyant and increasingly self-confident. But he remained approachable and attentive to others. Geoffrey Angold, a retired impresario, recalls being bowled over by Frank's style and charm when he met him about this time, writing of their encounter as follows:

I was still an impressionable schoolboy when I accompanied one of my teachers, Mrs Smith from Brentwood, to have Sunday lunch at The Cedars in Coggeshall. It was early 1960, and cold, gloomy and drizzly. We sat in the drawing room with Lady Baines over sherry. The room was comfortably furnished with pictures and books. Lady Baines was short and neat with her hair loosely bunned up. She was unpretentious and welcoming and conversation came easily.

Then suddenly, like a colourful Jack out of his box, the door opened and in swanned Frank, mid-forties and confident. He had fair, longish hair – artistic length – and was good-looking. I remember noting his strong bone structure and his baritone voice and extremely lively personality. He was artfully dressed in a pink shirt, a saucily knotted red-spotted neckerchief, snazzy baggy sweater, drainpipe trousers and suede shoes. For a conventional schoolboy from Brentwood this was for me a complete revelation; I had never seen anything like it! But he was a sweet man and did not make me feel like a boring mouse and was very warm and kind. He was also so nice to Mrs Smith and she seemed to revel in the glow of his charm, and so did I.[222]

In Coggeshall, while writing his books, Frank had also developed an interest in the antique trade, which was gradually growing into a significant local business. At the height of its boom, Coggeshall was to boast no fewer than 20 antique-shops. Frank built on his interest in Oriental art and became something of a local expert. He started buying and selling the odd piece and his circle of arty people and antique traders widened. He got to know dealers such as Ivor Weiss and Wilfred Bull and a local artist, Dorothy Butterfield.

Although homosexuality was not to be legalised in England until 1967, Frank was increasingly open about his sexual leanings and he seems to have schooled or introduced a number of young men locally into the arts of male love. He counted among such friends the local hairdresser, Lesley Driscoll, and the antiques dealer Mark Marchant.

'It was much more fun when homosexuality was illegal,' he would tell friends. 'Now it is virtually compulsory, and it has become rather common.'[223]

Indeed, Frank took pleasure in the louche side of his sexuality. His translation[224] of *Le Coeur Volé* (The Cheated Heart), a poem by the French poet Rimbaud,[225] which probably dates from the early 1980s when Frank was living in Coggeshall, is cheerfully indecent and scatological – the two writers had traits in common, not least in aspects of their sexual personalities:

---

222 Letter to the author, 2010.
223 Trevor Disley, a friend from Coggeshall, picture framer and local fire chief, interviewed by the author in 2009.
224 The original text is in the author's possession.
225 Arthur Rimbaud (1854-1891), who wrote most of his verse while still in his teens and later became a traveller and adventurer, was homosexual when young and had a tempestuous two-year relationship with his fellow poet Paul Verlaine, which started before Rimbaud was 17.

My wounded heart leaks at the poop,
My heart is swamped in fish-and-chips:
They launch upon it jets of soup,
My wounded heart leaks at the poop:
Beneath the horse-play of the troops
Which prompts to taking of the piss,
My wounded heart leaks at the poop,
My heart is swamped in chips and fish!

Footsloggers' jokes of standing pricks –
Their filthy jeers have sullied it!
Upon the taffrail, dirty dicks –
Footsloggers' jokes of standing pricks!
Oh magic waves – my launderette –
Receive my shame-soiled heart unzipped,
Footsloggers' squish from standing pricks
Have slashed upon it jet-on-jet!

When they have finally chomped their quids,
How shall we play it, wounded heart?
There'll be some bacchic hiccups yet,
When they have chomped their quids, I'll bet!
Yet I shall have some stomach fits
If I try choking back my shits:
How shall we act, then, wounded bum,
When they have shot their muck and come?

1. The cottage in Combroke (now converted into a single dwelling) where Rhoda Oldham, Frank's mother and the future Lady Baines, was born and raised.

2. Sir Frank Baines KCVO (far left), Frank's father, a distinguished architect who was born in Stepney Green.

3. Frank Baines as a boy at Trenoweth when he was still at Oundle School.

4. Trenoweth today.

5. The view to the sea from Trenoweth today.

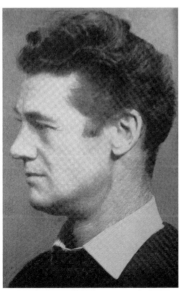

6. The picture of Frank from the dust jacket of *In Deep* (1959), the account of his voyage to Australia.

7. The *Lawhill*, on which Frank sailed to Australia as an apprentice in 1934.

8. Major-General Orde Wingate, leader of the Chindits, who was killed shortly after the start of the second Chindit Campaign behind enemy lines in Burma in which Frank fought.

9. Captain Frank Baines (in shorts) with the Chindits in Burma at field HQ in Mokso Sakan, from where he was despatched with his two defence platoons to hold the pass to Blackpool to the last man.

10. Major Jack Masters, the Brigade's brilliant field commander, who became the best-selling author John Masters and under whom Frank served as officer in charge of Brigade HQ defence platoons.

11. A column of Chindits advancing with a pack mule on a dusty track in Northern Burma. The Chindits marched up to 20 miles a day with loads of 50 pounds on their backs.

12. A drawing of the riverside docks in Calcutta by Desmond Doig, the artist and former Gurkha officer with whom Frank lived. Frank set up a tea-chest-repairing business in Calcutta before becoming a writer.

13. The author Frank Baines photographed at work down a hole at Victoria Station in 1958 shortly after the successful publication of *Look Towards the Sea.*

14. *Look Towards the Sea*, Frank's first book, published in 1958. The front cover was designed by the artist and print maker Julian Trevelyan.

15. The Cedars, Coggeshall, the Regency house which Frank inherited from his mother and which he sold in 1963.

16. A painting of Conca dei Marini by the artist Dorothy Butterfield. Frank moved to Conca from Sicily in 1965 and when he returned to England he lived with Dorothy until she died in 1972.

17. Portrait of Frank by his friend Matthew Screaton.

18. Frank with the author Brian Mooney in Coggeshall in 1977.

19. Frank in Dalhousie
with his two house-boys
– Raj and Pratap.

20. Frank in the grounds of his
stately alms-house in Coggeshall
in 1985.

THIRTEEN
DELUSIONS OF
GRANDEUR

FRANK'S MOTHER, LADY RHODA BAINES, REMAINED A FORMIDABLE presence, and when she fell ill with stomach cancer Frank looked after her with devotion. He arranged for her to be nursed at The Cedars, and, when she became too frail to manage the stairs, he had her moved to a room on the ground floor which overlooked the rose garden.

Lady Baines looms over – or rather looms out of – Frank's only published novel, *Culture of Bacillus*. With two highly popular and successful books in print, Frank was on a roll. But the success had gone to his head, and his third book was something of a disaster.

Published in 1962, the work centres on a dying nonagenarian chatelaine and a pallid 12-year-old heir who is saved from a rapacious aunt by the intervention of kindly servants and the unseen assistance of a tramp who turns out to be his father – not exactly gripping stuff. One reviewer caustically observed that Frank was either a writer of extraordinary talent or the architect of a book that read like an ill-digested Thesaurus.

Lady Baines, Coggeshall, and The Cedars waft in and out of the book in ghostly snatches of near-familiar character and half-recognisable scenery, but in *Culture of Bacillus* Frank is no longer grounded in reality. He has let go, and the result is a faltering narrative and an effusion of confused imagination. Frank, trying to find his way as a creative writer in a full-length novel, is simply less sure-footed than he was with auto-biography; and he has lost his sense of pace and that touch for story-telling which he had developed to such good effect in Calcutta.

Perhaps aware of the novel's inherent weakness, he tried to have the last laugh. 'I suppose some readers will find this an improbable piece of grotesquerie,' Frank wrote on the front cover. 'I enjoyed writing it, anyway.'

He possibly enjoyed writing it overmuch. *Culture of Bacillus* runs away with metaphors and almost drowns in recondite phrases and words.

The young boy, Jeremy, radiates 'something of the aura of sick-room'[226] and his nose is 'like a little piece of putty put on as an afterthought by a craftsman who was unfamiliar with the technique of creating faces, and who had only added this one as an inspired stroke and as a last endeavour in order to pull together and give meaning to a composition that might otherwise have failed'.[227]

The chatelaine, Selina Gloam, who 'had always been good with servants, horses, dogs and lovers, and in general with people whom she considered beneath her',[228] exerts on the house a 'largely unseen but often deeply felt presence'.[229] Metaphysical horror distills itself from the house, 'like from an alembic of poisons,'[230] and the presence of thousands of people 'whirled like a host of ghosts in a tornado of excitement, funnelling down onto the house in a typhoon'.[231]

Culture of Bacillus reveals something that Frank had always found hard to conceal: part of him wanted to be the little rich boy that he writes about. It was perhaps no accident that he had recently met and taken up with a winsome and well-to-do young Etonian called Jeremy.[232] In fact, all of his life he appeared to have been troubled by his social

---

226 *Culture of Bacillus* (Eyre & Spottiswoode, 1962), p. 6.
227 *Culture of Bacillus*, p. 7.
228 *Culture of Bacillus*, p. 77.
229 *Culture of Bacillus*, p. 82.
230 *Culture of Bacillus*, p. 114.
231 *Culture of Bacillus*, p. 147.
232 Jeremy Hill.

status – a sense of unease with his position in society no doubt exacerbated by the near calamitous collapse of his father's fortunes, which overnight turned Frank from being the scion of a rich, successful and highly decorated architect into being the son of a modestly well-to-do former housemaid.

Frank's creative writing often expresses this yearning. The early short story for the Calcutta *Statesman* – *Except the Lord Keep the House* – is set in one of the city's grandest mansions, which has been in the family since the time of Warren Hastings, the first British Governor of Bengal. Located on the fashionable Lower Circular Road, it is approached through gates, where there is a gatekeeper and lodge, and it is entered from a carriage porch where footmen are in attendance by the great doors. Inside the winged house, the countless rooms are enclosed by tall double doors, and above the living quarters is a warren of vaulted storerooms built onto the massif of the plinth. The ballroom upstairs has a *fauteuil* which was used by the Governor-General when visiting. The household is run by a major-domo and the house itself is surrounded by an enormous walled garden, and beyond the south front is a lake. The house, just like Trenoweth, has to be sold to pay the debts of the narrator's father.

This was a world which Frank at times longed to inhabit and which prompted him to say in *Look Towards the Sea*: 'The lower middle-class to which I belong ... oh, how I hate it!'[233]

In keeping with the characters, who are not quite what they appear, the chatelaine's house in *Culture of Bacillus* is on an almost mythological scale. It has two vast wings, many courtyards, primary and secondary front stairways, a ballroom, a Tudor great-hall, and 12 magnificent apartments in the so-called Tuscan rooms, and it is looked after by footmen, a butler, cooks, and a household of under-servants. The interior is embellished with frescoes, paintings, tapestries and marble statues; dazzling chandeliers hang from domed ceilings, and light pours

---

233 *Look Towards The Sea*, p. 175.

in through glass cupolas. The great mansion is set in extensive grounds leading off an immense avenue of limes, with gardens tended by an army of gardeners, and fountains, statues, columns and sarcophagi, and a large lake, extensive lawns and a labyrinth.

But it is not all fairy-tale. The chatelaine is a former high-class hooker, a favourite of a 'royal fornicator' who had made her fortune by blackmailing her husband, and there are servants with dubious characters, including the tutor, Mr Mills, who is an ex-convict. The boy, Jeremy, doesn't actually want his inheritance; and he is befriended by a tramp. The tramp, called Tancred, turns out to be his father, Rupert, who had long been presumed dead, a suspected suicide. Frank is here once again re-wiring his own life.

Frank grew up in the shadow of big houses, and the house in *Culture of Bacillus* has strong echoes of Compton Verney, the Adam-designed Palladian pile which his mother's Warwickshire village, Combroke, was built to service. Perhaps not coincidentally it was in Warwickshire that Frank had once masqueraded as an aristocrat by, as he put it, sporting an entirely non-existent title. This incident may have well have been connected with the Willoughby de Broke family – the 19th Baron had been forced to give up the family home in 1921 and he died two years later. Frank never again appears to have posed as an aristocrat; and, if anything, the unpleasant repercussions of that experience may have encouraged him into becoming in later life, and when it suited him, something of a class rebel.[234]

Trenoweth in Cornwall was the closest Frank ever came to living in a grand house, although it was more of a large estate than a stately home, and from it he was banished by his father's debts and sudden death. The Cedars, in Coggeshall, is a fine Regency house with a beautiful walled garden and is arguably the best house in the town, but for all that it was, in Frank's description, 'only a suburban villa'.

Frank nonetheless always had his eye for the big house – in one of Merlin's columns, he confesses his preference for living in castles – and

---

234 *Officer Boy*, p. 10.

he certainly grew up surrounded by and appreciating fine things. The furniture rescued from Sir Frank's creditors in Trenoweth, and moved to The Cedars, included a Queen Anne walnut double-domed top bureau bookcase, some Chippendale and Hepplewhite walnut frame armchairs, a set of Adam-designed dining chairs, and a Sheraton sideboard.[235]

In his Merlin column, Frank alluded to his gilded childhood, saying that he was brought up so 'stinking rich' that he never had to work. There was more than a grain of truth in this throwaway remark, because apart from his time at sea and his service in the army, Frank never held down a serious job. Careers, and full-time jobs, were for other people.

The only thing he ever stuck at was being a writer, and it was during his mother's illness, and while nursing her at The Cedars, that Frank wrote his second novel – *Place of Cremation*.

The novel, as the title suggests, deals with death, and touches on the nature of Frank's belief in God. Again, as with living in big houses, for most of his life this was as much an aspiration as a reality.

Frank was brought up by his mother as an Anglican – the Oldhams were church-goers – but his father, a founding editor of *The Realist*, had no time for religion; he was an atheist and he married Rhoda in a state Registry office. But for all that, Frank had a good grounding in Christianity and the Bible both from his mother and at school, particularly at Oundle. His writing often alludes to and quotes from biblical texts.

But from Frank's time in India onwards he was looking beyond Christianity, for something more, and this is what drew him to Krishna Prem's fusion of Eastern and Christian teaching. He seems always to have had a sense of God, or certainly of some divine presence, and there were occasions – notably when Dal Bahadur lay apparently mortally wounded by his side in Burma – when he 'found' God. But in the end, he saw God on his own terms:

God is present where and when He is realised to be present, and at no other time or place. Thus a realisation of His Presence makes Him available

---

235 Philips, Son & Neale auction catalogue, 17 July 1963.

even on the battlefield, beyond and above whom no other power or presence can exist, much less intervene to impose destruction and death.[236]

Ultimately Frank had no time for organised religion. He left the Ashram at Mirtola because he could not abide by, or live within the community's rules. Even in religion, he remained a rebel.

Talking about his time at the Mirtola Ashram, Frank told a radio interviewer that he realised on leaving it that one could dedicate one's life to God without doing anything quite so brash as living in a monastery.[237] 'But I think I have still tried to do so in my way. I have been faithful to the Cynara or whatever it is, after my fashion, very much after my fashion.'[238]

Frank got on well with individuals, regardless of race or creed, but he was never very generous about most of mankind; he railed in turn against the English, the Scottish, the Germans, the Americans, the South Africans, the Israelis, the Indians, and the Greeks.

His mother taught him in early childhood never to be prejudiced against people because of the colour of their skin. She gave him an almighty slap on the head when he initially refused to kiss his black cousin, Zoë:

I kissed Zoë as affectionately as anything and since then I have never been able to discover in myself one drop of colour prejudice.[239]

It was characteristic of Frank that he would rather have believed that Zoë's dark skin was somehow a throwback to Gypsies, rather than that she was the illegitimate daughter of an African or Caribbean Canadian soldier. He always wanted to be exotic; he couldn't bear the idea that he was ordinary, or in any way conventional. He also admitted

---

236 Original draft of *Chindit Affair*.
237 BBC radio interview, 1986.
238 A reference to the poem *Non Sum Qualis Eram Bonae Sub Regno Cynarae* by Ernest Dowson (1867-1900), with its recurring line 'I have been faithful to thee, Cynara! in my fashion'. See also p. 286 and footnotes 322-324.
239 *Look Towards the Sea*, p. 158.

to being a snob.[240]

Culture of Bacillus was not damned at birth, but it did not achieve anything like the success of the two earlier books. *The Times Literary Supplement* reviewer was arguably the most generous, writing on 24 August 1962:

> Mr Baines has an extraordinary talent. In his new book he is perceptive about the gripping fears and premature wisdom of childhood while at the same time being sensitive to the high-headed quality of old age. All this is combined in a tale for the imagination written in an unusual, tense prose.

> The story is that of a small boy after the Great War, brought up in a grotesque mansion peopled only by an army of servants and his strange great-grandmother whose heir he is. The narrative covers a short period during which the old woman is dying. Her middle-aged granddaughter strives to snatch the inheritance but forces human and supernatural thwart her.

> The centre of attention passes from the lonely conversations of the boy with the man whom he thinks is a warlock and befriends, to the semi-conscious dreams of the old women, to the house itself which is full of menace to intruders. As a creator of macabre atmosphere Mr Baines could hardly be bettered. The Evil Bird, endemic in the family, scrapes at the old woman's windows, the derelict banqueting halls of the mansion terrify the visitor who covets them, and in the end the establishment seems like a living organism to eject those who prey on it.

> But Mr Baines is also a first-class comic writer. The scenes in which the upper echelons of servants wonder what they should do about the situation are extremely funny and there is a superb description of a party thrown by the housekeeper who in her joy at playing hostess somehow – and how

---

240 *Look Towards the Sea*, p. 162.

exactly we never quite understand – takes on the being of her dying mother. This is a delightful romance.

Andrew Leslie, in *The Guardian*, was much less generous. He called it a 'sapling of a novel … atmosphere well evoked but short of narrative direction and purpose; heavy foliage, no stem'.

Frank had by now determined that it was his destiny to be a novelist, and by the end of 1962 he had completed two further novels, *Place of Cremation* and *The First Day of Adonis*, which both deal with homosexual love and death – themes to which he would return.[241]

Indeed death was never far from his mind during those months, as Lady Baines slowly succumbed to cancer. She died on 30 March 1963, aged 73, and she left the house and all its contents to Frank.

Frank determined to see out his mother in style. Stanley Haines, who was then Chairman of Coggeshall Parish Council, found him very demanding, and writes as follows:

He came into the parish office and announced that his mother would be wheeled out of the church on the funeral bier – and that there would be plenty of beer afterwards.

But that wasn't all. Frank insisted that she be buried in a prominent position, and not in the midst of all the other what he called 'common' graves. The only place that met his criteria was on the far north-eastern corner, an as yet unconsecrated area where there were no other graves.

It was explained to him that the Anglican Church would not allow burials in unconsecrated ground, and that the council would have to pay a fee to the diocese to get it consecrated. So Frank asked how much that would be and was told that it would cost £300, the equivalent of thousands today, which he readily agreed to pay.[242]

---

241 Frank destroyed the manuscripts of both novels.
242 Stanley Haines, in a note to the author, 2009.

Frank erected a very large Cornish granite tombstone over this mother, far larger than was officially permitted. He commemorated both his mother and father on its face, and left just enough room at the foot for his own brief memorial.

Shortly after his mother's death, Frank had The Cedars painted white with pink window frames and the tops of the metal railings and weather vane gilded in gold leaf, and in July 1963 he sold the house to Dorothy Butterfield's sister, Phyllis Storey. The house fetched £12,000 and the contents, which included a lot of valuable furniture and paintings, were auctioned off at a grand sale in the garden, making an additional £8,322.[243]

The sale was a major turning point in Frank's life. As if back in Mirtola as a Hindu monk, Frank auctioned off just about every possession, including his father's CBE and KCVO decorations, and a model of the *Lawhill* made from one of her deck planks. He told friends that he intended to get rid of everything except his toothbrush.[244]

The total of more than £20,000 was a lot of money in the early 1960s, and suddenly Frank was a very rich man. Farm labourers in England in 1963 earned just over £9 per week, some £500 per annum. In an act of spontaneous and lavish generosity, Frank is reported to have given a local boy in Coggeshall a jar full of gold sovereigns, which his mother had kept under her bed.[245]

---

243 Philips, Son & Neale catalogue, 17 July 1963.
244 Jeremy Hill in a note to the author, 2009.
245 Related in 2009 by Mark Marchant, Coggeshall antique dealer and friend of Frank. There is no other source.

FOURTEEN
HIGH LIFE IN SICILY

FRANK SET OFF ON HIS TRAVELS AGAIN, HELL bent on both enjoying and blowing his fortune – but this time he got no further than Italy.

He fetched up in Sicily and rented a villa (he called it a Palace) on Sicily's south western coast at Sciacca, a bustling fishing port with a fine old quarter and a spa that has been in use since the Phoenicians. There is no precise record of where the villa was; nor much about what he did. A friend from Coggeshall recalls Frank boasting that he was driven in a Rolls Royce in Sicily and that he had an army of mostly unwanted servants and his own pimp.[246]

It is, however, possible to glimpse Frank's life in Sicily through the pages of a novel he wrote about his time there – *Don Carlo to the Dark Tower Came*. Written in the same extravagant vein as his earlier novels, it deals unabashedly with male love and homosexuality in Sicily. The book was never published and the original manuscript is lost, but a synopsis survives,[247] as well as a generally positive reader's report:[248]

There are still subjects which are near-taboo for the writer – even in 1965. In the U.S. it is little girl love; in England, boy love. Writers who address themselves to such themes must either choose a kind of realism which, in the climate of their particular taboo-breaking, usually results in pornography, or rich circumlocutions of style which, if they are clever, and lucky,

---

246 Mark Stimson, a friend of Frank from Coggeshall, interviewed by the author in 2009.
247 David Higham Associates archive, Harry Ransom Center, University of Texas.
248 Dated 15 October 1965 (Random House archives).

may turn out to be 'literature', and thus morally unassailable. Mr Baines has chosen the latter method for recounting an intensely romantic and frequently most beautiful story about Sicilian pederasty. His model would seem to be the Corvo of *The Desire and Pursuit of the Whole*, with a dash of Nabokov. The result is very mannered, very original, very sustained and, I suppose, very moral. Searchers after eroticism – the vulgar kind – will have to read a long way before they reach the first kiss – nearly 400 pages. But those who can recognise the stimulus of language and who rise to the caressive power of its subtle, and frequently masterly, usage are going to be excited by this novel – even if they don't happen to be excited by beautiful Sicilian lads.

The plot of *Don Carlo to the Dark Tower Came* is as follows.

To the deserted princely palace of Arragosta comes a middle-aged millionaire Englishman, known to the locals as Don Carlo. Residence in the palace alone would constitute princely status, but Don Carlo, with his Rolls Royce and ability to employ a small town of servants (most of whom he doesn't want but whom he cannot get rid of because that vast ramshackle house is really their village), is a near-regal figure in the poverty-stricken place. He is in his early 50s (Frank was 50 in 1965) and is congratulating himself on being able to retire early and having sublimated his homosexuality to the extent that it hasn't inconvenienced him socially or bothered him emotionally. He feels that he is free, unenthralled, and able to read and talk and look at temples. He enjoys the company of women and has taken as his mistress a beautiful and not very young woman named Tizziana, who is from Trieste.

Quite unbeknowing, Don Carlo becomes the great catch for the boys of Arragosta, who court him by brilliant displays of roller skating in the forecourt of the palace. Their antics have a kind of innocence and are quite unpredatory and entirely charming. Don Carlo is able to see them aesthetically and with detachment. One extraordinarily lovely 15-year-old shows off to such a degree that he has a tumble and is allowed into the palace to bandage his grazed knee. Thus Fulvio and

Don Carlo meet.

But nothing happens. Fulvio is bewildered. His wounds are dressed and he hangs around, is allowed to sleep in some distant room, and is ignored. But Tizziana believes differently. She had her own plans for the rich and powerful Don Carlo – her own handsome teenage brother Amadeo – and she is furious because Fulvio is actually in the palace. Under her instructions, Amadeo eventually gets taken indoors also and, although he doesn't know it, Don Carlo is publicly compromised. Amadeo is not an evil boy and has more to offer the Englishman than Fulvio, in that he is fairly well educated and far less a child.

Don Carlo and Fulvio begin to fall in love, with the older man having as much difficulty in destroying his self-control as the young man has in maintaining his. The boy is all affection, all truth, and all openness, utterly transparent and unambiguous. The man is masked – and loathing his masks, so many of them. Fulvio is the nephew of the palace major-domo, Marcantonio; another uncle is the complex Don Raphael, a young man who has moved from one sort of Sicilian Slavism into another – the Mafia. Underneath the thin layer of conventional behaviour darker forces are at work. Tizziana, angry and disappointed because her brother has not captured the Englishman's love – and thus his power – accidentally sets the vendetta wheels turning. Don Raphael is immensely excited as the splendour of the victim occurs to him. The whole of Arragosta is tremulous with the superb and imminent assassination.

The Englishman senses disaster but believes that it is directed at either Amadeo or Fulvio. He gives a vast and fatalistic ball in the palace, using all the great rooms as in the old days, and taking care to show equal favour and kindliness to both boys. To Amadeo he gives an ornate dagger which is part of his fancy-dress costume. The knife delights the boy, who at once recognises Don Carlo as a good man. The next day, all preparations having been made, Don Carlo walks to his Rolls Royce and is about to drive off to Rome when a sudden and overwhelming love for, and fear for the safety of Fulvio, makes him bundle the lad into the car before the assembled servants and take him with him.

There follows a journey through Italy in which the boy slowly, deliberately and tantalisingly sets out to seduce Don Carlo. But throughout the holiday, Don Carlo resists his advances and never touches him.

Their tortured idyll is interrupted. A telegram from Fulvio's mother (tricked by the Mafia) brings the couple back to Sicily. There Don Carlo realises he must die. Like Socrates he is calm and philosophical. His only thought is for Fulvio. He extracts a promise from Don Raphael that the boy won't be hurt. He then drinks what he believes is a kind of hemlock but which is actually a powerful aphrodisiac.

The denouement is gory and lurid.

Fulvio is accidentally stabbed by Amadeo and takes all night to die, during which Don Carlo loses all control and enjoys his bloody lover with insane pleasure.

The reader for Frank's literary agents, while concluding that it is an 'exceptional, if strange' novel, takes issue with this sacrificial climax:

> It is in the concluding pages that events occur which are either less personally bearable (for me) or, as I suspect, are not presented with sufficient skill to make them bearable. For here, after 400 pages of delicate restraint, Don Carlo and Fulvio consummate their love in a horrible and quite unbelievable manner. Surely it would have been better comedy for Don Carlo, intensely sexually aroused by what should have been his suicide-draught, to have found the lover whose advances he has rejected for so long dead at the very moment when his own inhibitions have vanished and desire is at its height. Instead we have a sado-sexual mess of a dying lad with his dagger in his side being had all night by a crazed middle-aged man.

Had the reader known Frank better – not that it was either his job or remit to do so – he would have understood that there were darker things going on in this climactic scene. Apart from Frank's propensity for excess, he was here still dealing with his love for Dal Bahadur. The dagger blade in Fulvio's chest is the wound in the side of his beloved Gurkha.

On a less personal level, *Don Carlo to the Dark Tower Came* evidently drew on Frank's experiences of living and travelling in Italy – the landscape and architecture a far cry from the Himalayan foothills and Calcutta. But sadly we can only imagine what the anonymous reader enjoyed. 'The writing,' he says, 'is sometimes very wonderful, particularly in the descriptive passages on Italy and Sicily.' Frank destroyed the original manuscript.

Frank left few traces in Sicily. Mark Marchant, an antiques dealer and long-standing friend in Coggeshall, said Frank fell in love with a Sicilian boy called Andrea Gionfrida, and that he bought a house for him. Frank refers to Gionfrida in one of his letters, giving his address in Syracusa, but there is no further source for the story that he bought him a house.[249]

Frank left Sicily at the end of 1964 and he moved up the Italian Peninsula to Conca dei Marini, a tiny fishing village near Amalfi which clings to the cliffs, where he rented a house from the Gambardella family.

Despite his early success with creative autobiography, Frank was still determined on becoming a great novelist, but Temple-Smith at Eyre & Spottiswoode turned down his second offering, *The First Day of Adonis*. The rejection triggered a searching correspondence between Frank and his new literary agent, David Bolt, who had replaced Paul Scott at David Higham Associates. Frank wrote to Bolt from Conca dei Marini on 20 January 1965:

> You asked me if I intended to continue along this sort of line. As the matter obviously touches you very dearly – in so far as you certainly don't want to have to go hoofing round from publisher to publisher forever, carrying completely unsaleable manuscripts under your arm – I think I ought to answer your query.

---

249 In conversation with the author, 2009.

The answer, as far as I am able to give one at all, is – I think not. The present thing I am engaged in seems to be shaping quite differently. It is about a very rich, worldly and experienced man of the world who thinks he has got the measure of everything that could possibly happen to him – an Englishman – who settles in a small town on the south-west coast of Sicily. The town is imaginary, but it is shaped on the model of Sciacca. Gradually he finds himself surrounded and hedged in by a series of tiny incidents which develop an atmosphere of suspicion, peril and danger, but he is unable to imagine what the danger can be. Do these incidents mean that a conspiracy has been formed against him merely to steal from him – or to jockey him into a compromising position where he can be blackmailed – or are the so-called conspirators – if there really are such people – simply seeking to exploit him in the usual way in which all Italians exploit foreigners? He simply does not know—and neither do I, the author! This is as far as I've got, but it is enough, I think, to show you that the story is developing along essentially different lines from *Culture of Bacillus* and *The First Day of Adonis*.

I hope this will put your mind a little at ease; but it doesn't mine! I know too well from my experience of my own work how suddenly the dotty, the inexplicable – almost the occult – will leap out at me from the most ordinary or promising conventional story, and take over. Thereafter, it becomes a continual battle to keep the thing under control, or within limits.

Of course, if I were a good technical novelist, I might bring this sort of thing to a successful conclusion – but the trouble is that I'm not. I *hope* that I am gradually learning. You might help me here by telling me truly whether you think I am learning or not. *The First Day of Adonis* is a little better than *Culture of Bacillus*, is it not? Or is it? Tell me!

I suffer from the terrible disadvantages of all talented beginners whose first purely instinctive shots have gone home by a piece of pure good luck. But thereafter, one has to sit down and learn one's trade, and in the process of learning, one is almost bound to disappoint. The only thing is not to lose courage and self-confidence during that process of learning – which I confess I almost have!

Do you advise and encourage me to go on, or not? Do you think I've got what it takes?

I feel sorry for you. It's a thankless task you have undertaken in regard to my work, and one which does not pay you any reward. Thank you for saying that you're quite happy to go ahead with a lot of determination elsewhere, and that you like the book a lot. Ever, Frank.[250]

Bolt replied on 25 January:

I'm taking you at your word and writing absolutely candidly, and so shan't be surprised if you write back and say you're going to Curtis Brown! I'd like to say that I think *The First Day of Adonis* is a lot better than *Culture of Bacillus*, but it seems to me to present almost exactly the same difficulty, namely that quality which you call 'inexplicable – almost the occult' and which I would simply call 'fey'. Now this fey quality is something I like myself in a big way, but it's terribly hard to put over, and although I think there are many moments in both novels where you entirely succeed, I don't think you really appreciate just what a challenge you make for yourself in adopting this style, which so very easily slips into self-consciousness and becomes mannered. You've really summed it up yourself, you know, and I'm only paraphrasing what I say bluntly, that I think you've got an awful lot to learn still about the sheer mechanics and technique of constructing a novel. What you have got, is a hell of a lot of talent, which came out magnificently in the first two books, but which somehow tends to get buried in the novels and only comes out in occasional flashes, as it were. This is cheek on my part I know, but it's what I feel. I'm enormously encouraged by what you say about the next book, because although, like Maurice

---

250 David Higham Associates archive, Harry Ransom Center, University of Texas.

(Temple-Smith), I tend boringly to hark back to the famous first two, I agree that you can't go on in that vein forever, and I'm convinced it's only a matter of time before you find your true *métier* as a novelist.

Don't feel sorry for me personally, I get a great kick out of reading your stuff, and I'm very happy to offer *The First Day of Adonis* now. I expect to sell it, but I expect to sell it largely on your reputation (I'm trying Joseph first); when it becomes a best-seller in its own right, you can tell us what fools we are. Yours ever, David.[251]

Frank wrote back from Conca dei Marini on 30 January:

I don't consider your comments and remarks to be cheek at all, nor have I the slightest intention of going to Curtis Brown or anybody else. I'm sure they couldn't do any better for me than you are doing.

In fact, the way that you have written, and what you said, is precisely what I would have wanted from an agent, who has always seemed to me to be somebody *more* than just a selling machine.

I agree with what you say, and I can only add that the grasp of the sheer mechanics and technique of constructing a novel is proving a lot more intractable and elusive than I ever thought it would.

Your letter has convinced me that you really appreciate and understand my difficulties very well. You have stated the position perfectly when you said, 'I agree that you can't go on in this vein forever' and when you said further 'but I expect to sell it largely on your reputation'.

My position is a perfectly consciously adopted choice, and quite deliberate. After *In Deep* I had to either go on doing the same thing until I both wore out my material and my readers – but probably with the promise of main-

---

251 David Higham Associates archive, Harry Ransom Center, University of Texas.

taining a modest success, until I just faded out from sheer exhaustion, boredom of my readers ... Or, I had to use the small reputation I had already gained by the sheer good fortune, to tide me over the difficult period while I was learning how to write. The fact that this period is proving more extended than either of us probably thought it would does not really alter the facts upon which my decision was based in the first place. It merely means that I have all the greater need of my small, hoarded resources, in the shape of that reputation.

What I am saying is that my fate as a sort of professional autobiographer would merely be to end up as a worn-out, journalistic hack. To my mind, it is impossible to escape from such a conclusion with regard to my previous style of work.

My fate in my attempt to become a novelist may fail just the same. But my position in that case would be very much more uncomfortable than it would have been in the first instance, while in fact, I *may* even succeed in becoming a novelist. There is, in this mode, at least the possibility of *ultimate* success, although *present* failure. While, with the autobiographical mode, there was only the prospect of modest present success – but I'm sure that you agree with me that in that mode, without having learned the techniques and mechanics of constructing a novel, ultimate failure was equally inevitable!

About Joseph – it's interesting that I almost suggested Michael Joseph to you when you wrote; but then I thought that I had better leave it to your discretion, as it was probably your business to know who to approach. Why I nearly suggested Joseph was that I took that other thing of mine, *Place of Cremation*, to Joseph – having secured an introduction through Julian Trevelyan. He refused it, not, he said, because it was either improper or queer, but because it was not a good book. But he was obviously jolly interested all the same, and very sincerely, I thought, professed to want to see anything I had available.

I've only got one more thing to say, and that is that I feel so small that when I send you the next book, which is up to about 35,000 words by now and which does not *seem* to be going so badly (it is called *Don Carlo to the Dark Tower Came* – Don Carlo being an Englishman, and the Dark Tower, of course, Sicily) – when I send you my next book, I shall be just about as happy as a snotty-nosed schoolboy submitting his first English essay.

Thank you again, and *indeed*, for all the trouble you are taking. Ever, Frank.[252]

Frank plied on in Conca, finishing *Don Carlo to the Dark Tower Came* and at the same time holding an open house. Angela Pain joined him for a few weeks in the summer of 1965, and the following summer he invited his friend from Coggeshall, the local artist Dorothy Butterfield. Frank told Dorothy to bring her easel and paints and she left a splendid painterly record of her time on the Amalfi coast in a collection of water-colours of local landscapes and buildings that is widely regarded as being among her best work.

---

252 David Higham Associates archive, Harry Ransom Center, University of Texas.

FIFTEEN
RETURN TO REALITY

FRANK RETURNED TO ENGLAND AND COGGESHALL IN THE autumn of 1966 and moved in with Dorothy Butterfield. By all accounts, Frank and Dorothy had a happy partnership. Although heterosexual herself, Dorothy was more than understanding and sympathetic about Frank's homosexuality, and during his time with her Frank seemed to rediscover something of the carefree atmosphere of his youth.

Dorothy had first come to Coggeshall in 1958 following the death of her father, for whom she had cared at their large family home in Chalfont St Peter. Her focus now was to find a smaller house close to her married lover, a film actor. She alighted on the old guildhall in the very centre of Coggeshall. Her actor friend died not long after, while shooting a Western in Hollywood, and all she had left was half of his ashes – his widow kept the other half. Dorothy decided to stay in Coggeshall and she became involved in the local arts scene and got to know and enjoy the company of the town's small group of homosexuals – among them Frank. Sometime in the mid 1960s, Dorothy moved from the old Guildhall to 42 East Street, a larger property with a garden leading down to the back stream of the River Blackwater, and this was the home that she was to share with Frank until she died in 1972.

Together they turned both house and garden into a charmed residence. Dorothy was wealthy, and she and Frank indulged each other's penchant for collecting fine paintings and interesting pieces, and in living well. Although Dorothy appeared to be happy with the arrangement, as time went on this was increasingly at her expense. Dorothy was by this time a lady of stoutish proportions, with silvery hair swept elegantly into a French pleat, but with a girlish smile and a naughty sense of humour.

Kate Leatherdale, then a buxom young Coggeshall mother who used to clean for her, says that Dorothy Butterfield did things in style, and made a lovely home there, and that Frank, who was a man of great taste, made his contribution too.[253]

In fact they did things on an impressive scale. Frank got Dorothy to put up a statue on a plinth in the garden to commemorate her 16-year-old Yorkshire terrier, Peter, and when Dorothy decided she could no longer stand her neighbour, Frank persuaded her to have a 20-foot brick wall built between them, elaborately designed in a neo-classical style with curves and decorative balls. The wall bears the hallmark of Frank's own extravagance and grand style, and it is also a subliminal testament to his architect father. In the same vein, Frank also encouraged Dorothy to purchase and convert the now redundant warehouses of E W King's seed company in the centre of Coggeshall into a small block of modern flats – a conversion that won an architecture prize for sympathetic restoration.

Disheartened by the lukewarm response to his novels, Frank stopped writing altogether for a while. He turned his energies to East Anglia's by now booming antique business. He specialised in oriental *objets d'art* and opened his own little shop in Coggeshall – in the basement of the Post Office – which he filled with very good pieces of porcelain and art from the Far East.

Frank's approach to commerce often baffled his fellow antique dealers in Coggeshall, and utterly confused his customers.

Richard Goss, a journalist who lived in Coggeshall at the time, says that, unless would-be buyers came up to scratch, Frank imperiously refused to sell them anything. A surprisingly large number of people including collectors, enthusiasts and other dealers alike, left the cave

---

253 Interviewed by the author, 2010.

empty-handed because they hadn't quite matched Frank's own intellect and knowledge – or because he simply didn't like the look of them. His tenure in the shop also led to the village's only regular traffic hazard at a time before its by-pass when it was on a very busy route from the Midlands to the East Coast: Frank, complete with flowing robes and carrying an ivory cane, was always too impatient to wait for a gap in the traffic and simply launched himself from the kerb, brandishing the stick and daring startled motorists to run him over.[254]

Frank also helped out at a store in the Bures Antique Centre, but, much as he enjoyed the antique business and the opportunity it gave him to engage with customers, he found a lot of those who worked in the trade boring and shallow. Little did he imagine that it was soon to land him in such trouble.

Frank dabbled as well a little in painting; producing a series of lurid portraits in oils – a few of which still hang in back rooms in Essex – and he hadn't altogether give up his ambition to be a writer. In early 1970 he resumed contact with his publisher, this time dealing directly with John Bright-Holmes, who by now had replaced Temple-Smith. Aware of the failure of *Culture of Bacillus* and warned off by reports on his subsequent fiction which had been turned down by Eyre & Spottiswoode, Bright-Holmes persuaded Frank to return to surer ground and resume his autobiography.

Frank wrote to him on 23 April 1970:

About another book on the lines of *Look Towards the Sea* and *In Deep*, well I am rather in agreement with you, that I ought perhaps to have a shot at it. I'm certainly quite willing to have a try, particularly as my circumstances and the line of country which I am furrowing at the moment would make another book fit in extremely well.[255]

They met for lunch on 8 May and shortly afterwards Frank started

---

254 Interviewed by the author 2010.
255 Random House archives.

work. 'I am finding so much material stowed away in my mental attics, much of it very useable,' he told his publisher.[256]

A note to the editorial committee at Eyre & Spottiswoode underlines Bright-Holmes's thinking:

> I have just made fresh contact with this wayward genius for whom E. & S. published two volumes of 'imaginative biography'. They both had stunning reviews ... We called the books 'imaginative biography' not because the author lies but because he sometimes does tell more than the truth ... Baines has not published for ten years, although he has written novels. His talent is not for invention so much as for raising truth to the power of 'n'. He is a natural autobiographer. So I have encouraged him to continue his autobiography, and he has sent me 25,000 words. I had in mind that this would cover the war period when he was in the army in India, became a Chindit, and up to the end when he went to a Burmese monastery.[257]

Bright-Holmes evidently had to 'sell' Frank to his editorial colleagues, so there is some top-spin in what he wrote to them, but what is clear is that he was still expecting, or at least hoping for, a best-seller from his 'wayward genius':

> My colleagues who (mostly) will not remember Frank Baines will want to know how he compares to Spike Mays.[258] Baines is a much more imaginative, much better educated, much more brilliant writer and with the danger inherent in all that of plumbing greater depths. All going well (and Baines will need a lot of editing from me) we should sell him better – the potential best-seller is in him in a way that Mays will probably never quite achieve. Both are colourful characters, but Baines is flamboyant and showy.[259]

---

256 Random House archives.
257 Random House archives.
258 English author, brought up in East Anglia, who served in the army in India, and like Frank wrote a series of colourful autobiographies also published by Eyre & Spottiswoode
259 Random House archives.

In a letter of 27 October 1970 to Frank's literary agent, David Bolt at David Higham Associates, Bright-Holmes announces almost in triumph that he has reached agreement with Frank to publish a new instalment of his autobiography:

I promised to let you know if I got anywhere with Frank Baines. I am glad to say that I have done and we have agreed terms for a third volume of autobiography which will cover his time in India during the War and will broach his Chindit period. It is going to be very good.[260]

Bolt's reply of 30 October 1970 is revealing:

Many thanks for letting me know about Frank Baines, which sounds like good news to me. I think that you deserve a good book out of him from sheer persistence! If you have persuaded him to return to the style and theme of his earlier books, that's quite an accomplishment.[261]

Apart from the collective persuasion of Bright-Holmes and Bolt, another powerful incentive seems to have been at work. Frank had virtually run out of money. In less than a decade he had spent or given away the entire proceeds from the sale of The Cedars and its contents, and by the early 1970s letters from Frank mention for the first time that he is having trouble with his bank manager. In fact, the letters become increasingly insistent. On 21 September 1970 he wrote to John Bright-Holmes:

I am enclosing some letters from my bank manager, from which you may see that he is pressing me to reduce an overdraft of £1,200 down to less than £1,000 or more. Rather unwisely, I suspect, I showed him your letter to me dated April 20th 1970, in which you mentioned that I ought to be thinking of continuing the autobiography. Of course, he was on to it like a stoat after a rabbit.[262]

---

260 Random House archives.
261 Random House archives.
262 Random House archives.

If I remember correctly, when I lunched with you on that occasion on May 8th, you did just mention the word 'money', but I rather grandly waved it aside, saying I didn't want any.

Well it now looks as if I was being decidedly premature and that I can no longer afford to adopt quite such a magnificent and disinvolved attitude!

My reason at the time was that I didn't really know whether, or how, or even if, the book would go, and after all it's bad enough owing the bank money, but it would be simply terrible owing you money as well, without being able to fulfil my obligations.

I am now, however, up to about 25,000 words of the book, and I do see that it will go. Angela (Pain) has read it and likes it.

May I, in this case, take up again the question of money and ask if you are prepared to advance any?[263]

Bright-Holmes wrote back by return with a promise to read the first 25,000 words and to come up, quickly, with a firm offer and a 'decent advance'. He enclosed the letters Frank had received from his bank manager, commenting, 'They read a little similarly to some I have had recently.'
Frank replied on 24 September:

Thank you for your most encouraging letter. I am sending it off today to my bank manager with a little letter saying how grateful he ought to be for thus dragging him into the world of the arts, from out of the rag trade (my bank is in W1, in Mortimer Street), and that alone ought to be worth twelve hundred![264]

Frank wrote again to Bright-Holmes on 9 November 1970: 'Do

---

263 Random House archives.
264 Random House archives.

please let me have the contract to sign; I want the money.'

The final contract arrived later that day with a note explaining that Bright-Holmes would be away in New York. Frank replied by return to Bright-Holmes's assistant, Mary Todd, enclosing the duly signed contract, and deployed brazen cheek to try to conjure up speedy payment of the advance for his new book.

Dear Miss Mary Todd

As I daresay you are aware, John Bright-Holmes has instructed me to return this agreement, duly signed, which herewith I do – and incidentally make it sound all rather like part of the marriage service!

I always like to visualise my correspondents, so accordingly I am visualising you with horn-rimmed spectacles, protruding teeth, and 'ear-phones'! Am I right to do so? Or do publishing women affect a similar swinging image to female advertising executives? On second thoughts, probably they do. Yet who knows, you may be just a lovely little woman with a bun, a boy-friend in a good position at the bank – and both members of the Surbiton tennis club!!

Or alternatively, are you the mysterious MHT – only referred to by cipher – who follows JBH when it says 'in reply please quote'?

I hope so, because I am relying on your already having read my most recent letter to your boss about money. After all, Clause XI F does say '£300 on signature of this agreement', thus I sincerely pray that you may possess sufficient executive power to squeeze a cheque for this amount out of your employers at once, and send it to me enclosed with your part of this agreement signed.

I shall be quite unable to wait until John Bright-Holmes gets back, for by that time I shall be in Newgate.

Don't get me wrong – I am terribly earnest about the money, so please start hoofing around the building now in search of someone who can sign that cheque.[265]

As well as with money, Frank was also having problems with his writing. He seemed to have lost his sure touch. His two first books had virtually flown from his pen, much as Frank talked. The novels had also gushed out freely, but this third volume of autobiography, *Officer Boy*, proved to be a struggle.

There were tussles over content, length, style and the title, and also about potential libel, particularly over suggestions that one of Frank's fellow officers, Peter Bentham, had homosexual tendencies. In the book, he becomes Toby Pastoe.

From the outset, there was an issue about where the story would end. Frank had early on envisaged a sequel – the story of his time with the Chindits – and he mentions the possibility for the first time in a letter on 24 September 1970. But Bright-Holmes thought he needed at least part of the Chindit story to sell the book.

Bright-Holmes wrote on 22 October 1970:

It is possible that the logic of this book may demand the inclusion of the Chindit material (or quite a bit of it) rather than its delaying to a further volume.

In publicity and sales terms too I certainly put a lot of weight on the Chindit part because it gives a point of reference that will be immediately understood by the trade and fairly easily communicated to the public ...

You know, I imagine, that the Japanese have said that the Chindit operation did more to cause their defeat than anything else, until the Bomb?[266]

Bright-Holmes also betrayed anxieties that Frank, who hadn't

---

265 Random House archives.
266 Random House archives.

written for several years, had gone off the boil and that his indulgence in fiction had somehow blunted his gift for lively narrative, writing on 16 October 1970:

> I really am delighted that you are writing again, because it is clear that a good book is going to result ... You have certainly not lost your way with words. The only general observation I would like to make at this stage is that too often I feel you are nudging the reader in the ribs. Your writing is, in fact, quite vivid enough to make your points for you without this being necessary.
>
> I admit I do have reservations about the Wimbledon section and the whole political agent stuff. It seems to me not to work very well at the moment, although I am not certain why. It might be because the material is a little thin compared to the other experiences you are relating. It might also be a combination of this with your eagerness to make it appear very funny and strange, which (as they say nowadays) tends to be counter-productive.
>
> Perhaps I could add one other point which I hope will not offend you in any way – I do, though, feel it could be a tactical error to be too frank sexually until the book is well under way. I am speaking not in literary terms but commercial ones. There is a plentiful audience for your book in Essex and Wimbledon, for example, and it could conceivably be put off if not inducted gently.[267]

Bright-Holmes wrote again on 22 October:

> To revert to the book again, I agree with you that from the literary point of view it is going to be OK. I quite agree, too, that a lot of your nudging of the reader was by way of getting the writing wheels running smoothly again. I don't see any basic problem in taking a lot of that out and making the text more literary, in the best sense of that word.[268]

---

267 Random House archives.
268 Random House archives.

Frank replied on 23 October: 'Sorry about nudging the reader in the ribs. It's probably nothing more important than a sort of nervous "tick" due to beginners' nerves.' He added that he was not offended by the remarks about sex and that, in general, he was inclined to agree with Bright-Holmes on all points.[269]

The only outstanding issue at this stage remained the cut-off of the story, and Frank wrote again the following day:

I find I am quite an old technical pro when it comes to the flinty-eyed realities. [I can] write the material, assemble the material in such a way that it could either end where I suggested to you in my last letter, at 60,000 words, or go to about 80,000 and include some of the Chindit training (but it would have to be only training) leaving the real operations for a further volume.

He ended the letter with a flinty rebuff to his publisher, which despite its apparent bravura reveals quite how difficult he was finding this return to autobiography:

May I ask you, although it sounds a funny request, not to write me any more letters, as I really have to get down and concentrate. I think we have covered the business and literary points quite fully for the moment and if I need your help, or I think you should see some more of the typescript, I will write to you myself. Please don't be offended either at this, but I am suddenly becoming horrifically aware that there is an enormous amount of work to do in, for me, a comparatively short time; and, also for me, much of the quality of the work seems to depend very much on just loafing about without feeling that there is very much to do, and then it all seems to flow quite naturally. I mean, I just want to *avoid* a feeling of crisis or deadline!![270]

---

269 Random House archives.
270 Random House archives.

The correspondence did indeed stop, and Frank completed and delivered the book on time in February 1971. But, for Bright-Holmes, the result was far from satisfactory. He wrote to Frank on 31 March 1971:

> What I have been doing is reading and editing your MS as I went. In my opinion it needed quite a lot of this for different sorts of reasons – for I felt you often spoilt some marvellous material by nudging the reader too hard in the ribs, for example, or by letting sentences go on for too long, or by unclear punctuation (five dots is not the best form for clarity or the look of a printed page), or too many exclamation marks, a bit too much over-writing, or whatever.

> Apart from this I like the book very much indeed. It is very lively and amusing and interesting and picks up perfectly where you left off twelve (!) years ago. I particularly like the opening scene in Montevideo, the air attack on the ack-ack site and the Ipis cannon ... so please don't be depressed if I seem to be saying and marking a lot.[271]

Bright-Holmes, however, asked for some cuts and in a letter the following week, on 5 April, he requested further cuts, saying that it was 'a bit on the long side, and sometimes over-dramatised'. To push things forward and help Frank with the editing, Bright-Holmes even asked him to come to London and stay at his home in Wimbledon. In the event Bright-Holmes came down to Coggeshall because Frank was temporarily immobilised as the result of a bicycle accident in which he had injured his leg.

Following this visit, Bright-Holmes wrote to Frank on 19 April 1971:

> I very much enjoyed coming and seeing you last Wednesday, and could you kindly thank Miss Butterfield again on my behalf for giving me such pleasant hospitality.

---

271 Random House archives.

I hope you are really by now feeling much better after your accident, and that in particular your leg is beginning to get easier.

I am most grateful for your help over the script and for accepting much of what I suggested as you did. It is a very entertaining book indeed.[272]

On the sidelines, Frank was also still trying to get his fictional work published. He still believed passionately that he was a novelist.

He had mentioned the unpublished novels to Bright-Holmes at their meeting on 8 May 1970 when they had agreed that Frank should return to his autobiography, and, in a letter of 22 September that year, and by now well into his new book, Frank was still fighting their corner:

At our meeting on May 8th, I also mentioned two other typescripts of novels, and I asked if you wanted to see them, and you said you did. *Don Carlo to the Dark Tower Came* is frightfully long – about 120,000 words – and is about Italy. The other one is quite short, 60,000 words, and is called *Place of Cremation*. You read it about 10 years ago and were incredibly guarded in your comments. You gave me the impression you were frightened.

Well, we are all 10 years older now, and a good deal more world-weary. The book has been read by several critics in typescript, and much praised to me to my face. I've no reason to suppose that these critics were lying. My own opinion is that you at least owe this short book your very serious consideration. David Robinson, the film critic of the *Financial Times*, who lives in Coggeshall, read it and was much impressed by it. Paul Jennings,[273] who lives in East Bergholt near here, when talking to a friend of mine about it, said that Frank Baines's tragedy was that he was far in advance of his time.[274]

---

272 Random House archives.
273 Paul Jennings (1918-1989), British writer and humourist.
274 Random House archives.

Bright-Holmes promised to look at the shorter book, *Place of Cremation*, and said he would send the longer Italian novel out to a reader, adding 'All of us publishers would like to be able to read everything we get with the attention it deserves, but unfortunately life is just not long enough.'

Frank sent him the typescripts of both *Place of Cremation* and *Don Carlo to the Dark Tower Came*, and, to speed things up, he even included the reader's report on the Sicilian novel which his agents David Higham Associates had commissioned in 1965.

A month later, in a letter of 21 October, he took Bright-Holmes to task for not acknowledging their arrival:

> I thought, therefore, that I would just mention that I hope your non-acknowledgement doesn't imply that you are going to adopt Maurice Temple-Smith's technique of embarrassed, slightly askance-looking silence, when dealing with sodomite 'Grand Guignol'.[275]

Bright-Holmes replied that was not trying to fob Frank off and apologised that he was a slow worker. However there was no follow-up, and a few months later, in a letter dated 12 January 1971, in which he announced that he had finished *Officer Boy*, Frank became still more insistent, indeed almost abusive:

> I still think that you ought to get down and read *Place of Cremation*. I mean, I think it is your *duty* to do so, not to me, but to the firm that employs you. After all, you publishers are always bellyaching about the dearth of original fiction, but when a bit of original creative fiction falls into your laps, you all make a sour face. It's true, isn't it, that none of you would recognise a piece of original, creative fiction – not even if you found it wandering around wearing a dressing gown in your own home before breakfast?

---

275 Random House archives.

Well you've got a piece with you, full of splendid prose and wonderful surrealist imagery, and all you are going to do, I can see, is make a wry face, as if you'd bitten into a lemon – but if you'd only realise it, this is the effect that all original and creative writing always has.

Alright, John, the last thing you want to be lumbered with is originality and creativity – they are too damned uncomfortable. What you want is good plastic copy or clever imitation – something that you can't pretend to yourself and to others is original and creative, but which quite simply is saleable.

And as you know, nobody buys originality or creativity except in minute quantities – and a minute fragment of the population at that. Pity! Ever, Frank.[276]

Frank was being far from fair with his editor. Although he specialised in history, including the Monarchs series on the kings and queens of England, and scholarly historians such as Robert Blake, Jack Scarisbrick and J. H. Plumb, Bright-Holmes had by now been in publishing for more than 20 years and he had looked after and edited a distinguished stable of creative writers – among them John Braine, author of *Room at the Top* (Braine dedicated a later book, *How to Write a Novel*, to Bright-Holmes) and Bernice Rubens, who in 1970 became the first female writer to win the Booker Prize, with *The Elected Member*. When Bright-Holmes moved from Eyre & Spottiswoode to Allen & Unwin as editorial director in 1972, taking Frank with him, he introduced influential American authors such as Bernard Malamud and J P Donleavy to Britain.

George Greenfield, in *A Smattering of Monsters*, described Bright-Holmes as 'one of the three or four best post-war book editors, a man of commanding stature and presence with a solid off-drive'. This was a reference to Bright-Holmes's life-long passion for cricket. Bright-Holmes wrote two books on the game, and also edited a volume of

---

276 Random House archives.

the diaries of British journalist and author Malcolm Muggeridge.

On 21 September 1971 Bright-Holmes finally got back to Frank with an encouraging note:

> I have had a report on *Place of Cremation*, which is really quite a good one, and I will get down to proper consideration of it once we have seen how *Officer Boy* goes. I have not forgotten.[277]

Writing *Officer Boy* and persuading his publishers to take his fictional work seriously were not Frank's only problems in 1971. The tax authorities – or rather the Ministry of Social Security – were after him. Frank's life-long dislike of bureaucracy and his reluctance to pay tax, which had forced him to flee Calcutta in 1956, had caught up with him again.

Once again it was running a business, not writing, which ensnared him. When he opened his little shop in the basement of the Post Office in Coggeshall, he had been forced to register as self-employed and he had been given an Insurance Card on which he was supposed to buy stamps and stick them in each month to show that he was paying his regular contribution to the State's social welfare system.

The Insurance Card was started in March 1969, but when Frank was visited by a Social Security inspector 18 months later in September 1970 there was only one stamp on it. Frederick Frost, the inspector, was less than impressed and reported Frank to higher authorities.

Frank was sent a succession of letters threatening him with the full consequences of the law if he refused to pay the arrears. In characteristic style, he ignored them, telling friends that he wasn't going to pay because he didn't plan to be using the welfare system in his old age. He was determined to dig in his heels.

Frank was summoned to the Magistrates Court in Witham on 2 March 1971. A local landowner, Christopher Parker, was the presiding magistrate. Frank defended himself and did his best to turn the

---

277 Random House archives.

proceedings into a show trial. The case was fully reported in the local papers.[278]

'The people of my generation have been asking ourselves how Germany, Italy and Russia came to find themselves in the position they did under Hitler, Mussolini and Stalin,' Frank told Parker. 'Looking around at this country now, I think we are going the same way. I feel I must make a stand. In 50 years time people will ask the same questions in this country as we have asked of Germany, Italy and Russia.'

He gave his address as The Basement, Post Office, Coggeshall, and told the court that he was an antiques dealer 'who had never made a deal' and that his operations at the Post Office basement shop were minimal.

'In actual fact, I am a writer,' he added.

Parker was not amused.

'We are here to interpret the law and see that it is not made a fool of. If you are not prepared to pay the arrears we shall have to send you to prison. I hope that by giving you a period of time to think about it you will end up by paying the amount you owe.'

Frank stood his ground.

'I realise this and am perfectly prepared to go. Bring on the gyves.'

Frank had pleaded not guilty to failing to pay his National Insurance contributions but was duly found guilty and convicted. He was fined £8 with £5 costs and ordered to pay the arrears of £101.58 within three months or go to prison for 90 days.

In private, Frank riled against the 'administration' – he refused to use the word 'government'. Friends rallied round him. Bright-Holmes, when he heard about the court appearance, signed off his next letter with a robust message of solidarity. 'All the very best,' he wrote, 'and to hell with social security.' He later, at Eyre and Spottiswoode's expense, sought legal advice from Rubenstein, Nash & Co about protecting Frank's earnings.

---

278 News reports in *East Anglian Daily Times*, 3 March 1971 and *Braintree & Witham Times*, 5 March 1971.

'What a pity that this interesting character must drag his publishers into his public spirited protest,' the lawyers wrote, helpfully but inappropriately suggesting that Frank could assign his rights to his wife![279]

The *Financial Times* film critic David Robinson even wrote to the Ipswich based *East Anglian Daily Times* complaining that they had 'traduced' Frank in their report on the proceedings at Witham Magistrates Court by describing him as a 'writer' between inverted commas. Robinson demanded an apology on Frank's behalf. Tony Miles, editor of the *Daily Mirror* and another of Coggeshall's resident journalists, promised his support.

In the interval, while the law was slowly preparing to exact its toll, Frank embarked on another new career. He made a brief appearance in one of the very bawdy scenes in Italian movie director Pier Paolo Pasolini's *I racconti di Canterbury* (Canterbury Tales), which was being filmed in Coggeshall.

An episode from *The Pardoner's Tale* was shot in Coggeshall's 12th century barn, an imposing remnant of its great Cistercian Abbey. The barn was turned into a tavern interior in which the extras, dressed in extremely uncomfortable medieval stage costume were let loose as roisterers. Frank was one of them. They roistered so well that one of the villagers fell backwards over her stool and split her head open. The scene involved an actor urinating on the assembly from a balcony above. For the shots of the roisterers below, water was squirted from a bottle. The actor himself was supplied with quantities of beer, coca-cola and tea, and at intervals the extras were sent outside into the cold wind while he did his close-ups.

'What was the name of the director?' asked Frank. 'Pissolini?'

Frank had meanwhile started work in earnest on the story of his service with the Chindits, the planned sequel to *Officer Boy*, for which he had received a contract from his publishers at the end of May 1971, for delivery by February 1972.

---

279 Random House archives.

Frank was hauled before the magistrate once again on 17 August, and this time the *East Anglian Daily Times* was more respectful in its reporting – 'Author Prepared for Prison as Protest', its headline read. Following Robinson's letter, Frank had been promoted from 'writer' to 'author'. The paper reported: 'An author who refuses to pay National Insurance contributions repeated yesterday that he is prepared to go to prison as a measure of protest.'

Frank told the court that he could not co-operate with a system which liked to knock people down to have the emotional satisfaction of picking them up. The medicine of National Insurance contributions, he said, was a harsh tax which was worse than the sickness it was supposed to cure. They could not expect him to collaborate with such a system.

As in their previous encounter, Parker was unyielding.

'We're here to administer the law,' he said. 'You are entitled to your own opinions, but you just can't opt out of the laws of the country.'

He gave Frank a further 14 days in which to pay up. Frank said he wouldn't and he then asked: 'What will you do? Come and fetch me from home?'

'Arrangements will be made,' replied the assistant clerk.[280]

In an interview with the Colchester *Evening Gazette* after the court hearing, Frank said: 'At the age of 56, I am quite prepared to spend the rest of my life in prison rather than conform with this iniquitous system. Anyway prison will be a new experience for me.'[281]

He wrote a long letter to Bright-Holmes on 1 September, bringing him up to date on his draft of the Chindits story and saying that he was ready for prison:

> From tomorrow, I must be prepared to be carted off, although I expect it may be a couple of weeks yet, since, like the trains, these affairs never seem able to run on time. However, I ought to try to get all my business done in time, hence this letter.

---

280 *East Anglian Daily Times*, 18 August 1971.
281 *Colchester Evening Gazette*, 18 August 1971.

Frank gave details of the journalists who had taken an interest in and written about his case, and he ended with characteristic humour:

> I've done my best from the publicity point of view, and short of getting myself shot as an infamous fellow, I can't do anything further. I leave everything, with complete confidence, needless to say, to you.[282]

He wrote again on 7 September, insisting that he did not want any prison visits:

> I'm not particularly keen on being visited in jug like a preparatory schoolboy by his loving parents. I have always rejected emotional or sentimental sympathy in the English meaning of the word. It makes me want to puke. But of course I have never rejected sympathy in the French or Italian meaning. The fact that the English have attached such a loathsome interpretation to this fine word is just another example (if any were needed) of just how low the English can get.

> But if it's a question of business, of arranging a jail break, or bringing me a huge cake (baked naturally by the lily white hands of your loving Rose) enclosing a file, a hand-saw, and a coil of nylon rope, or even bringing a group of visiting journalists – if it's a question, that is to say, of publicity for the book, then I am all for it.

Frank got to see the dust jacket – 'the best I have ever had'– but by the time *Officer Boy* was actually published, he was behind bars. The Essex police had finally come for him in early October. They swooped somewhat theatrically on 42 East Street before dawn and drove him away to Brixton. Frank had taken the precaution of shaving his head, commenting: 'I shall deprive my jailers of that pleasure at least.'

Frank's publishers, meanwhile, had drawn up a list of influential people to whom complimentary copies of *Officer Boy* were to be sent.

---

282 Random House archives.

The list is an impressive tribute to Frank's friendships and to his rep-
utation, and included the novelists Simon Raven, Colin Wilson and
John Masters, the Oxford scholar A. L. Rowse, the yachtsman Eric
Hiscock, and journalists, George Gale (editor of *The Spectator*), Tony
Miles (editor of the *Daily Mirror*), David Robinson (of the *Financial
Times*) and James Cameron.

He had close links with them all, except perhaps Gale, whom he
had met in unexpected circumstances, explaining to Bright-Holmes:

> I have been to his house at Wivenhoe, near Colchester, but not as a writer,
> simply in the humble capacity of helping another antique dealer deliver
> to his wife a hideously ugly and very heavy clock which she had ill-advisedly
> bought.[283]

They all responded – Wilson with a warm note praising Frank's
style, and Masters with a glowing endorsement:

> Frank Baines is a powerfully evocative writer with a brilliant nervous style.
> He is a very funny man and his descriptions dazzle like fireworks at close
> range. *Officer Boy* is a wonderful book.[284]

Reviews were positive, but not glowing.

'It is one of the last first-hand accounts (of Frontier Operations)
that we are likely to get and, when Mr Baines curbs a certain over-exu-
berance, one of the best, with evocations of bivouac, march and action
under wide skies that is lyrical as well as ribald,' wrote Christopher
Wordsworth in *The Observer*.

The Times Literary Supplement said Frank had told his story 'in
a highly individual mixture of gusto, humour, observation and personal
idiosyncrasy':

---

283 Random House archives.
284 Random House archives.

Mr Baines is not the kind of man to whom ordinary things seem to happen. As an historical account of India and the Indian Army during the 1940s, *Officer Boy* can only be classed as a picture in a distorting mirror, but the distortions are so amusingly grotesque and the surface has everywhere such burnish and sparkle that many people should thoroughly enjoy these far from plain tales from the hills.

Frank spent two months in Brixton prison – an experience which he hated. He never wrote about it, and nor did he talk much about it, except to reveal that while inside he was assigned to work in the prison library.

His incarceration was noted in the diary column in *The Times* on 14 October:

Frank Baines, English eccentric extraordinary and author, is celebrating the publication of his third work of 'imaginative autobiography', *Officer Boy*, in prison. He is there on a matter of principle: Baines refuses to pay his National Insurance contributions ... He is much given to the grand gesture.

Dan Sansom, Frank's solicitor and former neighbour in Coggeshall, said that, though it was a matter of principle for Frank, he found it very chastening. He said that it had changed his view of human nature, and was an experience he did not want to repeat.[285]

After Frank was released at the end of November, Dorothy, without his knowing, paid his debt and his fine. She had come to rely on Frank and had found the whole prison episode very upsetting; she did not want to go through it again either. Moreover, she had something much bigger to worry about – she had been diagnosed with liver cancer, and her doctors had told her that she would be lucky to live another 12 months.

Frank returned to 42 East Street, determined to look after Dorothy in the same way that he had cared for his dying mother. They resumed

---

285 Interviewed by the author in 2009.

their domestic life as best they could under the shadow of Dorothy's incurable cancer, and Frank went back to working on his book about the Chindits.

The story of his 'love affair' with the Chindits, which at its heart is about his love for Dal Bahadur, was to prove to be perhaps the hardest challenge in his literary career.

SIXTEEN
LOW LIFE IN ESSEX

FRANK STARTED ON HIS CHINDIT BOOK AS SOON as he had finished and despatched *Officer Boy*. He warned his publisher that it was going to be a highly emotional undertaking, and that he was by no means sure that it would flow easily.

He wrote to Bright-Holmes on 27 May 1971:

> I want to be prepared for some blind stroke of fate leaping at me out of the subconscious ... You are an excellent editor, and I am very grateful to you for it. You have transformed those first two chapters out of all recognition.[286]

Initially, Bright-Holmes was encouraging, writing back the next day:

> I posted the contracts before I had read through your chapters which I did last night and I think they work splendidly. I really am delighted and agree with you that you have got it right ... It does look like being a very good book indeed and a memorable one.[287]

But Frank was assailed with doubts, and he compared writing about the experience to the agony of re-living it, writing to Bright-Holmes on 1 June:

---

286 Random House archives.
287 Random House archives.

This was the sort of mission which by my obsessive insistence, I had taken upon myself. I imagined I was sufficiently tempered as a soldier to cope with it. I had not bargained for the frightful demands which it would make upon my moral fibre, nor the fearful inroads it would carve into my mental stability. Nor did I realise, in my naivety, that I was setting myself on a par with mighty professionals of war like Joe Lentaigne, the commander of 111 Brigade, and Jack Masters, the Brigade Major – people who, by virtue of their training, that is to say, their carefully cultivated callousness, were much more essentially entitled to foresee a successful outcome to the campaign than a mere spectator such as I was. For with my facile enthusiasms, I was fundamentally half an amateur.

They were the new men, the men of destiny, representative of that sort of person who would shortly start winning the war for us in this theatre of operations, and assuredly among some of the earliest of their species to make an appearance in South East Asia. They elevated all of us to a similar status; for we too, the incurable civilians in uniform as well as the enthusiastic amateurs, were ennobled by being able to join such an illustrious company.[288]

Frank concluded by proposing two titles for the book: *Men of Destiny* or *Illustrious Company*. Bright-Holmes was not so sure and a few days later, in a letter dated 5 June, Frank came up with: *Big-Shot, Gun-Shock, Soldier-Man*:

Difficult to say, I admit. But it comes well after *Officer Boy*, which in any case is going to be difficult to cap. Big-Shot stands for General Wingate and the other mighty professionals and protagonists like Joe Lentaigne and Jack Masters. Gun-Shock stands for the impact of battle, which is what we all without distinction suffered from. Soldier-Man stands for me and the other fighting foot-sloggers.[289]

Bright-Holmes had suggested to Frank that he send his draft to a

---

288 Random House archives.
289 Random House archives.

Chindit expert, and Frank ended the letter on a note of high conspiracy:

> You had better suggest to your biographer of Wingate that he investigate the air crash very thoroughly.[290] Facts are not so easy to come by. At least one sergeant in 111 Brigade Headquarter thought he had been murdered (I suppose you would call it assassination) when news came through of the manner of his death ... Smouldering resentment burns like a slow match to a barrel of gunpowder.[291]

He followed up with another letter on 6 August, complaining that he was finding the new book slow work but that he was pleased with the result:

> I am afraid that it is going awfully slowly. However, I think the quality is extremely high. It's solid, taut, you might say tensile in the sense of high tensile steel (whatever that is!). What I mean to imply by this word tensile is a sort of elastic quality. In a way, what I have written is some of the best stuff that I have done yet. Although the subject matter is not yet particularly intense, I feel that the writing certainly is so. It is quite different to my other stuff. I confess to being rather intrigued by it.

Frank returned to his proposal for the title, only this time adding 'Corpse' at the end, which he said was self-explanatory – 'it stands for what we were all universally in danger of ending up as'.

> And if you want to repeat the *Officer Boy* technique with the jacket, I have a splendid photo of the author, almost completely naked and looking decidedly thin, standing beside an elephant accompanied by its Burmese *mahout*,[292] and wearing on one end of his body a very large-looking head (on account of this body being emaciated, I suppose) and on the other end, a huge pair of boots![293]

---

290 Orde Wingate died in a plane crash in north-east India on 24 March 1944.
291 Random House archives.
292 Elephant driver.
293 Random House archives.

Bright-Holmes responded diplomatically to the suggested title, in a letter of 9 August:

> The only possible doubt I have is whether it might seem a little lightweight for the subject … Sorry you're finding the Chindit book going rather slowly, but you half expected that, so it doesn't seem all that much of a bad sign in itself. It's likely to be your most important book so far, so it's worth all the trouble you can take over it.[294]

Just before he was taken to prison, Frank was complaining again in a letter of 23 September that he was having to 'rewrite the bloody thing about a dozen times. I've never had this sort of trouble before.'

The spell in prison and its effect on him, together with the time he dedicated to Dorothy after he got back home, slowed the writing even more, and Frank missed the February 1972 deadline. He finally delivered a draft in the late spring. By now the working title was *Wringing Wet*.

Overall Bright-Holmes was not impressed, as he indicated to Frank on 6 July 1972:

> I had in fact read *Wringing Wet* by the time you rang Mary last week, but I was still trying to work out what I felt was wrong about the book. Because, unfortunately, I do not feel – and I am very sad indeed to be saying this – that it comes off.

> Of course I was greatly entertained by a lot of what you have written and felt at first that there were no greater problems than we had, and solved, with *Officer Boy*.

> And the whole passage of your affair with the recalcitrant mule is not only hilarious but one of the best passages you have written. The further, though, I went into the book, the less satisfactory I found it and by the end, although I could see well enough why you chose that point for the end, I felt that

---

294 Random House archives.

you had stretched out one fairly brief sequence of experience too far for its content. I appreciate, I think, how you need space to convey a feeling of breakdown, but too often it seemed to me you were elaborating both your story and its style so much that it lost the crispness and clearness of your best passages. Possibly this happened because of the long interruption you suffered in prison after you had written nearly one half. I may be wrong, but I felt that it was in revising this part you lost freshness and cohesiveness through your effort to describe your state of mind more exactly. I do not feel incidentally that this is a matter for verbal editing, like we did before; it is a matter of the *scale* of the book.

He then comes to the nub of the matter:

And here, if I may, I would like to digress a moment and raise a different but related problem. I was tremendously disappointed, like you, at the lack of attention given to *Officer Boy* which I really thought was damn good even though it lacked the ideal 'unity' that *In Deep* had by nature of its subject. However it was not widely reviewed and has not sold widely either (1,678 copies is the present tally) and this means we have to be particularly careful with the content and launching of Baines IV.

Bright-Holmes continued with a host of suggestions, urging Frank to start off the book with the 'big guns' of the Chindits and Orde Wingate, and he added that he did not think *Wringing Wet* was a good title. He told Frank bluntly that he thought the subject of the book had become inflated beyond its natural limits and that this was perhaps a result of too great a concentration on himself and his feelings at the expense of the narrative. Frank had become too self-indulgent. Bright-Holmes said that, while autobiography was of course a self-centred art, it tended to succeed best where it least appeared to be so.[295]

Frank accepted the criticism and fired himself up for a major re-write. Bright-Holmes wrote to him on 14 July:

---

295 Random House archives.

Very many thanks for your call last week. I am so glad that you don't feel too depressed at my reaction to *Wringing Wet*, and I am indeed very pleased that you feel you can write a book to which the events you cover are the prelude and which ultimately will reach to the Chindit operation. As I said in strictly marketing terms I believe it is necessary for us to be able to talk about Wingate and the Chindits, and I believe too there is a market, mostly amongst old soldiers, for a book specifically on this subject.

He concluded by offering Frank a revised contract with a new delivery date of 31 May 1973.[296] A note was circulated internally sanctioning an additional £100 advance to Frank, but with the proviso that it was issued as a money order: 'I queried why we should be put to the additional trouble of paying by money order instead of a cheque and was told that he is having problems with his bank.'

Dorothy died on 17 November 1972 and Frank had the immediate problem of finding somewhere to live; 42 East Street had only been rented. In her Will Dorothy left Frank an apartment in Gravel Court, behind the old King's Seed Company warehouse in the centre of Coggeshall, but it would take time for probate to be granted.

In the interim, Frank moved to East Bergholt to live at Fountain House with an Essex antique dealer, Lionel Evans. Evans ran an antiques shop and restaurant from the house, and, while staying there, Frank became involved – at least peripherally – with one of the 20th century's most colourful art fraudsters, Tom Keating, who used his talent for copying great paintings to make fools of the sale-room establishment and earn himself a lot of money.

Keating, who died in 1984, produced forgeries on an industrial scale – Turner, Degas, Van Dongen, Matisse, Modigliani and the English visionary painter Samuel Palmer. He called them his 'Sexton Blakes'. For much of the 1970s, he and his partner Jane Kelly ran a highly successful operation, selling sold some 2,000 of Keating's fakes. Lionel helped them.

The law did not finally catch up with Keating until 1979 when he and Kelly were arrested after their sale of a series of fake Samuel Palmer landscapes was exposed by the journalist Geraldine Norman, then sale-room correspondent of *The Times*. The two were put on trial, along with Lionel who was accused of fencing a fake Constable.

Julian Birch, then a local antique dealer, remembers meeting Frank at Fountain House in 1973 together with Keating and Kelly:[297]

> Lionel had Tom and his girlfriend staying with him at the time. They were living in the Canaries but were very short of money and Lionel had offered to put them up in East Bergholt while they tried to raise some money. Tom painted in the back room and Jane, who was a very unpleasant girl, was out a good deal.

> Tom and Jane went back to the Canaries but it was obvious that their relationship was on the rocks, even to me, so I was not surprised when Tom came back alone to stay with Lionel.

> Tom was a great talker. He talked about the war and being a stoker which he had never got over. He also had a huge chip on his shoulder about anyone who had been more successful than him. He disliked, he said, anyone posh, anyone who had got on through their family connections. In fact he was a very embittered man for half the time, and the rest of the time he was a great raconteur and good company.

> One day in the back room at Lionel's, Tom said that he could easily copy Van Dongen. Since we were not remotely interested in Van Dongen we laughed it off and Lionel kept offering us Van Dongens to sell. This was all conducted in a semi-jocular way because we all knew who had painted the pictures and I assumed that Tom was giving them to Lionel *in lieu* of rent or cigarettes. Lionel's exuberant personality when describing these 'great masterpieces' was extremely entertaining. I can only think that if anyone was taken in by it they were either extremely naïve or greedy.

---

297 Note to the author, 2010.

Lionel was an expert antiques dealer; he was very knowledgeable and an extremely good salesman. He had a wide network of friends among the local dealers, including Ivor Weiss, Geoffrey Compton Dando, and Wilfrid Bull, who was for a while the uncrowned king of the trade in Coggeshall before he was sent to prison for murdering his wife.

Many of them had been good friends with Dorothy – and she in turn, encouraged by Frank, had bought antique paintings from them and also some works by the Jewish artist and dealer Ivor Weiss. Lionel returned the favour and in 1973 he and Frank held a retrospective of Dorothy's paintings at Fountain House.

Birch continues the story:

The atmosphere there was always convivial and it was a pleasure to drop in – everyone was welcome.

I became involved in the fake Samuel Palmers when we went there one day and Lionel was having histrionics in the attic with a lot of paintings. Most of them appeared to be Van Dongens, but he then produced four small pictures which were instantly of interest to me … they looked like Samuel Palmers.

I asked Lionel if I could borrow them and he initially said 'No', and that he wasn't sure where they came from.

It was at this stage, I think, that Lionel decided to play innocent about the origins of the paintings. He asked Tom if it was anything to do with him. Tom told him that Jane had placed various pictures in salerooms to raise money for them both, and that they had come from the attic of a relative.

These 'Palmers' were in fact part of the Keating production line; Lionel had shown them to a London dealer who told him that Palmers like them were fetching upwards of £20,000.

Another friend, the City fund manager Jeremy Hill, recalls a dinner at East Bergholt when Lionel and Frank seemed to be more than aware of what was actually going on:

> We went to a remarkable dinner there with Frank when the conversation centred on the duplicity of London art dealers and the impossibility of selling pictures that hadn't been authenticated by a small ring of self-seeking, self-appointed experts.

> It so happened that they had a Modigliani in the shop which they couldn't get authenticated which was going to deny them a substantial profit. After dinner we had a chance to examine the Modigliani which was as fine an example of the artist's work as I have handled. We went home convinced of the iniquity of the art dealing world.[298]

Keating and Evans faced trial soon after.

The trial was a major news story and the object of intense interest. Kelly turned Queen's Evidence against both Keating and Evans. Keating pleaded not guilty, and when the case was dropped because of his poor health he emerged from the courtroom a celebrity. Evans also avoided prison – he was given an 18-month suspended sentence – but the trial broke him and he lost everything as a result, except his many loyal friends who stood by him, among them Frank.

Julian Birch has a final memory:

> After the trial I asked Lionel why he had tried to sell fake Palmers. He replied that he had never actually made a decision to market them, but things had got out of hand and he had gone along with it. Lionel only discovered at a late stage that Tom's pictures actually sold as originals, but Tom of course had known all the time.

The tale continues to work its magic in Essex and beyond: there

---

298 Jeremy Hill, note to the author, 2009.

are now fakes of Keating fakes in circulation, and the Essex town of Manningtree has named a street after him.

Frank did not stay long with Lionel, and there has never been any suggestion that he was ever directly or personally involved in Keating's fakes – although he clearly knew what was happening. When Dorothy's will had been settled, he moved back to Coggeshall, taking up residence in a ground floor flat she had left him, No 5 Gravel Court.

Frank turned the flat into an oriental Kasbah. He put an oleander in a pot by the door alongside his bicycle, and crammed the sitting room with spectacular Japanese and Chinese antiques. Julian Birch remembers the flat as being 'massively uncomfortable'.

It was not a good period for Frank. He changed literary agents, or rather his literary agents changed. David Bolt, who had looked after him at David Higham Associates, left in 1972 to set up his own agency, Bolt and Watson. Bright-Holmes had also moved. He joined George Allen & Unwin after Eyre & Spottiswoode was taken over by Methuen, but he took the contract for Frank's Chindit book with him. A new draft was finally submitted in 1975; but it was never published.

Meanwhile, Frank had totally run out of money.

But he didn't seem to mind. He took a job at the White Hart Hotel as a kitchen porter and dishwasher. Following his hero George Orwell, he became a *plongeur*. The White Hart was perfectly located for him, just across the road from his flat. It was an old post inn that had been pulled into the 20th century and made over into a comfortable hotel by expanding into the adjoining properties through the enterprise of Braintree-born Ray Pluck, who would dress in the evenings in a white dinner jacket in symbolic salute to his own social elevation from village inn keeper to country hotel proprietor.

Pluck says that Frank was the kitchen porter for about five years, turning his hand to whatever tasks needed to be done. He was an excellent worker and good fun, and, off-duty, they became good friends.[299]

Frank also continued to dabble in oriental antiques. He occasionally

---

299 Interviewed by the author in 2010.

accompanied one of his young friends, an antique dealer called Elizabeth Cannon, on trips to London where he would help on her stall at the Cutler Street jewellery market in Houndsditch. She says that Frank enjoyed the busy cosmopolitan 'wheeling and dealing' atmosphere on Cutler Street, and the opportunity it gave him to show off and entertain and interact with people from all over the world. His smart British 'toff' voice went down particularly well, and he had a special way of clinching sales with American ladies: he would simply tell them that such and such a piece was far too good for them, after which they always bought it.[300]

At the White Hart, Frank met one of his final English boyfriends, John Grimsey, who was the trainee chef and 40 years his junior.

Grimsey says that he was still at college when they first met. He was living at home and Frank used to shower him with very racy letters which he had to destroy in case his parents found them. When Grimsey came to the White Hart full-time in 1975, he moved in with Frank at Gravel Court and they were together for the next four years. Grimsey remembers Frank as very warm-hearted and very loyal, and says that Frank was faithful to him.

Grimsey recalls a trip to London in 1975, when Frank delivered the first revised draft of his Chindit book to his publishers and remembers that it was rejected. Afterwards they went to see one of his old friends from the tea industry in Calcutta. Frank very rarely talked about his past and the closest Grimsey ever came to it was on a trip they made to Italy together. They went to Rome and then drove down south to the Amalfi Coast to visit Conca dei Marini where Frank had lived for quite a time.[301]

Gail Turner,[302] Dorothy Butterfield's great-niece who was living in Rome at that time, recalls the drama of Frank's return to Conca. Gail was with him on that trip, and can never forget seeing a beautifully-preserved middle aged woman, who would have been just a young girl

---

300 Note to the author, 2010.
301 Interviewed by the author in 2010
302 The wife of the author, who was working in Rome for Reuters.

in the 1960s, come rushing out of the church as if onto an Italian opera stage when news of Frank's return spread around town. The woman propelled herself towards Frank, embraced him in the main piazza and implored him to stay. 'Resta, resta un po'di giorni con noi,' she begged him. 'Stay, stay a few days with us.'

Frank wrote an amusing account of his journey home from Rome, but beneath his jocular descriptions of travelling through Italy and France on a very crowded train there were hints of a deeply troubled person:[303]

The train consisted of 16 coaches, was three quarters of a mile long, and carried at least 3,500 people. It travelled at a steady 80 mph all the way to Paris, with occasional brief stops at Pisa, La Spezia, Genoa and Torino where more and more people were packed on board by a – by this time – completely distracted train staff. Little old ladies were lying full length and sleeping in the corridors, and to get to have a pee required the training of an army obstacle course. During the night someone pushed someone else through our lavatory window which was steel-reinforced plate glass. There was blood on the window frame and the toilet-bowl was full of you-know-what. John and I decided there was little we could do except take it all philosophically but I can tell you that balancing yourself on top of that loo-seat and supported on either side by several suitcases, while an 80 mph wind howled in at the splintered window, was an experience I do not want to repeat.

We arrived exactly on time at Victoria Station and were duly whisked off by our hired taxi to Coggeshall, where we partook of a traditional British high-tea of fish-and-chips.

Emotionally, we were two completely broken men. Still are, for that matter! Neither of us can settle to anything.

---

303 Letter to the author and his wife, 7 September 1977.

Frank went on to explain that he was very restless and was thinking of selling up and moving on – perhaps even to Rome:

Alternatively, there is the possibility of simply selling up everything, concealing the proceeds in gold or diamonds under the scrotum, and hoofing off around the world to see the sights. They tell me that white cranes still take off from the emerald green of the Bengal paddy fields and wheel on an updraught against thunderheads. They tell me that great breakers still surge south of Cape Horn, 100 feet high and over half a mile between their crests. The moon still rises round and red as an apricot across the Gulf of Salerno over against Conca. Kisses are still sweet, they say: champagne is still sharp and *frizzante*; lips, they say, are still red, and although all these things face and lose their vivid fragrance, there still remains, so they say, a sort of ashes like the dried rose petals of carefully prepared *potpourri*, which is imperishable.

Don't you think we ought to try for that imperishable … that eternal?

Or must I be content with the never-ending horror of Coggeshall fetid-bourgeois living?

What am I searching for … ? The Crock of Gold or the Fountain of Youth or just another sensation? Don't ask me, I don't know. I've always been like this; it's too late now to confront me with a list of my inadequacies. I and my friends will just have to learn to live with them.

In the meantime, as our holiday proved, it **is** possible to experience brief moments of pure bliss … tiny fragments of heaven. The moon did rise dead on time, and red as an apricot, across the bay from Conca! It ought therefore to be possible to fit these brief scattered moments, these shattered heavenly fragments, ultimately into the complete picture, the pure, perfect, golden, apsidal mosaic of the risen Christ ... which is all our lives. Isn't that worth trying? Isn't that some sort of achievement worth aiming for?

Well, no doubt, you think Rome has turned my head, but I'm deadly serious ... Society is breaking up (or down, whichever way you like to look at it). The old conventional modes of good form are no longer sufficient. Unless, therefore, I express myself this emotionally you won't believe that I have any feeling at all.

The trip to Italy was the beginning of the end of John's relationship with Frank, and John moved out of Gravel Court shortly after they returned.

A few months later, Frank announced that he was indeed going back on the road. He entrusted his flat at Gravel Court to his friend, the local solicitor Dan Sansom, and bought a new British touring bicycle, packed a few clothes and a sleeping bag into the panniers, and then one day in early June 1978, aged 62, pedalled over the old brick bridge crossing the River Blackwater and set off for India.

SEVENTEEN
PEDALLING THROUGH EUROPE

IT WAS EXACTLY TWO YEARS LATER, IN JUNE 1980, that Frank reappeared, at least in terms of the written word. He sent Dan Sansom a 40-page letter, intended not just for Sansom's eyes but also to be typed out and distributed to his other local friends; which Samson duly did.[304] The account of Frank's adventures that it contains is so interesting and vivid – and so charmingly and naturally written – that it is reproduced here in full (and for the first time).

* * *

My trip has been absolutely fabulous, and I certainly regard it as the best thing I have ever done! For sheer danger, endurance, humour, adventure, it has been far better than the great sailing ship voyage of my youth, or the Chindit adventure with Wingate! Who would have thought that at the age of 62 I could set out on a bicycle for India and actually arrive! I can hardly credit it, and looking back on my adventures, or some of the nasty bits, I should certainly never have attempted such a feat in the first place, nor would I dream of ever doing it again.

Of course I had the luck of the devil. I set out almost completely

---

304 The original hand-written letter is in the possession of Dan Sansom.

unprepared. I spent the first night in Canterbury, and the following day, after doing the Cathedral which was vibrating like a violin to the boys of King's School practising for Sunday Matins, it suddenly occurred to me that I needed some maps. So I went along to Smiths and kitted myself out with some half dozen charts to take me as far as Istanbul. Then I set out for Dover where I boarded the ferry at 1pm, landing in Boulogne at 5 pm. Throughout my whole trip I found that the citizens of one country invariably warned me against the wickedness and thievery of those across the border. It started at Dover, where the dockers told me that my bicycle and all my kit would be promptly stolen as soon as I reached France. Of course nothing of this sort happened, but that didn't stop the French from warning me against the Swiss (such virtuous people against whom, one would have thought, nobody could have said a word), the Swiss from warning me against the Italians, the Italians against the Yugoslavs, the Yugoslavs against the Greeks, the Greeks against the Turks (between whom there really is still a great deal of active hostility), the Turks against the Iranians, the Iranians against the Afghans, the Afghans against the Pakistanis, and of course the Pakistanis against the Indians. As it happened it wasn't until I reached India and was staying in a holy place intended for the repose and refreshment of pilgrims and attached to a temple, that I lost anything at all (my bicycle lamp and dynamo, which I had expected to get stolen in any case and had come to regard as expendable). It speaks volumes for the honesty of all those countries and the countless strangers I had to deal with that my bicycle lamp and dynamo survived as far as India. It was at Brindaban that it went, a particularly holy spot dedicated to the worship of Shri Krishna![305] Later on I had 500 Rupees stolen by a very holy woman while staying at another very holy place, but apart from incidents in Kurdistan, in the wild unpoliced country between the last Turkish town of Dogubeyazit and the Iranian-Kurdish town of Tabriz (during which trip I was frankly terrified) these were the only things I lost.

---

305 A group of temples in Uttar Pradesh believed to have been the scene of one of Krishna's most notable exploits.

The trip across Europe was lovely (the weather was foul) it was also infamously expensive (five days staying at the cheapest doss-houses cost me £300) and most of the time I was drunk! As I crossed the border into Switzerland, with romantic Rhine-and-ruined castles looming down at me on every hand, I began to wonder how to cross the Alps. Did one just walk over them, or what? I hadn't, you see, prepared myself for any such eventualities, nor given a single thought to the technique of my journey. I imagined that as soon as I arrived on foreign soil I should see a signpost saying 'to India', or 'to the East'. I assumed it would be like it is when you get on the Italian *Autostrada del Sole* from Milan and at every intersection leading off to little town like Poggibonsi (a real name – I haven't made it up) you see the one huge word above and covering all – '*Sud*'! And at 200 kilometres an hour you tear south.

But not at all!

In fact I had to sit down with my Smith's maps and work at my route with the greatest exactitude.

I went along the French / Low countries border – First World War terrain, through Arras, Rheims and then into Franco-Prussian 1870-71 War country and through Metz and Sedan. Just outside Louvain (a fine city with a superb palace – have I got the location right? – it can't be Loudun where the devils came from, that's the other side of the country), I had my first puncture. I can't mend a puncture, just like I can't type. I regard it as my business to compose the words and ride the bloody bike, not meddle with mechanics, and this was in the midst of the most blissful, agricultural country with only a lawn-mowing machine in sight!

It was being operated by a very small boy on the lawn of a rather pretty house built of some cream-coloured stone that looked like a sort of nutty nougat. You could actually see the hazel nuts sticking out at the side. I asked him, could he mend a puncture? 'Yes, Monsieur.' Would he mend mine? 'Yes, Monsieur.' And that is exactly what he did, and all he said.

Modern French roads are not built for bicycles. They are ten lanes wide (five one side and five the other) and defended with crash-barriers, anti-tank traps, inset glass marbles the size of tennis balls (presumably to discourage horses) and those little rubber pylon things that make such a lovely noise when you knock them down doing 200 kilometres an hour. I was willy-nilly forced to use them. My Smith's maps (also not meant for bicyclists) hardly showed any other. And I will say that the French motorist who uses these roads is really charmingly companionable. I had no sooner got on to the great fairway leading into Metz than everybody started waving me welcome! People on buses, lorry drivers, private motorists, the lot. I responded with a great surge of affection. How warm these Continentals are!

Suddenly a helicopter appeared overhead, ten black-leather-coated breeched and legginged motor cycle police drew up all round me, and a lorry load of soldiers de-trucked just ahead, all carrying the very latest automatic weapons, and took up their position, but they didn't actually drop parachutists!

The motorists hadn't been welcoming me. They'd been warning me off!

Well, thereupon commenced a long parley, which I finally won. *They* insisted that I lifted my bike over the crash barrier and into the adjoining waste land where thickets of thorny thistles six feet high competed for living space with bramble bushes the size of houses. When I pointed this out, even the police looked doubtful. I followed up my advantage by saying that, instead of having a living bicyclist on the *autoroute*, they would end up by having a dead tourist in the morgue. The ten policemen looked even more doubtful. Finally their commandant reached a decision and gabbled into his radio set. He then implored me to be 'tranquille'. I *had* been getting upset.

Eventually the accident emergency ambulance arrived, complete with doctor, medical orderlies, and a blood transfusion apparatus. They bundled me and my bicycle inside and took me into the centre of Metz — a fine old city with some noble architecture. It seemed to me somehow to be an entirely equitable solution.

But in Switzerland, cycling along beside the Rhine (I don't know how the Rhine got into Switzerland, but there it indubitably was) I still hadn't solved how to cross the Alps. On the other side of the road was a railway line and of course *that* was the answer. I would go by train.

Hastily consulting my maps, I confirmed that the point of departure must be Zurich. I wasn't far from it and was in the outskirts that afternoon by half-past-three. I'd no idea in which direction the railway station was, but a line of track ran beside the road and, by consistently following it, I reached one of those blank walls covered with time-tables and advertisements for far-off places which are unmistakeable. It was it all right, and hordes of people were pouring into it and out of it like Hell's Mouth, to make it even more unmistakeable. I propped my bike against the wall and dashed into the nearest *bistro* and downed two double brandies to give me courage, and entered too. By comparison, Liverpool Street Station at the rush hour was like a sleepy country market town. It was PANDEMONIUM! I was completely panic-stricken and didn't know what to do. Ahead of me a huge board hung from the roof – the arrival and departure indicator – which seemed to include every city in the world. Names like Berlin, Copenhagen and Barcelona loomed giddily down. Suddenly an inconspicuous little name caught my attention, Chiasso, and I knew where I was. It was on the line to Milano.

Now when I sent my heavy luggage by rail back from Salerno in Italy, I happened to notice that it went via Chiasso, and never having heard of the place, I took the trouble to inquire where it was. It is a frontier town on the railway line to Zurich from Milano, and just the destination that I wanted. The train left at 4 pm and it was now five minutes to. I rushed to the ticket-office (there were a line of twenty windows all fully manned and in complete working order, so that not more that a waiting line of one or two people ever formed at any particular window), and got my ticket. 'Hurry,' yelled the man in French-German-English. 'The train goes in three minutes' (finally settling for English with a trace of accent). 'You pay for your bicycle from the chef-du-train. *Binario numero cinquanta.*' I fled to *binario numero cinquanta* with thirty seconds to spare, successfully passed the barrier while a series of whistles were furiously blowing, and the *chef-du-train* (there are no platforms, only a raised footway about six inches above the track) hauled me aboard. I sank exhausted into cushioned comfort while outside a rain squall beat against the windows. At eight o'clock I de-trained at Chiasso and stayed at an Italian-speaking boarding house on the Swiss side but within sight of the frontier check-post. I had entered Switzerland at dawn that very morning from France and now was a good as in Italy. My journey across Switzerland had taken just 15 hours!

This lucky, exact timing was a feature of the whole trip.

I pass over Northern Italy in silence, as we are all so familiar with that it hardly merits a comment, except to say that I was still drunk, only more so. I passed through Trieste and entered Yugoslavia. Trieste, to my eyes is still recognisably Austrian – still decidedly Habsburg. In fact, the shadow of the Habsburg double-headed eagle, to my mind, still hangs very heavily over the whole of Yugoslavia and, in spite of Tito, modern developments have not succeeded in exorcising it. Split is pretty up to the minute in a sort of Mussolinyish way, but Turkish pashas – to say nothing of Philip of Macedon and the Emperor Franz Joseph, a pair of rather appropriate twins – have left a sort of psychic impress upon the atmosphere which to me is as strong as the smell of tobacco in a long-abandoned room. Do you know that in the rock-cut temple of Ellora (I'm in India now) which was abandoned for purposes of worship about six or seven hundred years ago, the scent of incense is still so strong in some portions that it is positively over-powering until supplanted by the smell of piss – yes! People pull out their pricks and urinate in the sacred premises where erstwhile you weren't even allowed to wear your shoes. Isn't the world strange?

Incomprehensible!

In Trieste all roads naturally lead to Vienna, to Salzburg, to the

Tyrol while one road – the road I entered by – leads around the head of the Adriatic into Italy, and it was while travelling on this road that I crossed the battlefield of Solferino, a carnage that had almost the same effect on the young Emperor Franz Joseph as the Kalinga war (back in India again now, please excuse me popping back and forth) did on the Emperor Ashok. One of his famous (Ashok's not Franz Joseph's) rock-cut edicts is near here. I've never seen it. Everybody else on the tourist bus wanted to get on into Bhabaneshavar, but I insisted on stopping and peering through the grid gate that protects it, like those sliding grills that protect all the shop fronts from Istanbul to Hong Kong. Most unimpressive – the edict, not the grille-gate. That was terrific!

But to return to Trieste, since it is oriented in the directions I have indicated, it's pretty difficult to find the road into Yugoslavia. In fact, nobody seemed to have heard of the country and its frontier post whose name I had culled from the map, although it's only a short cycle ride from the city – certainly not more than 15 kilometres. Up a steep incline through an old and unsmart part of the city, past a crumbling waterfront area where the houses still bore the crests and coats of arms of a forgotten aristocracy, then the city suddenly ended in neither slums nor suburbs nor unkempt allotments, but in a great, big, bare, deserted, barren hill. It was evening time and a bit eerie and it had also started to rain. There were many signs of abandoned fields and cultivated plots that had been left to return to nature, but whether this indicated an unfertile soil or reflected the aftermath of some political upheaval, it was difficult to say. I passed through customs and immigration easily enough – my bicycle and attendant rolls of sleeping bag and panniers astride the rear wheel have always caused these gentlemen at every frontier post to giggle, and I have always been waved onward with the very minimum of regulations.

I thought I was going to like Yugoslavia but in the event I didn't. I ought to have liked it, with the sea on my right hand, bright and sparkling, and high mountains on my left. But the sea is completely empty and absolutely devoid of boat or sail or fisherman, and the off-shore islands look entirely uninteresting, being bleak and barren. I never saw a single boat on the sea for the whole time I was there! On the left-hand side, the wind blows down gullies from the mountains towards to sea in fearful gusts. Being unprepared for this on my first day, I was cycling blithely on the edge of the road and paying attention to nothing when a hurricane blast blew down a gully and hit me and nearly knocked me over a hundred foot precipice. I saved myself by throwing myself off my bicycle away from the fall and into the face of the wind. Only just averted was unidentified corpse at foot of cliff!

Another thing that made me regard the country with extreme dis-favour was that the Germans have taken over the southern part of it and turned it into a sort of second-rate version of Rimini. Principally those people who haven't enough money (or *savoir faire*) to go some-where really smart for their holidays over here, and swank in front of each other, pretending that they are on the *Promenade des Anglais*. The Germans are pretty dreadful whoever or wherever they are, and don't they know it! They have become almost as masochistic and guilt-ridden as their pals, the Jews. Except that I detect a subtle change of roles here. Since the last war, the Jews have become more and more Prussian. Israel is a distinctly (though it's thinly disguised socialism) Prussian-style military state like Assurbanipal's Assyria, or Sparta! Germans, on the other hand, are rushing about and washing their dirty linen in quite unnecessarily public places, while complacently bleating '*culpa mea*'. In spite of this, funnily enough, on my trip I have met several young Germans who were absolutely stunning from the point of view of intelligence, and emotionally also highly sympathetic, and that is certainly more than I can say for my compatriots.

Yugoslavia is curiously empty. It's as if nobody has been able to fill it. Nothing significant ever seems to have happened there, and the dead insulated nature of the place even kills genuinely significant events, so that Sarajevo and the Archduke Ferdinand are like very indifferent spec-imens of history badly preserved in poor quality pickling vinegar, so that they have entirely lost their savour. Tito was only an imitation great man, out of courtesy given that title, just like India is only an imitation state, simply flattered by the West with a pretence of recognition, whereas everyone knows it's only a hollow shell ... and this, merely for purposes of cold-war realpolitik.

Yugoslavia's essential nature, its inner substance and consistency, is to be brigand country. That role it could, and would, fill superbly well. But now all the old bad men want to reform and become bourgeois, with the result that one feels much the same as when in the presence of some brilliant old whore who has embraced religion and become a supporter of Mother Church. Tito himself exemplified this, and the old bandit, corseted into his absurd suits, with his blue-rinsed hair, was frankly ridiculous, whereas he was OK while he was wearing the Phrygian cap, the cap of liberty, his chest strung across with a bandolier full of bullets, and carrying a not very reliable gun.

The first thing I saw in Yugoslavia was a tree! It was the largest tree I have ever seen in my life – a maple or plane tree, like in Grosvenor Square where the nightingale sang.[306] Now I suppose they've been scared away by that fucking great cold, American eagle!

This tree was so old it must have stretched back to Diocletian, who was born in Yugoslavia and also retired and died there. It was in superb health, its leaves large, abundant and glossy, and it didn't show the slightest sign of decay. It might have been a young sapling of an early, giantesque age of colossal grasses like giant bamboos, and of tree ferns and of Californian red-woods.

It wasn't as big as a Californian red-wood, but round the base it was all of 60 foot in girth. Nearby an ancient conduit conducted a stream of ice-cold, crystal-clear water into a colossal reservoir constructed of Cyclopean slabs, down into which, to the water's edge, a flight of worn stone steps descended, where some ancient market women were sitting selling vegetables, and one old crone beckoned me and invited me to drink, which I did. The water tasted as if charged with subtle

---

306 Frank's Grosvenor Square bird was perhaps a distant cousin of the more celebrated nightingale that sang in Berkeley Square.

flavours which it was impossible to distinguish, and was slightly oxygenated.

I was pretty surprised to come upon this magical, classical spot more appropriate to Italy than to boring, bourgeois Yugoslavia, but it gave me hope. It did prove that the old gods are still alive, and have moreover every intention of continuing in what superficially looks like a very unfavourable environment for them and that furthermore, they have the capacity to do so. The tree was the sigma, sign or external symbol of the presence of the god – a very healthy and active one. It was this sort of evidence that I left England to find. Do you detect the presence of a god in Coggeshall – up Tilkey perhaps, on the Honeywood Estate? I'll tell you where there still is one. At Markshall. You go up there alone on a winter's day and walk through those woods and you'll feel it alright – maybe even see one flitting through the trees on goat-hooves![307]

Fifty kilometres from Dubrovnik I stayed in a place where I couldn't find accommodation, it was so crowded with Germans, so I had to apply to the Tourist Information Office for help. A few telephone calls and they fixed me in no time. While I was there, talking to other travellers, I learnt that the local boat to Corfu and Greece called in at Dubrovnik at four in the afternoon on the morrow, and I was strongly advised to take it.

On the Dalmatian coast there is a sort of camaraderie of the road almost as there must have been in the great days of the camel-caravan routes across Asia. A lot of people were travelling – young men and girls on motor-bikes from Holland and Germany, one or two Americans hitch-hiking to Greece, a van-load of school boys from Sunderland or one of those frightful places in the North, in charge of a couple of adventure-playground school-masters, bent on climbing Ararat. And, of course, the inevitable old jalopy done up in psychedelic colours and crammed with the advocates of the alternate (or underground) society

---

307 Tilkey is an area of Coggeshall where the earliest bricks were made in the Middle Ages; the Honeywood is a housing estate; Markshall was a large house demolished after WWII.

– a group gathered from all nations. In its way it was rather exciting and made me feel young – certainly the reverse of OAP!

These people thought I was frightfully funny and kind of adopted me. The word went forth down the road that an ancient, eccentric Englishman was cycling to the other side of the world. When I arrived at halts or bars or eating places I found that I was already well-known. They didn't actually erect the traditional arch of flowers that is by custom accorded to visiting notabilities, but nearly. At all events, I was invariably greeted by the query: 'Are you the mad Englishman?' It was like being confronted by the accusation: 'Are you the Christ?' And I had no alternative but to answer: 'I am!'

In France, I constantly met bands of cycling youths going the other way – their arses in the air and their noses to the ground. Recognising from my panniers that I was a long distance traveller, as they were, they always greeted me, waving their arms forward and shouting grandiloquently '*A Paris!*' When, in reply to their questions, I answered '*Aux Indes!*' they simply didn't believe me and thought I was pulling their legs.

But the boys on the Dalmatian coast did believe me, and they went out of their way to be helpful, by putting at my disposal their fund of experience, which was considerable, for they were all much more seasoned travellers than I. In this way I learnt that my originally intended route down to Titograd, on the Albanian border, and then inland, wending my way through the mountains of Montenegro until I eventually came out at Thessalonica, was hopelessly untenable. Not only were the roads terrible, and practically impassable for even motor traction, but there was nowhere to stay. Some of these youngsters had actually done that trip, and they assured me that I would not survive.

So the information about the boat from Dubrovnik to Corfu and Igoumenitsa on the Greek mainland was an absolute godsend. It was an example of that fantastic luck I was attended by, which I have earlier mentioned; and my arrival within 50 kms of its calling port at Dubrovnik was an example of the extraordinarily close and exact timing (pure luck!) which was a feature of the whole trip. In fact, on a bicycle, it is impossible to plan your arrivals and departures exactly because all sorts of unseen eventualities intervene, like punctures, 10 mile inclines up mountains which you have to negotiate on foot and which are not indicated on the map, and mechanical defects of every type and description, for pieces were constantly dropping off my bike without my noticing, and precipitating me onto the road, where I was forced to complete the journey to the nearest blacksmith on foot. (These are, of course in the town's garages, but in the country districts I found nothing but blacksmiths to do my repairs, and jolly good they were, frequently refusing payment!)

Accordingly I swept the 50 kilometres to Dubrovnik on the following day, arriving in the town about mid-day, in good time to get my ticket and loaf about.

While thus loafing, my attention was attracted by two charming old ladies, obviously belonging to the *ancien regime*. They were dressed in elegant silk two-piece suits with floral design, and flowering flower-pot hats (it was the height of summer) and carried hand-bags and shopping baskets. They stood out from the shabby proletarian crowd by whom they were surrounded and looked entirely out of place. I watched fascinated, as they tottered across the road towards me in their high-heeled shoes, obscurely obsessed by the idea that I was watching a piece of theatre, and wondering who they were, and how on earth they had strayed into – for them – such an unlikely environment, although they appeared to be at ease and entirely at home in it.

Suddenly, before any of us – we, the bystanders – could realise what was happening, there was a scream of tortured rubber and the squeal of brakes. A car rushed around the corner and down the road much too fast – the ladies saw it and panicked, neither advancing nor retreating but dithering in the centre of the road – and it hit them square in the middle with the most frightful splat!

One of the ladies, fearfully injured, was killed outright. The last I saw of the other was lying on the sidewalk, her bodice and blouse open and her breasts exposed, while her heart was massaged by a lady in black – black skirt down to her ankles and black shawl over her head, a peasant. They couldn't find an ambulance and eventually a private car drew up and with considerable difficulty they manipulated her into the back – she was unconscious – and drove away. The flower-pot hats, the shopping baskets and the handbags remained in the middle of the road as a testimony to what had happened – these and a gigantic pool of blood – as if the local people feared to touch them. Then, after half an hour some kind official came and collected them and took them away.

The boat to Greece was very civilised, clean, painted white, and altogether like a miniature liner. I omitted to mention that it was a car ferry and was able to accommodate quite a considerable number of trailer caravans, of which there were a lot. My bicycle was stowed below on the car-deck along with the Mercedes, the BMWs and the Peugeots. We got underway about five and everybody proceeded to get acquainted. The promenade desks were thronged with masses of American females, all talking in very nasal voices and I was determined I wasn't going to speak to any of those. Eventually I palled up with a very nice New Zealand couple about my own age, and we had an excellent dinner together and several bottles of heavy, ruddy Montenegrin wine and (refrain) I got slightly drunk and went to bed in the scuppers. My God! But I was enjoying myself – I was happy!!!

Greece was a different kettle of fish – unbroken ground and an entirely unknown country. While in Yugoslavia I was able to speak or respond in Italian and got by, God knows what language I should have to communicate in Greece – as it happened I succeeded with English and French. German, of course, would have been better and I discovered that German is a sort of universal language from Greece, right through to Turkey, to Iran and if ever I do any more travelling I shall have to learn it.

I travelled across northern Greece for about a week. It's old Macedonian Turkish country, and still very Turkish in feel. I saw many abandoned mosques and ruined wooden, Turkish-style houses and there was another distinctly Turkish feature which was definitely sympathetic – the wayside drinking fountains, each with its little marble plaque saying it was donated by whom, although of course it wasn't until I had travelled in Turkey, where the country is full of them, that I recognised this feature for the Turkish legacy that it is.

I was a bit nervous about my first day, which was a 100 km journey across the mountains to a town called Janina, and I actually asked the receptionist at the Government rest house where I was staying whether he thought I could make it. 'Course you can! Why, when I was a boy I used to cycle once a week to Janina to visit the cinema, *and* back!'

'But I'm 62!'

'Nothing to it!'

For the first time in my trip feeling really discouraged, I set out. Actually there were two mountains, up 3,000 feet and down – up 5,000 feet and down! Half-way up the first mountain I was so exhausted I had to stop at a peasant's house and ask for a drink of water and then, just round the corner from that place, I discovered a house where an old man was selling fried ham-and-eggs and hot coffee. The peasant must have thought I was dotty.

I reached Janina about 6pm, having been 13 hours in the saddle!

I was pretty interested in this town and still am. Unfortunately, travelling as I am, I haven't been able to look up the appropriate references.

It is mentioned by Dumas in *The Count of Monte Cristo*, as having been the place where Ferdinand (Mercedes's ultimate husband, but I cannot remember the aristocratic pseudonym he masquerades under in the latter part of the book – General something-or-other), the mercenary military commander, betrays his Turkish overlord, someone called Mehmet Ali, to the attacking (?) Habsburgs (?) while all the time pretending to put up a brilliant suicide stand. When I read *The Count of Monte Cristo* as a boy I assumed that the story of Ferdinand's treachery at Janina, as revealed by the Count of Monte Christo to encompass Ferdinand's downfall, was simply a fabrication concocted for the purpose of the plot of the novel. While I was in Janina, however, I saw enough evidence to prove at least that the town had been an important Turkish port. There is a citadel containing a governor's palace, a very large principal mosque splendidly situated on a bluff overlooking the lake, and the whole place reeks of independent, self-maintained principality, for it occupies the central position in a very large, fertile vale watered by several rivers which drain into the big lake, teeming with fish – the marshes abound with waterfowl and there are deer and wild goat in the hills. It is a jewel of a place for a marauding Turkish prince, and I wouldn't mind having the run myself.

The next day was going to be the most difficult, according to the map. I had to cross over a high pass of 8,000 feet, where is situated the winter-sports centre of Greece – skiing and all that jag, so it must have been high. I had no alternative but simply to go at it and hope something would happen. I have a private motto in my life which has on countless occasions proved of inestimable value. It is 'Walk on!' When confronted with apparently impenetrable obstacles to progress, I have remembered this and walked on boldly into the midst of them. Of course, it sounds a bit school-marmish when put into writing in cold blood, but I can assure you that when you get close enough to them, the obstacles invariably vanish. It is like seeing in the distance a thick forest of trees. It looks solid. But when you get near it you find you can walk between the individual trees quite easily.

So leaving the Vale of Janina, its lake, its reedy marshes, and the minarets of its mosques, I passed down a splendid avenue of trees by the edge of the water – all looking peculiarly unreal in the dawn light – and assailed the round green shoulder of this bloody great hill.

When I am very exhausted or have a particularly demanding physical task to perform, my mind goes blank. It was so in the present instance. I remember negotiating the first and second hairpin bends as the road snaked up the hill (of course, I was walking, pushing the bike with its 60 lb load) and looking out over the plain. The sun was just above the horizon and it had already started to get hot. The next thing, it is eleven o'clock and I am down in a valley. I must have come over the mountain in a state of cataleptic trance, but it is still not the main obstacle. That lies yet ahead and this is merely a foothill.

I am in very pretty undulating country with little wooded hills, small fields given over to the cultivation of cantaloupe melons or sunflowers, and stone houses looking indefinably and modestly prosperous. There is quite a broad river spanned by a war-time Bailey bridge, while the original mediaeval stone construction stands breached by its side − surprising still to see the scars of war so long afterwards! I meander through this idyllic countryside very contentedly and put up at an inn. Two young men are repairing a Ford tractor while a third sits under a tree and strums a mandolin and sings. An older man fiddles under the bonnet of a pick-up truck. I order my favourite drink when on the road and thirsty, because it prevents you from getting too hopelessly drunk, what they call in France a *panache* (I always thought it meant a plume of feathers − the Prince of Wales's crest is a *panache* − but the French − and they ought to know, after all, it's their language, insist that it means a mixture), and the English publican a lemonade shandy. Nobody at the inn had heard of such a thing and the older man showed a certain amount of curiosity (he spoke some war-time English) so there was nothing to do but sit down and order one for him too. It turned out that he was a *padrone* and the young men were his sons.

In Northern Greece they drink beer, which at the rate at which my thirst demanded that I consume it soon rendered me incapable, or two kinds of wine. Now my smart friends (if I still have any friends, let alone smart ones!) who loll about on Lesbos or wherever, are always going on about the marvellous Greek wine! But I found only these two kinds were available in Northern Greece and both had distinct limitations. The first is the well known Retsina, but you can't quench your thirst on the taste of turpentine. The second is a sort of supermarket brand and comes in two colours, red and white. It is called *Domestos* or *Domesticos* − a name redolent of lavatory cleaner and the kitchen sink. It is perfectly disgusting, hence *panache*.

Well, my friend and I soon passed from *panache* to straight beer and pretty soon we were drunk. In this euphoric mood I interrogated him, and he answered about the road ahead, and my worst fears were confirmed. He assured me that on a bicycle the very idea of assailing such a massif was absurd. I must have looked pretty cast down at this information because he suddenly threw out the suggestion: for the payment of a certain sum (I forget how much and anyway it would have been in dinars and so untranslatable, but under the circumstances it was quite modest) he would put the bicycle on the pick-up and take me to the top. And this is what he did. Once again my motto of 'Walk on!' had been marvellously vindicated.

After a terrific swoop down the obverse side and a suitable period for sobering up, I found myself on the lip of a deep-cleft gorge. By now thunderclouds had gathered and it threatened rain. As usual, the inevitable hostelry was in evidence just ahead and, as I felt rather fragile and in no mood to get wet, I took shelter there. The *padrone*, a man of about my own age, asked me if I was English, and when I answered yes, he launched into the story of a war-time encounter that had taken place there and which he had witnessed as a boy from that self-same hostelry. The English forces were withdrawing up the gorge towards the mountains down which I had come and, when they reached the gorge's lip, exactly where I was, they had laid an ambush for the pursuing German column. Some obstacle placed at the mouth of the gorge had caused the German tanks to bunch, and then, while the thunder rolled and rattled in the surrounding hills, the rain poured down and the lightning flashed, my companion, with blazing eyes and histrionic gestures, proceeded to recount the incidents of that memorable battle.

I have since come to the conclusion that he must have been mad. Only such an hypothesis could explain the extraordinary vividness with which he conjured up the encounter. Of course the scene was peculiarly sympathetic to such dramatics – the wild hills of harsh, limestone outcrop; the dark sinister cleft of the gorge like some entrance to the underworld; the raging storm; and my companion like some demented Lear, a re-incarnation of Tiresias or an Old Testament prophet inveighing against the Germans and (horribly!) exulting in their doom. It was too much for me and like a craven I fled. The storm had passed (I could never be sure that my companion had not actually produced it as an accompaniment to his story) and I entered the cleft.

It, too, ought to have been a magic place, for it was clothed with all the appropriate appurtenances, but a notice board at the entrance announcing in English and Greek that it was called 'The Gorge of the Nymphs' effectively banished any god. All the same, it was very pretty. Beautiful maple trees grew there in profusion and a crystal torrent rushed in a deep gully to my left, making a most agreeable sound, and every so often there was another notice board in two languages announcing that this was the way to the Grotto of Venus, this the way to the Grotto of Cupid, each provided with parking-spaces, litter-baskets and similar conveniences of civilization – really, Dan, it was weird, after that man been declaiming his hatred of the fallen enemy, to come upon such evidences of middle-class niceness and I think I should have preferred a spoor of broken bottles. As it was, it was like being back in Clapham Common (I was born there – remember)!

Eventually I surpassed this little picnic enclave in the midst of an untamed vastness (for this, I suppose, is what it was – I mean a picnic enclave) and came out onto a wide sloping valley. The torrent, spanned by a very modern, architectural-looking bridge, passed under the road and became a river and it was obvious that I was at the beginning of the coastal plain, at the end of which stands Thessaloniki, as yet 300 miles distant. Away ahead a very curious pink-coloured lump stood out of the plain like gigantic jujube (it's a sort of sweet we used to suck in our boyhood, made of the same stuff as those disgusting jelly babies they advertise on television, but you're too young to remember!), and as I approached it – slowly, oh, ever so slowly – it revealed itself as being an enormous rock.

It was a huge mass of pink granite thrusting out of the plain like a rude gesture, its summit about 1000 feet about its base. It was as smooth and rounded as a baby's bottom and in shape not unlike it. At its foot was a little town about the size of Bures with several streets about 50 yards long, in one of which was an eating-house where they did an excellent roast chicken. But most interesting of all was its church. This dated (according to a brochure which I found at the hotel) from 600 AD and I could well believe it. It had obviously never been cleaned since. Strangely its filth lent it its principal charm, and I am sure that had it been clean it would entirely have lost its fascination. As it was, with its stubby tower constructed of Cyclopean blocks, the bell-cage supporting a very untidy stork's nest, its surrounding courtyard paved with granite slabs worn smooth as silk and perambulated by some shabby priests at whom, every so often, admiring peasant women threw themselves in an ecstasy of devotion to kiss the hems of their exceedingly grubby garments, it was straight out of the fairy-tale story-books with which my devoted parents used to provide me in my youth, complete with illustrations in glorious verisimilitude, in order to stimulate my imagination, of folk legends from European Hinterland – folk legends which invariably incorporated a stork's nest, although this was the first real one I had ever seen.

The similarity of this actuality in front of me to the well-remembered stories (with their accompanying pictures) of my youth made me indeed feel very light-headed. I half imagined, but no, of course, I hadn't seen it before; neither was this a dream; yet the whole – not the place, but the surrounding psychic ambience in which it was bathed – was strikingly familiar.

Sadly, this interior was a slight disappointment. I suppose I had been so struck by its outside that I had been expecting some interior revelation. Instead I had to make do with a perfunctory inspection of some soot-grimed icons and content myself with marvelling at the incredible lay-out where everything had obviously been planned with the maximum symbolic value in mind, but which produced the minimum convenience.

All the same, it was a magical place and the rock, the church, the stork's nest testified to the presence of a god. It was not until I was leaving that I noticed that the stork's nest had, in fact, been abandoned. It was an old one. Had the god, then, departed too? I was forced regretfully to conclude yes! There is little doubt that those notices further up the road, those parking-spaces, those litter-baskets must have wrought havoc among the last of the Olympians and done a fearful work!

On the following day I found myself on the main road from Athens to Thessaloniki and actually cycling past Olympus on my left, which was as usual covered in cloud. It would vouchsafe absolutely no indication of what its majestic inhabitants might be thinking.

This day I did my longest run, 205 kilometres, 120 miles, and 15 hours in the saddle! I passed the night in a squalid sort of holiday-camp run by a couple of seedy Greeks and occupied entirely by Germans, on the coast. While I was eating an extremely tasteless cutlet of some sort, garnished with sawdust, for supper, I was seized by a frightful cramp in the legs. My muscles knotted up into iron bands and I jumped to my feet to try and relieve the tension, my face distorted with pain. Everybody looked at me as if I had done something improper, but a young German sitting across from me and wearing spectacles understood what had happened. He seized my legs and began to massage the muscles very capably and succeeded in dispelling the knots. Twice more I was attacked by cramp during that meal and twice more this young man massaged me until at last the spasms subsided and I was able to stagger off to bed. I shall always be grateful to him; he was one of the better ones.

Bed was my sleeping-bag on the rock hard ground beside the little hut which served for an office. I retired at eleven and got up at half past three and was on the road by four.

That night, while I had been asleep, there was an earthquake but I knew nothing of it. I was only apprised of the fact when passing through Thessaloniki at noon. When on the road to Thessaloniki in the morning, a lorry coming in the opposite direction lost its load.

There was a very high cross wind and this lorry, which was piled with round plastic water pots like melons contained in a net, got caught in it. The net burst just opposite me and I was deluged with these round, dangerous looking objects which for one mad moment I mistook for bombs, for they *looked* exceedingly heavy but were in fact as light as a feather. I was in two minds whether to stop and help the driver retrieve his cargo, but when I noticed that all the other traffic on the road ploughed relentlessly on, crushing the plastic water-pots indifferently, which exploded with a lovely squash, I continued too. Obviously it would have been considered eccentric to help!

Out in open country beyond Thessaloniki, I noticed the freshly-demolished houses. A feature of the damage was that where two houses were standing side by side, one was completely destroyed while the other was apparently untouched. That night in another squalid holiday camp, I met an Austrian schoolmaster accompanied by two of his pupils who were cycling from Salzburg to Istanbul. The boys were then going home by train and he was going to India 'to meditate in Bombay'!!! I should have thought it would have been easier to meditate in Salzburg than in Bombay (of all places!), but I didn't say so. He was riding a lady's bicycle and was obviously as mad as a hatter. I slept in my sleeping bag on the rock-hard ground, under a tree, and woke up before dawn, covered in sparrow shit! On the road by half-past three to avoid the Austrian schoolmaster.

Another holiday camp, this time in the town of Kavali, on the coast, whence the boat goes to Lesbos – very big, well-run camp, bog, showers, running water, cafeteria (shit, shag and shave – tuppence!), laundry, the lot. Plenty of exotic shrubs, oleanders, crotons, bougainvillea, hibiscus, campsis grandiflora (the Californian climbing tiger-lily – orange head of flower, flowers August-September, later in the UK – Manuel has a plant – fantastic thing – very gaudy!). Also fresh-water swimming pool as well as private beach.

In the cafeteria a very brassy middle-aged red-head was presiding, who was obviously (pro-tem at any rate) queen of the place, for everyone, even the waiters, deferred to her. She was the centre of a group of young, working-class English boys, one of whom turned out to be her son. Apparently she had a house in the town and (God knows why!) was merely visiting here. Anyway, after we had eyed one another once or twice, she made a gesture indicating I should join her table, which I did. She was knocking back brandies as fast as they could bring them, but they didn't seem to be having any effect. I made one or two conversational gambits in an attempt to establish my co-ordinates, and found out that she ran a fleet of buses between London and Istanbul. She certainly knew her Turkey, particularly the eastern part, and I pumped her for all I was worth. What she told me was not encouraging. In fact, it was so *dis*couraging that I very nearly abandoned my trip on the strength of it. You see, for a European traveller by land to the Far East, Istanbul is a sort of Rubicon. Once beyond it, and you more or less have to continue, for going on is as easy, or easier, than turning back. But while you remain the European side of Istanbul, you can always take the train to Victoria and disembark on No 9 platform in a couple of days.

However, this woman didn't want to put me off. She told me that although I would certainly lose all my possessions, I should probably escape with my life!!

The next morning, while cycling out of Kavali on the last lap of my journey through Greece, my bicycle finally threw in the sponge and collapsed.

British bicycles are nowadays obviously no longer made of metal, and although I paid £100 for mine, it was unquestionably constructed out of spaghetti. About three miles outside of Kavali, in a very pretty spot on the coast road and immediately in front of the main gate of an army depot, my front tyre gave a little whimper and went flat! The whole of the Greek army turned out to participate, but they weren't of much help, although very charming in other directions, and I finally had to admit defeat and wheel the damned thing back into town. There I put up at a very large and imposing-looking garage, on the outskirts, whereupon a man came forward, whom I took to be the proprietor, and to whom I explained my difficulty. He nodded wisely and appeared to understand. He then threw himself on the bicycle and before I could stop him, promptly took it to bits. I watched in consternation while piece after piece came apart, but he had such an air of authority, he exuded such an attitude of efficiency, that it was impossible to believe that he did not know what he was doing. When he had taken everything to pieces that would come apart, wheels, tyres, inner tubes, valves, chain, sprocket, handle-bars, saddle, he laid them tidily on the ground, regarded them for a moment with a brief look of affection, then walked to a juggernaut lorry that was parked nearby, got in and drove off. He wasn't the proprietor at all, in fact he had nothing to do with the place, and he left me in a bugger's muddle.

When I finally found the garage mechanic he was anything but sympathetic. In fact he rejected outright the idea that he should have anything to do with a bicycle, saying such things were for babies. He also had some extremely unflattering things to say about the English, insisting that none of us wanted to do any work.

So there I was, with the bicycle in bits and me almost in tears of rage and frustration. Remarkable to relate, I did manage to re-assemble it, but it never worked again. It wasn't that I'd put it back wrong, but that all the threads, as soon as I attempted to tighten the nuts, simply braised. As I told you, British Bicycles are made of butter and this one was no exception.

I thought I should be able to get some nuts in replacement but no such luck. The cycle shop where I finally landed up either couldn't or wouldn't find any to fit. To complicate matters, its proprietor spoke no foreign language and all our business had to be conducted via an interpreter in French. He offered to sell me one of his cycles, of which he had a large stock, and I had to decide on the spot what to do – whether to buy one and go on, or to admit defeat, confess failure, and crawl back to the UK with my tail between my legs. My principal difficulty was in the matter of budget. I had no idea how expensive my trip was likely to be or what anything would cost. My great fear was to land say, somewhere on the Iranian-Russian frontier and there run out of money. What the hell did one do then! Consequently I was inclined to be rather mean with expenditure. In this particular instance, I postponed a decision, found a very cheap hotel where I shared a room with what looked like two young Army deserters, and relaxed.

The Greeks are the most plebeian people that I have ever met – not proletarian but plebeian. They are real plebs. Obviously the legend about the Dorian invaders who became the Hellenes and created Classical Greece, is true. They have not survived and have mysteriously disappeared. The present population is composed entirely of Helots, the original Mediterranean inhabitants of the place (a type which you get all round the Mediterranean basin) and whom the Spartans in particular, as well as other city states, enslaved. They are small, dark and hairy, with oily skins. In fact they *look* like apes – very endearing apes like the ones who perform on television for the Brooke Bond (or is it Liptons!?) tea-party. They have no more connection with ancient Hellenic culture than the present-day population of India has with Rig-Vedic or Upanishadic culture. Both peoples are like the bugs on the rose bushes; they seem able to survive long after the roses are dead.

Indians are similarly non-aristocratic and are as common as mud. They seem to lack entirely all trace of noble or patrician instincts and are willing to wallow in base practices with a perverse pleasure which it is positively compelling to watch, as for instance at the zoo one sometimes cannot tear oneself away from watching filthy creatures like hyenas and alligators. This used not to be true of the English, but I am inclined to think that the present generation of English is entirely base-born (and this hasn't anything to do with class or conventional social standing). Of course, we live in a very anti-aristocratic and anti-patrician age!

When I was last here in India, twenty three or twenty four years ago, there were still recognisably one or two Indian gentlemen. Now the type has entirely vanished. They are all slaves, but not slaves like the Italian lower-classes who pander entertainingly to one's more shameful vices out of a feeling of fun and a sense of participating in the enjoyment of one's money, which one does not deny them.

These people are slaves in the sense that they cringe and whine when they feel they are inferior, and are ruthlessly arrogant when they feel they are on top. Unfortunately, although I have tried bravely, it is impossible to have the slightest respect for them.

In spite of my unfavourable assessment of the Greek soul, I really enjoyed this place Kavali and stayed there several days. It was a small, thriving harbour where strange little vessels were constantly coming and going (for your Greek is incurably busy) at all hours of the day and night. Consequently there was always something to see. Moreover the fishing fleet brought daily to the quays a selection of mouth-watering delicacies which the restaurants were not slow to exploit. I used to dine daily at a bistro on the waterfront off *moules marinières*, fried oysters, a selection of crabs and lobsters, a prawn-and-chicken *pilau* (or *pilaff*, according to the way you pronounce it!), baked squid cut into rings and braised in butter, a fresh salad, a capsicum and cucumber yoghurt, and goat's milk cheese! Next door there was a huge fruit and vegetable stall where one went and chose one's dessert – bunches of luscious grapes, peaches the size of footballs and every variety of melon. But I still couldn't get any decent wine.

Kavali has an old crusaders' citadel and very fine specimen of a Turkish house which is open to the public and preserved (although not very well). It belonged to Mehmet Ali Pasha (not the same one who ruled at Janina – at least I don't think so – but alas! I am miles from my reference books – of which I really do feel the lack – and so cannot guarantee to be accurate), who was Viceroy of Egypt and who more or less took Egypt out of the Ottoman Empire and made it semi-independent. He was very famous in his time and contemporary records are full of him (period 1850-60?). I went all over the house and it really did give me an insight into the Ottoman Empire's upper class: comfortable, clean, commodious but not showy, convenient (the lavatory and bathing arrangements were most impressive) and I could have settled down and lived there in complete content. In front of the house, which was situated just below the outer wall of the citadel on a sort of bluff which looked towards the Greek mainland in the west and towards Istanbul in the East – it was undoubtedly the governor's house when the citadel was not under duress – was a paved square, always completely deserted, in the centre of which a white marble equestrian statue of the famous man, wearing an enormous turban like the pantomime version of Ali Baba, charged recklessly forward, waving a curved scimitar which miraculously had remained unbroken. It speaks volumes for the good will of the Greek people (who really do loathe the Turks) that they have left this statue and this house intact. In contradistinction, the Indian people have pulled down every statue of Britishers – some of considerable aesthetic distinction, viz that equestrian statue of Outram at the entrance to Park Street – and then replaced them with replicas (in most cases a frank crib or incredibly bad copy) of local worthies, of mind-boggling insipidity, executed in white marble and realistically tinted and all invariably wearing spectacles. I don't know why, but the sight of a statue wearing spectacles is to me always indescribably ridiculous!

But the main feature of Kavali, which dominated the eastern part of the town, was a mediaeval aqueduct. It looked authentically Roman, but I am assured that it wasn't. It was constructed about 1200 – 1300 to bring water to the citadel and a marvellous monument it is. The road in and out of town in that direction towards the Turkish frontier and Istanbul passes beneath it through the arches, and it forms, as it were, a triumphal gate. It is a good 200 feet high above the roadway, built in red Roman-style storeys and clerestories of arches of gradually diminishing size. Of course, in marvelling at this late though authentically classically-designed aqueduct, I had forgotten that at the time it was constructed, all this territory formed part of the Byzantine Empire, where the ancient engineering techniques still survived up to the dawn of the Italian Renaissance. Doesn't it seem amazing that, as the Byzantine Empire crumbled and Byzantium the city fell in 1492, Columbus was discovering America and Donatello was casting in bronze his marvellous young David – the first nude in the round to appear since the fall of the Western Roman Empire, and which heralded the birth of the New Age?[308] The curtain falls in one theatre, only to be raised in another. I wonder now, as Western civilization totters into senility and decay, where the new dawn is breaking and whereabouts in the world we may look for a fresh inspiration: toward China, towards Russia, towards America?

Every evening I took up my station at a cafe table underneath these arches to enjoy the evening game. It was a game played between about 200 swallows. They used to swarm in densely-packed flocks out to sea and round the headland where stood the citadel, then swerve inland and swoop through the arches at vertiginous speed, all the time keeping up an incessant twittering. Round and round for over an hour, always keeping to the same way and always flying in the same direction. There were so many of them that there was no interval where one swarm ended and another began. It was wonderful to watch them, so graceful, gay and carefree, like happy holiday-makers on a roundabout. (I mean a fair or circus side-show roundabout not one at a road intersection! I don't think you're going to find many happy laughing holidaymakers at the roundabouts and road intersections on the way to Clacton!)

Finally I came to a decision and bought my bicycle. I had decided to soldier on. Curiosity simply to see what would happen next, what the following town, country, day had to offer, overcame me as it always has. It was a French ten-speed racing cycle and cost me £50 in Greek currency – an equivalent machine in the United Kingdom being in the neighbourhood of two or three hundred! The man at the shop assured me that it was an excellent machine and he was right. It is still with me, having done upward of 5,000 miles, as well as knocked about on the tops of buses.

At the time, however, I had never ridden a ten-speed racing bicycle and the changing of the gears is quite a different technique to what you

308 The city actually fell in 1453.

have to do with a Sturmey-Archer three-speed. The proprietor of the cycle shop tried to give me some instruction but in French, through the mediation of an interpreter, and while trying to steer the machine through Kavali's awful traffic, this was not very effective. I fell off, broke the chain, and nearly killed myself in the process of trying it out. Eventually I decided that at my age I just could not manage those racing handlebars and was about to cancel the whole proposition when the proprietor suggested he change the handlebars from my original bike to the new one. This did indeed simplify things, for with those drop handlebars I had absolutely no control and kept on steering under the wheels of buses. I paid him his money, packed my bags and set off for the Turkish frontier, but although I could now control the thing a bit and keep roughly to the middle of the road, I still didn't know how to change gear. I kept pausing in my peddling when I changed gear as you do with a Sturmey Archer. But with a ten-speed it is the reverse. As a result, the chain kept coming off and getting jammed between the rear sprockets, and a good deal more besides. While I was lumbering along the road like this, about five miles out from Kavali, and quite desperate, who should heave alongside but another cyclist, an American, riding an identical bicycle. After we had exchanged greetings – Dr Livingstone, I presume – he proceeded to give me a course of instruction while riding at my side – 'pull that lever, tighten that screw a bit, keep pedalling' – until I had properly mastered the technique. I never did find out anything about him, or what he was doing, and I have come to regard him simply as one of the gods – after all, they are capable of taking strange disguises – who had descended from Olympus on purpose to help me.

The Turkish frontier was fifty miles distant and I reached it about four o'clock, after riding through fields and fields of sun-flowers. It is amazing how this plant always manages to face the sun, for when the sun sinks in the evening, every plant is facing towards the west. Yet the sun never manages to catch it out, for when it rises at dawn, damned if every plant is not ready for it and facing east. I only noticed one exception and that was in Turkey where in a field of fifty acres one single plant was holding out against the universal hypnotism (it is surprising how quickly you notice!), but whether its mechanism had gone wrong or it was a deliberate deviationist I was not able to say.

Hereabouts there were masses of storks' nests on the roof tops, in chimney pots, and even in the overhead electric cables. I have seen somewhere a map of the distribution of storks' nesting places, and their concentration, but I have forgotten it, and I should very much like to refer to it again.

The Turkish frontier was demarcated by a river across which ran an old stone bridge. Greek sentries patrolled one half and Turkish sentries the other, both lots taking great care not to show by the flicker of an eyelid that they had noticed the other's presence. There was a sort of United Nations rest camp immediately on the other side and there I put up, promptly falling in with the van-load of Sunderland schoolboys and their two schoolmasters whom I had last encountered on the Dalmatian coast. They had been climbing Olympus or some other madcap adventure and were now hoping to go onto Ararat if they could get insurance cover – for which purpose one of the schoolmasters had gone on to Istanbul by bus to make the necessary arrangements.

The other one, a very experienced traveller and a mountaineer to boot who had already done Ararat twice, proceeded to enlighten me about Eastern Turkey and entirely confirmed what the brassy red-head in the holiday camp at Kavali had said. It seemed madness to continue.

I was even more discouraged when the other schoolmaster returned, having failed in his mission and saying that no respectable insurance company would dream of issuing a comprehensive policy in Turkey where the standard of driving was so appalling that it was suicide to venture out on the roads.

The schoolboys therefore departed for Africa where their Cicerone decided that they would climb in the Atlas. I know this sounds crazy but it's literally true, although how they expected to get from the Turkish frontier to Tunisia or wherever in the time available and with the money at their disposal, beats me! But the schoolmaster was one of those perpetually sanguine types and the schoolboys at any rate were enjoying themselves.

I set out for Istanbul.

There are three principal highways from Europe and the Balkans into Istanbul, each of which claims for itself the dignity of being the Trans-Asian Highway. One comes in from Munich via the Austrian Tyrol and Thessaloniki and this was the one I was on. Another comes in from Poland, through Czechoslovakia and hits the road from Thessaloniki about ten miles inside the Turkish frontier. The third (the busiest, I found) comes from Moscow through Bulgaria (picking up tributary roads from Romania on the way) and enters the unified stream of the other two about 30 miles from Istanbul, where the three roads make one busy, hectic artery and this really *is* the Trans-Asian Highway which stretches across Asia Minor to Teheran then Afghanistan and into the Indian sub-continent. Of course, since the Russians have closed Afghanistan, you now go from Teheran through southern Iran into Baluchistan and enter Pakistan via Quetta, but, at the time I was travelling, this route was reputed to be dangerous, several Americans having been killed on it and their vehicles looted.

I soon came to the second of these roads, at the junction of which there was a primitive but pretty thatched eating-house, with benches and tables set out under trees. I ordered a big meal (the food at the United Nations camp was not very good, being what I call poor-quality international – even good quality International, as you probably know, is entirely tasteless) by the simple expedient of going inside and pointing to the dishes I wanted. This method of ordering your meal is practised by the entire international travelling fraternity in Turkey and is not resented. Indeed, it is the only way you can get anything to eat, Turkish being an extremely difficult agglutinative language which has not been rendered any easier to pronounce by the simply extraordinary transliteration into Roman script from the Arabic carried out by the German expert hired for that purpose by Kemal Ataturk when he was modernising Turkey in 1923!

While I was eating this meal a young German drove up, coming from the other way, that is from Istanbul, and joined me. He slumped down on the bench beside me without any ceremony like the survivor from a battle and gasped out, 'I couldn't stand it any longer. I had to get out! Get me to Greece or I shall perish!'

'You mean you find Turkey unsympathetic?'

'It nearly killed me!'

'But what happened?'

'Nothing in particular. It's just that everything's so tough and so entirely uncivilized. One simply longs for a little urbanity!'

He was by no means an exquisite and if this young man couldn't take Turkey in his stride, I began to wonder how *I* was going to survive in the environment.

I think now is the time to state quite definitely that I didn't find Turkey at all like this, but at the time, entirely inexperienced as I was, it was pretty off-putting constantly to be arraigned by these gloomy prognostications, and my experience of the road I was now travelling did nothing to set my mind at rest.

Turks, although no doubt devoted fathers, faithful husbands and loyal friends, become madmen when they get into motor-vehicles. Indeed, it is by no means Turks alone who are like this, as we all have experienced, but Turks seem to suffer from the psychological syndrome in the extreme.

To make matters more difficult, from my point of view, Turkish drivers do not recognise the bicycle. It has no right to exist. The proper attitude for a cyclist, I soon established, when confronted by a bus or a lorry, is to dismount and stand by the side of the road salaaming respectfully while the superb creature sprays him with grit and gravel.

This was not at all in line with my own ultra-arrogant attitude and a confrontation became inevitable. It is very interesting how a bus / bicycle or lorry / bicycle confrontation can be conducted. On the face of it, the bicycle doesn't have a chance, but in actual fact a determined cyclist endowed with a certain amount of courage can create chaos on any busy thoroughfare. All you need is a steely eye and the obstinacy of a mule.

As soon as you see a confrontation approaching, stick firmly to the middle of the road. Don't allow yourself to be deflected for anything. Then, as soon as your antagonist is able to see that you are looking at him, engage him in eye-contact and hold his gaze till the last minute. If you pursue this course with confidence, you will find that your antagonist very soon slackens speed and pulls in to the side of the road, or does whatever else is necessary to let you pass on your way unimpeded. I have known some very impressionable antagonists who have even saluted me!

Of course you do sometimes encounter the occasional rogue elephant. In this case you just have to gamble on the unwillingness of most drivers to knock down and kill a foreign cyclist on the open road. I have on several occasions brought a bus or a juggernaut lorry to a raging standstill, its steaming snout within two inches of my front wheel. Once you know that most drivers' pretensions are pure bluff, you are home! All you have to do is to call it. Once you know that most of LIFE'S pretensions are also pure bluff, you are equally home. The world becomes your oyster. However, there *are* exceptions and I have encountered some very intelligent lorry drivers who realise that I am also bluffing, and who have driven straight at me. When this happens, there is nothing to do but get quickly out of the way; however, I have never know any of LIFE'S vaunted pretensions to behave in a similar manner. Walk on and they vanish. Or rather, they simply fall apart on either side, leaving the way ahead clear. Naturally, it does require a good deal of courage and self-confidence to behave in such a fashion, but I have been subjected to what I can only call a gruelling initiation in such matters (not just now, but throughout my life) and having survived to come out the other side, I can state categorically that all of LIFE'S terrors are mirages and that the secret of success is knowing this, in which case, when death or disease or some other disaster threatens, one does not react. One does not react with love, or hate, or fear. Then those particular mirages disappear, always of course to be replaced by other mirages, for LIFE is a series of pictures – the greatest show on earth!

Sorry to go on about LIFE! I apologise. Let us return to the road. It was characteristic of all roads in Turkey, specially designed, I opine, to make cycling difficult if not impossible in all but urban built-up areas. Firstly, although a main international artery, it was only two lanes wide, one coming and one going. Secondly, the so-called hard shoulder was composed of large diamond-hard and glass-sharp stones about the size of one's fist. No attempt had been made to put a roller over them and impact them so that, except where heavy vehicles had drawn off the road and flattened them into the soil, they were loose and sharp and absolutely impossible to negotiate with a bicycle. Along this highway charged juggernaut lorries from Cracow, Prague and Budapest, going to Iraq. There were also British, French and German juggernauts going to Istanbul and all stations east. On top of this lot, there was the Turkish traffic between the little towns, and the local farmers' tractors with their trailers taking that year's grain harvest to market in sacks.

The juggernaut lorries used to snake behind me with a whisper of exhaust (for it was not the oncoming traffic that now proved difficult – although I have been actually waved off the road by some of those arrogant bastards – but the traffic overtaking me). These damned juggernauts were as long as a train. First of all the cab passed you, way up in the air and so high overhead that it was impossible for the driver to see what was happening at his feet. There was I wobbling away amateurishly (I have never learnt to ride a bicycle really efficiently like a butcher's boy, and have always been frightfully unsteady). Once the front wheels had passed, I used to sigh with relief, but then came the really tricky bit. There was this huge space, large enough to pitch a tent in, between the front set of wheels and the rear set, and I don't know whether the slip-stream was really strong enough to pull one physically in, or whether this space exerted a peculiar sort of hypnotic fascination – I suspect the latter – at any rate, I was always getting sucked in, and it was a real struggle to keep straight.

Istanbul was fifty miles ahead. I was almost within sight of my objective. But I had not gone ten miles beyond the intersection where the Poland, Czechoslovakia road meets the Munich, Thessaloniki highway, than I had diced with death twice! The second time it was such a near shave that I felt the blood draining out of my extremities and concentrating itself in the heart, and I nearly fainted from terror. My knees were weak and I was panting from fright, so that I was forced to dismount and sit down at the side of the road where I gave a bit of thought to my predicament. I couldn't *walk* the fifty miles to Istanbul, and I tried flagging down buses but they simply wouldn't stop. I couldn't communicate with anyone because the only European language spoken seemed to be German, which I have always resisted like the plague. And no habitation in sight.

Actually, I was mistaken. There was a small thatched hut a little way down the road, and I wandered towards it in a desultory sort of way, trying to resist the temptation which was becoming ever more insistent to pack the whole thing in and admit defeat. The hut turned out to be a liquor shop and I had a peg. (It's called *raki*, is colourless, and is made from rice. Variations of it are drunk in all of Asia – you find it in the *saki* of Japan – and it's potent as hell.)

I felt better and had another. You can guess the rest. I got pissed as a fart! Well, to cut a long story short, that is how I reached Istanbul – on *raki*! It is a curious fact to which countless inebriated incidents in my life have testified that once you are well and truly intoxicated, although you are always falling down, you never get hurt. It was so in the present case. I hesitate to enumerate the number of times I fell under the wheels of lorries, but nothing seemed to happen. I appeared to bear a charmed life.

Istanbul is a genuine gateway to Asia and I found it a magical place. I could quite happily live there and the food and wine are magnificent. Istanbul is largely vegetarian in its staple diet, rice being a common commodity which is extensively grown in the lowlands round about the city, right up the mountains which support the central Anatolian plateau. In their cookery they use it in the most imaginative fashion, mixed with all sorts of intriguing herbs and vegetables which give it the subtlest of fascinating flavours. Ankara on the other hand, being the centre of a vast grassland and wheat-growing country, is entirely bread and meat.

The two cities are so different in inner essence, psychological and physical structure and in their architectural and urban orientation that is difficult to credit that they belong to the same country. Ankara, although quite impressive, is still decidedly provincial, whereas nobody could accuse Istanbul of being other than entirely metropolitan. There are several of these big cities, Palermo, Naples, Alexandria, Calcutta, which partake of this strong psychic smell. Istanbul is one of them. I can only attribute it to something in the mental make-up of their inhabitants – a little breath of tomb-odour, possibly from altogether another dimension – which makes these places stand out in retrospect as being quite unique.

After travelling through the suburbs, you enter ancient Byzantium through the original Roman or Greek walls. Nothing in any of the illustrations I had seen of these walls prepared me for the monumental size and impressiveness of this defensive system. They are in a class by themselves. The walls of the Mother City, Rome itself, are tiny by comparison and one gains a powerful impression of the might and majesty of this amazing empire which endured for just over a thousand years. From the breach in the walls by which one enters, one travels in a straight line for two or three miles direct to Santa Sophia which is the heart of the city. Here, on the bluff overlooking the Bosphorus, is the gigantic cathedral of Justinian which has served as a model for all the mosques of Istanbul. Here also is the original fortress-palace of the Emperors of Byzantium and of the Ottoman Sultans, and here is the superb Blue or Sultan Ahmed mosque as well as masses of other monuments, both Islamic and Greek, all crammed into a comparatively small space and lying about unnoticed and uncared for with that careless abandon so perfectly captured by Piranesi in his series of eighteenth-century engravings of Rome. The centre of Istanbul is exactly like these engravings of Piranesi. I have several Piranesi engravings in No.5 Gravel House (they are quite valuable – about £80 to £100 the piece) and you should go down there and take a look at them if you want to get an idea of what I say.

I personally found it positively weird while going about my ordinary commonplace business, to encounter acanthus leaf capitals and fluted marble columns lying about on the sidewalks of what ostensibly were busy modern streets, while all sorts of interesting ancient fragments accumulated in the gutters or protruded from the earth as if they were growing, in exactly that fashion which Piranesi depicts as being so in eighteenth-century Rome's Forum before archaeologists got digging. In the event, the overall impression created by such a state of affairs is infinitely more authentic than excavations.

I stayed in Istanbul five days. I had a raw backside from riding the hard racing-saddle which I had not got used to, so I had to wait for that to heal. I saw most of the monuments and I can only repeat that Istanbul is a place to come back to again and again.

Stuck in suffocating England as I often was, I never for once imagined in those miserable moments that I would be privileged to see such marvellous things as I have on this trip. For instance, just in front of the Sultan Ahmed mosque, a twisty, black, bronze, barley-sugar-shaped pillar sticks up out of the ground in an inconsequential manner and is so little regarded that I was hard put to find a reference to it in any of the guide books. It stands at one end of a very unkempt garden in the shape of a rectangle about 300 yards long with rounded, apsidal ends. Do you know what it is? It is the original turning pillar round which the chariots had to race; the rectangular garden is the original Roman amphitheatre – infinitely more impressive than the amphitheatre of Maximus or is it Maxentius at Rome, because it has been left in the original ruinous condition and almost intact. The spot evidently had such strong historic associations that the Sultans never built on it. You don't come across relics like that every day.

Dan, if I am ever to get this – I can hardly call it a letter – off to you, I shall have to close. If I ever have occasion to write to you again I will continue in my next.[309]

---

309 The letter was finished on 19 June 1980. The further letter about the rest of his journey, which he promised friends, was never written.

EIGHTEEN
BACK IN INDIA

FRANK COMPLETED THE JOURNEY OVERLAND, MOSTLY BY BUS, through Turkey, Iran, Afghanistan and Pakistan, and he arrived in India, bike in tow, on 30 August 1978. He then cycled several thousand miles around the Indian sub-continent, before settling in the Hindu temple city of Puri in the eastern State of Orissa – it is also a sea-side resort – to live in a simple beach house on Chakra Tirtha Road. It was from here that he sent his long letter to Dan Sansom in June 1980, which also included a brief account of his new location:

The enclosed photograph is of the beach. It is 300 yards from my door. Right in front of the open window where I am writing the sand stretches out to the sea. To my right is an ancient temple on a sand dune. Now the monsoon has arrived and it is beautiful weather. The cloud effects are spectacular. Great breakers roll in from the Bay of Bengal and I can hear their roar. I am well and happy but this doesn't mean that I shall *never* return. The political situation may alter and whereas at present I can live in India unmolested without a visa, Mrs Gandhi may well bring in an ordinance whereby citizens of the United Kingdom will be required to have one. In which case my stay would be limited to three months. Of course, you can buy a certain number of extensions (corruption) but that won't go on forever, if only for the reason that after a time it begins to look suspicious. So we shall see!

From this beach at dawn I have counted as many as 200 sailing log-catamarans setting out for the fishing grounds 30 and 40 miles out to sea.

Lovely fish to eat, especially lobsters and prawns.

My house is only a cottage (£6 per month) but it is very pretty and I have two servants. I have a magnificent collection of potted exotic plants in my courtyard and I am experimenting with growing plants in the sand.

Frank also corresponded at about the same time with another friend in Coggeshall, Prue Turner (the niece of Dorothy Butterfield), who was then living in his old house, The Cedars. In a letter from Puri dated 30 June 1980, he wrote that he was well, happy and enjoying himself.[310] He enquired whether Dan had circulated his letter about his bicycle journey to other friends and said that he planned to complete the account of his trip in a later letter. He continued:

Of course India is unspeakably awful and most of the Indians are even worse, but at least in this country one does not find the suffocating atmosphere of housing-estate England which I found so stultifying. There are no laws, or rather, there are laws but nobody takes any notice of them, and one does as one likes, which suits me.

As an old man, an Englishman and an ex-officer of the defunct Raj, I occupy a privileged position which I would never have in England. People (that is, people of my age who remember it) look back to the period of British rule as a golden age!!! This may surprise you, but it is absolutely true!!! The young, of course, like the young everywhere, are so ignorant, backward, inferiority-conscious aggressive, uneducated, uncultured, that I cannot even begin to describe them!

Frank ended the letter by asking what had happened to Lionel

---

310 Airmail letter in possession of Prue Turner.

Evans at end of his forgery trial, and whether he had got off.

In another letter to Prue Turner, in August 1980, Frank announced that he was leaving Puri:[311]

> The hour has struck and I am off on my travels again, into Central India and Tribal territory, and consequently I shall no longer be at this address.

> My trip continues to be packed with hair-raising experiences and every sort of adventure, mishap, disaster, catastrophe that can be imagined. But it is also very funny and sometimes beautifully, breathtakingly, heart-warmingly rewarding. I think I had better stop this effusion or we shall be back with the 'rich tapestry of life' – than which nothing is more revolting.

> I have just bought my third bike! I feel like one of those heroes of legend – 'How they brought the good news from Ghent to Aix!!! – who keeps on killing horses under him! But really, the roads – and the trip generally – seem to knock hell out of bicycles, if not out of me!

> Actually I have stayed in Puri so long (over a year) because I was so mentally and physically fatigued that I was unable to go a step further. I did not choose this place because of any virtues it had (it has none), but simply because I arrived there and flopped. I couldn't drive my body another inch forward. Better now, and raring to go.

Frank set off again and eventually fetched up in the Himalayan foothills in the North of India. He had returned to his old hunting-ground. This time, he settled in the former British Raj hill station of Dalhousie on the borders between Himachal Pradesh and Kashmir, and rented rooms in an old colonial-style house with a name to match – Shanti Kung Snowdown – where one of the greatest figures of modern Bengali culture, Rabindranath Tagore,[312] wrote his first poem. Frank

---

311 Airmail letter in possession of Prue Turner.
312 Rabindranath Tagore (1861-1941), Bengali poet, novelist and musician, and Nobel Literature Laureate, stayed in Dalhousie with his father in 1873 and began to write while he was there.

went native: he grew a moustache, dressed in a lungi and took up with a local boy called Rajindra Rana.

Raj was still a schoolboy when he first met Frank, whom he ended up calling 'Dad'. He gives this account of how their acquaintance came about:

> I was on school holidays at the time and I needed a job. Somebody told me that up there on the hill there was an Englishman who needed a servant. I knocked on the door and asked if he needed a servant, and he said yes. We sat down and tied up the salary and I got the job. He took me on as a servant and treated me like a son. But he didn't give me a salary, just pocket-money.[313]

The arrangement seems to have worked well. Raj was deputed to take on another boy, and he thus became Frank's major domo – and his lover. Pratap, the other boy of about the same age, did the cooking and household chores. Raj stayed with Frank for four years, and Frank evidently delighted in educating him. That winter they went on a two-month tour of Northern India, visiting Delhi, Agra, Nagpur and Hyderabad.

Raj says that he had never seen a big city before, and that Frank wanted to show him the big cities and the people who lived there. Thanks to Frank, he saw many Indian cities. Over time, Frank was to send or accompany Raj on trips to Calcutta, Amritsar, Bombay and Goa.

A letter to Jeremy Hill's wife, Virginia, gives a few insights into Frank's state of mind during those years, and shows that he had lost neither his devilish sense of humour nor his penchant for exclamation marks. Virginia Hill had written a Christmas card from Essex in December 1982 to propose that she and Jeremy pay him a visit, and she had commended him for retreating into a spiritual life. 'I envy your ability to cast yourself into the arms of God,' she wrote, probably not fully aware of the actual state of Frank's life.

---

313 A letter from Rajindra Rana to the author, 2010.

Frank wrote back in February 1983:

This is a *dreadful* country, and pray be under no misapprehension that you are visiting Disneyland!

You use a very highly charged phrase – 'Cast yourself into the arms of God'.

How incredibly clever of you! And how did you know! This is precisely – almost in your very words – what I articulated to myself about what I was doing! But I never visualised that somebody would pick up my idea as easily as you appear to have done. As a matter of fact I am a bit embarrassed to have been found out, just as if you had caught me with my trousers down in *delicious fragrance*! Are my motives so transparent? And do you read me that well!

What I have really been doing is trying to grow old! You know how cats crawl into a lonely hole to die! Well, I have crawled into this hole to get the aging process over with, out of sight of my friends. Needless to say, it has been a total failure, as I persist in thinking of myself as young, dashing and handsome!!! You can imagine into what farcical situations such an attitude leads me! I thought I would finally return to England after several years as a beautiful old man, having at last achieved the final metamorphosis from butterfly into caterpillar. However I see now that it's not going to be like that. I seem to be totally incapable of aging decently and respectably, and am still inclined to outrage people by the idiosyncrasy of my ideas or my conduct. While this is so, don't you think I'd better continue to keep out of the way?

Frank had in fact been visited a few months earlier. Dan Sansom and his son Hugh had flown to India to see him in September 1982. Frank sent Raj to meet them at Delhi and escort them up by bus to Dalhousie.

Sansom says that Frank was living in a very pleasant location, but he wasn't doing much, just existing. He thinks that Frank had moved from eastern India to Dalhousie because he felt more secure and more at home among the Tibetans there.[314]

Sansom recorded his impressions of Dalhousie in a journal he kept of the trip:[315]

Dalhousie is delightful with a small bazaar centre and houses dotted about all over the surrounding hills, and with glorious views of the snow-capped Himalayas.

We walked up to the town centre accompanied by Mr Jootla whom I had sat next to on the bus. He was obviously a local worthy and was extremely pleasant and knew Frank well. Raj organised an old jeep to take us up to middle Bakrota and Frank's house. The Tibetan centre is quite large with a school, a carpet factory and a number of houses.

Frank has part of a bungalow near the school, adjoining the little restaurant looking out on a yard with a ramshackle little shop opposite. He has three rooms, one quite large with an entrance lobby used as a kitchen, and is quite comfortable. There is electricity but no running water and the loo is a little distance away (you have to take the key) and is the hole-in-the-floor variety. It is also used as a bathroom by taking a large bucket of water in!

Frank was dressed in a lungi and old cardigan and looked very fit and weather-beaten, though rather older. He was thrilled to see us and obviously greatly excited by our visit, and the umbrella was greatly appreciated. He has kindly put us in his room where there are two charpoys[316] and plenty of blankets. He has two boys living with him, Rajindra and Pratap, both about 18, whom he took under his wing and who do the cooking, shopping

---

314 Conversation with the author, 2010.
315 A notebook journal, *India 11-29 September 1982*.
316 Wooden bed strung with light rope.

and chores for him. They are both pleasant and jolly chaps and the arrangement seems to work well.

After a rest, I walked with Frank down into Dalhousie to look around – about 15 minutes down a steepish path. Every afternoon the clouds build up and it rains – the tail end of the monsoon – and we had to shelter from a violent hailstorm for a bit. When we got back up, there was a violent thunderstorm with tremendous lightning which rumbled on all evening. We enjoyed a simple but pleasant evening meal, Indian style.

The following day Sansom accompanied Frank on a tour of Dalhousie:

Walked down with Frank to the bazaar and down further to the bank. Had a walk round Dalhousie itself, which spreads over three hills, the main shopping part being quite a bit higher than the bus terminal section where the bank is. We had quite a nice lunch – all Indian food here, simple but pleasant – and then walked back up to the Tibetan centre.

A large number of Tibetans have been permanently settled here by the Indian government and Frank rents his rooms from the headman. From December to March most of them go down to Dharmsala, where the Dalai Lama lives, as Bakrota gets almost buried in snow. In the afternoon we walked to Upper Bakrota where there are magnificent views of the neighbouring valleys and hills, all thickly wooded, and there are bears and wolves around.

The remainder of the journal recounts a two-day jeep-trip which Frank and his boys organised and includes further notes on Dalhousie, and how Frank, a caring and anxious host, went to the trouble of helping them arrange their onward train journey so that they could see other parts of India.

Writing on the day of his and Hugh's departure, Sansom summed up Frank's situation:

It has been great fun staying with Frank, and he has been to considerable trouble to entertain us and to make our stay as comfortable as possible. He is certainly in a delightful place and plans to stay there hopefully until he is 70 (in three years' time) and then to consider whether or not to return to England. He looks and obviously is pretty fit and tough (he had to be to cycle all over India, let alone out here), and the Tibetans are quite a pleasant lot. Although he has virtually adopted the two 18-year-olds, Raj and Pratap, they look after him well and are nice lads. He seems quite happy doing nothing and can't even be bothered to write.

Frank had still described himself as a 'writer' in his new passport, issued in Delhi in February 1982, but he had in fact stopped writing, and he never even started on the promised sequel to his long letters about his bike journey to and travels around India. His final years in India appeared to have sapped him of much of the energy and zest which had once driven him, and he had finally come to a stand-still; he was doing virtually nothing. He was calm – possibly for the first time in his life.

But once again, Frank was forced to make a hurried exit.

Raj says that in March 1984 Frank got a letter from the Government telling him to leave India within 15 days. The order to leave India could well have been partly connected with his over-staying his visa, but Raj believes it mainly stemmed from the events that were unfolding in nearby Amritsar, where Sikh militants had occupied and fortified the Golden Temple Complex in open defiance of the Government of Prime Minister Indira Gandhi. He says that Operation Blue Star was about to start, and thinks that the decision about Frank stemmed from a concern for the safety of foreigners.

Blue Star was the controversial operation which reached a bloody climax in June 1984 when the Indian army stormed the Golden Temple

Complex and recaptured it, killing an officially estimated 500 civilians and quite possibly many more. These were unsettling times in India: two of Gandhi's Sikh bodyguards took their revenge later that year by assassinating the Prime Minister. By then, Frank was back in England. Raj says that Frank wanted him to accompany him to England:

> Frank wanted me to drive him to England by Jeep, but it was a very long drive for me and far too difficult. He then offered to take me by air, but I said I would go with him next time. Sadly, there was not a next time.

NINETEEN
END OF THE ROAD

FRANK RETURNED TO COGGESHALL IN EARLY APRIL 1984. He was seriously ill with a stomach problem – a recurrence of the amoebic dysentery that had dogged him ever since the Chindit campaign in Burma – and he looked gaunt. However, although he recovered quite quickly, he was virtually penniless. He had spent almost all his money, and despite his defiant stand at Witham Magistrates' court 13 years earlier railing against Britain's welfare system, he was now dependent on the National Health Service and on his state pension. Dan Sansom came to the rescue, and he found Frank lodgings in one of the modest almshouses opposite the church in Coggeshall, No 10 Church Green.

'Of course, being Frank, he quickly turned it into a stately almshouse,' says Sansom.

With whatever money he could scrape together or borrow, Frank furnished his one-bedroom apartment and laid out the 'grounds' in his customary grand style. He installed an elegant Chinese chair and a statue of Buddha in the living room; and outside he built a mound, like an old Sarum barrow, on the small strip of grass between his back door and the railings along Church Street. Around it he erected a 10-foot high 'barley-sugar' twisted column topped with a Corinthian capital, a substantial stone pineapple, a large classical urn and a stone cherub – all mounted on plinths – and a stone seat. In the warm summer months, he entertained his guests with tea in the garden, holding forth while striking statuesque poses by his pillar. No one asked what the neighbours thought.

Once again he became a popular figure in Essex. He strutted around Coggeshall as if he were the local squire and would sit on a bench in Market Hill, the town centre, and swap gossip with one of his long-time local friends, Mark Marchant. He would stop and banter with anyone who had time for him, and talk his talk wherever and whenever he found an audience.

Frank continued to cycle and he kept his bicycle in the bathroom of his little home. He would set off on long trips to visit his cousins, Jill and Roy Baines and Avis Baines, who still both lived some 15 miles away in North Essex. (Ralph, Avis's husband Hubert's other son, had died.) He would also cycle over to Bures to see Jeremy and Virginia Hill.

He found a new friend in Matthew Screaton, a young artist from Cornwall, with whom he took up with enthusiastically. They had a close platonic relationship; Frank had found another young man to educate.

Screaton writes:

He had a very fine eye and he liked my painting, but he loved above all the idea of teaching me and opening my eyes to new experiences. He commissioned a portrait and he thought I should expand my horizons, so he paid for me to travel to Sicily, his own former Hellenic stomping ground.[317]

Raj, meanwhile, showered him with affectionate letters, with news about his various jobs and a taxi business he was running; and in each letter he avowed his love and implored Frank to return.[318]

'Next month,' Raj wrote in August 1985, 'your birthday. God give you long life.'

In November 1985, he signed off a letter: 'I love you, I love you.'

Wishing Frank a Happy Christmas in December 1985, Raj said that he had a plan to become a rich businessman and make enough

---

317 Note to the author, 2010.
318 The letters, in the possession of Dan Sansom, are transcribed here with a minimum of correction.

money to come to England: 'In my plan I will be rich in a five year up to 1990. If I am rich I want to you back with me. I prayer the god – God give you a long life, then I will return your debt. Dear Frank, I love you and a few days ago you are coming in a dream.'

'I am waiting for you, or you should wait for me,' he said in January 1986.

'Thanks very much for sending the photo,' he wrote in April 1986. 'I am very sorry for you and I hope now the weather is better in your country. Beautiful weather in Dalhousie. These days many people is asking about you are coming back to India, and where do you live. Everybody say you are a very good person. I am not going to marry in my life. What do you think? It is a good idea. Sometime I think I don't like this life.'

A letter in July 1986 starts 'Dear Dad' – Frank's all-but-last identity.

In early 1987, Frank hinted that he had heart trouble.

'I got your letter on May 16th,' wrote Raj. 'I feel very sad you are sick. I know heart trouble is very bad.'

'Well make up your mind and come to see me,' he wrote in July 1987. 'You don't remember me, but really I remember you too much. Sometime I feel very sad. But what can I do. I haven't got the money to come to see you in England.'

Frank, meanwhile, had not completely lost hope of getting his book on the Chindits published, and in the summer of 1985 he worked through the surviving draft – itself a rewritten version of the original – and edited it once more. This was the only draft of an unpublished work which Frank had kept; he destroyed all other manuscripts. Trevor Disley, a young friend from Coggeshall who was just starting a picture-framing business, helped Frank by reading and correcting the new draft, and he arranged for his aunt to type the manuscript. All Frank's handwritten books had been typed out in similar fashion over the years by willing helping hands. Frank never touched a typewriter and to have done so would have been – in his eyes – 'frightfully common'.[319]

---

319 Note to the author, 2010.

Frank called the revised version *Prisoners of Hope*, and he sent it to David Bolt, who was now working as an independent literary agent, but he found no serious takers. The only publisher who expressed any interest was one who specialised in gay literature, but Frank had no wish to reduce his experiences as a Chindit to a sort of romantic homosexual novella. The story of his time in Burma – the biggest event of his life – remained unpublished until 2011, when it appeared, following rigorous editing as in the case of his other books, under the title *Chindit Affair*.

Frank also wrote a short piece about The Cedars, the house in Coggeshall where he and his mother had moved in 1935 and which he walked past daily as he set off down Church Street to shop – invariably dressed in rolled-up blue denim jeans and sandals, carrying a wicker basket on his back, and with a cane in hand.

'The Cedars was always known as the best house in Coggeshall,' Frank wrote in November 1986. 'Probably it still is! Its prestige and pre-eminence have in no wise diminished, during these latter degenerate days, for the fact is that it is among the small number of Coggeshall's "great houses" still in private occupation, whereas so many of them have been divided, demolished, vandalised, or become business premises or offices, continues to assure it distinction.'

Frank stayed in The Cedars the following summer, house-sitting for the owners[320] for two weeks in August 1987, and again he saw and wrote about ghosts.

'Consenting to dog-sit, I thought memories of the past would have no effect on me,' Frank wrote in the *Visitors' Book*. 'Vain thought!!! My mother, clothed in a bright summer dress of pink-and-red stripes, continually peeped out at me from every bush. The whole occasion was traumatic, and made more so by Brian's sister telephoning and trying to persuade me that the tapestry room (as she called it) was haunted.'

But he wasn't just contending with ghosts. Only a month away from his 72nd birthday (23 September 1987), Frank was still struggling

---

320 The author and his wife Gail Turner.

with his identity – he signed the *Visitors' Book:* 'Francis Baines, sometimes known as Frank Baines'. And this was not all. The heart condition that had felled his father when he was only 56 was also stealing up on him.

Raj continued to write lovingly. His last letter was dated 18 October 1987:

Dear Frank

I received your letter a few days ago, which is very nice. But that is not good news – you didn't come back to India. Please try to come back. I very well. I am not going down to Punjab yet. If I am going down before I will give the address. Today is a very bad day, windy rain and hailstone, getting very cold. How is the weather in your place? Maybe same like Dalhousie. You are coming in a dream last night. You are coming with two to three coolies to carry your luggage up to my place. How are you these days? Mr Kapila died 2-3 months ago. Do you remember me sometime in the bed? I remember you in Dalhousie. How about my jeans? I didn't get them yet. Dear Frank I love you too much. But what can I do? I am not able to come to England – too far from India.

Your Raj with sweet kisses.

Frank never saw the letter. By the time it arrived in England he had been dead for over a week. Following a ferocious hurricane in southern England and a global collapse of equity markets, Frank succumbed quite unexpectedly to a chicken. He had cooked a meal for himself and Mathew Screaton using a half-unfrozen bird, and the resulting food poisoning triggered a fatal heart attack. He was found dead at his home sitting in his oriental chair on the morning of 22 October 1987.

The doctor who attended Frank was Robert Jones, who had been at the centre of a highly-publicised investigation into the mysterious and still unsolved murder of his wife in 1983. Dr Jones gave three causes of death – as if one wasn't enough – cardiac arrest, cardiac failure and gastro-enteritis. He listed Frank's occupation, appropriately, as 'Author (Retired)'.[321]

* * *

Frank originally ended the account of his last meeting with Dal Bahadur that occupies the final chapter of *Chindit Affair* with the first verse of *Non Sum Qualis Eram Bonae Sub Regno Cynarae,*[322] a poem by Ernest Dowson[323] which was itself inspired by a line from the Roman poet Horace.[324]

Frank's choice of these lines tells us much about him – about the way he saw himself as different and apart; about his sensual and emotional nature, with its lapses into sentimentality; and about the sadness he felt about the imperfect and impermanent nature of love. It is apt that his biography should end with these lines – words that obviously moved him greatly, and spoke to him intensely of his long-ago love for Dal Bahadur:

Last night, ah, yesternight, betwixt her lips and mine
There fell thy shadow, Cynara! Thy breath was shed
Upon my soul between the kisses and the wine;
And I was desolate and sick of an old passion,
Yea, I was desolate and bowed my head:
I have been faithful to thee, Cynara! In my fashion.

---

321 Frank's death certificate.
322 I am not the man I was in the days when Cynara was queen over my heart.
323 English poet (1867-1900) associated with the decadent movement.
324 Horace, *Odes,* IV, i.

TIMELINE: FRANK BAINES 1915-1987

1915   Francis (Frank) Trevean Baines born in Clapham (September 24)
1929   Sir Frank Baines buys Trenoweth in St Keverne, Cornwall
1929   Sent to board at Oundle School
1933   Leaves Oundle
1933   Sir Frank Baines dies at Trenoweth (December 25)
1934   Sails to Australia on the *Lawhill*
1935   Returns to England
1936   Lady Rhoda Baines moves to The Cedars in Coggeshall
1938   Footloose in South America
1938   Back in England, becomes a Conservative Party agent
1939   Enlists and joins an anti-aircraft gun battery in East Anglia
1941   Transfers to India for officer training
1941   Posted to North-West Frontier, sees action
1942   Assigned from North-West Frontier to Kirkee Camouflage School
1943   Joins General Orde Wingate's Chindits
1944   Fights with the Chindits in Burma
1946   Demobilised and returns to England
1947   Enters Mirtola Ashram
1950   Leaves the Ashram and moves to Calcutta
1956   Returns to England
1958   *Look Towards the Sea* published
1959   *In Deep* published
1962   *Culture of Bacillus* published, writes *Place of Cremation*
1963   Lady Baines dies at The Cedars (March 30)
1963   Sells The Cedars
1964   In Sicily, writes *Don Carlo to the Dark Tower Came*
1965   Moves to Conca dei Marini on the Amalfi Coast
1966   Dorothy Butterfield visits Frank in Conca dei Marini
1966   Returns to Coggeshall and moves into 42 East Street with Dorothy
1971   *Officer Boy* published; spends two months in Brixton Gaol
1972   Dorothy Butterfield dies
1973   Becomes the kitchen porter at the White Hart Hotel in Coggeshall
1978   Sets out to cycle to India
1984   Returns to Coggeshall from India
1987   Frank Baines dies in an alms-house in Coggeshall (October 22)

INDEX